European Perspectives on Environmental Law and Governance

This book provides a range of perspectives on some of the most pressing contemporary challenges in EU environmental law and governance from some of today's leading European environmental academics and practitioners.

The book maintains a focus on three key cross-cutting issues, each of which is carefully analysed through the lens of governance. The first theme to be addressed is that of climate change and the problems it poses for EU governance. The second issue explored concerns the challenge of integrating environmental considerations into other policy areas, as is required by the Treaty on the Functioning of the European Union and the EU's Charter of Fundamental Rights. Finally, the third theme centres on the important challenge of improving environmental enforcement within the EU, and considers issues such as the Aarhus Convention and the evolution of the Commission's work on implementation and enforcement throughout the past twenty years. Each of these three themes is situated within the broader ongoing debate about the changing nature of European environmental governance post-Lisbon and the ways in which developments in this area fits within broader trends in European governance theory and policy generally.

European Perspectives on Environmental Law and Governance contains contributions from experts in the field including Mary Robinson, Alan Boyle, Ludwig Krämer and Liam Cashman, and will be of interest to academics, students and practitioners of EU environmental law.

Dr. Suzanne Kingston is a Lecturer at the School of Law, University College Dublin and a barrister practising at the Irish bar. She has appeared, *inter alia*, on behalf of Ireland and the European Commission before the EU courts and has published widely on EU law issues.

Routledge Research in EU Law

Available titles in this series include:

Forthcoming titles in this series include:

European Perspectives on Environmental Law and Governance

Edited by Suzanne Kingston

Routledge
Taylor & Francis Group

LONDON AND NEW YORK

First published 2013
by Routledge
2 Park Square, Milton Park, Abingdon, Oxfordshire OX14 4RN

Simultaneously published in the USA and Canada
by Routledge
711 Third Avenue, New York, NY 10017

First issued in paperback 2014

Routledge is an imprint of the Taylor and Francis Group, an informa business

British Library Cataloguing in Publication Data
A catalogue record for this book is available from the British Library

Library of Congress Cataloging in Publication Data
European perspectives on environmental law and governance / [edited by] Suzanne
Kingston.
    p. cm. – (Routledge research in european union law)
  ISBN 978-0-415-50006-7 (hardback) – ISBN 978-0-203-09656-7 (e-book)
  1. Environmental law–European Union countries. 2. Environmental policy–
  European Union countries. I. Kingston, Suzanne, 1977-
  KJE6242.E95 2012
  344.2404'6–dc23
                       2012009988

 ISBN 978-0-415-50006-7 (hbk)
 ISBN 978-1-138-80968-0 (pbk)
 ISBN 978-0-203-09656-7 (ebk)

Typeset in Garamond
by Taylor & Francis Books

Contents

Notes on contributors

Joanne Blennerhassett has been lecturing in environmental law at the University College Dublin on all aspects of domestic, European and international environmental law since 2003. Joanne graduated from Trinity College Dublin in 1998, with an honours degree in law, a year of which was spent at Assas, Paris II, La Sorbonne, specialising in European competition and international law. She holds a master's degree in European Law from UCD. Joanne trained as a solicitor and previously worked with Arthur Cox, specialising in commercial law, corporate finance, commercial litigation and insolvency. She was admitted to the Roll of Solicitors in May 2002. Joanne is also an arbitrator and a member of the Chartered Institute of Arbitrators, and holds a Diploma in Arbitration and a Diploma in International Arbitration. She is also an accredited mediator and holds a Diploma in Commercial and Civil Mediation from Friary Law and ADR Groups' mediation training. Joanne's current research is focused on her doctoral research which examines class actions and multi-party actions as a route to justice for mass harm, particularly environmental harm.

Alan Boyle is Professor of Public International Law at the University of Edinburgh School of Law. He teaches international law, international environmental law and law of the sea. He was General Editor of the *International and Comparative Law Quarterly* from 1998–2006. Publications include *International Law and the Environment* (with Patricia Birnie and Catherine Redgwell) (3rd edn, Oxford University Press, 2009) and *The Making of International Law* (with Christine Chinkin) (Oxford University Press, 2007). He practises international law from Essex Court Chambers, London. Cases include *Pulp Mills on the River Uruguay* (ICJ 2006–10), *Aerial Spraying* (ICJ 2009–), *Bay of Bengal Maritime Boundary* (ITLOS and PCA 2009–); *Japanese Whaling* (ICJ 2010–).

Liam Cashman joined the European Commission in 1988, having previously trained as an Irish solicitor. For a large part of the period since then, he has dealt with complaints from and infringements concerning Ireland in Directorate General Environment. His case-handling experience extends to litigation in the European Court of Justice and subsequent follow-up of judgments. He is currently deputy head of a unit devoted to compliance promotion, governance and legal issues.

Javier de Cendra de Larragán is Senior Research Associate at the UCL Energy Institute and the Faculty of Laws, University College London. He holds a master's degree in law and economics, an LL.M in international, European and comparative energy and environmental law, and a PhD on climate change law and policy. He has done consultancy for the European Commission, DECC and industry. His main task at UCL is to integrate legal research into the work carried out at the Energy Institute. Javier publishes regularly on different aspects of international and European energy and environmental law. Key topics include EU climate change law and policy, legal frameworks for the promotion or renewable energy and energy efficiency, the interface between climate laws and trade laws, the interface between industrial and environmental laws and policies, state responsibility in international and EU law, and carbon governance.

Suzanne Kingston is a Lecturer at the School of Law, University College Dublin and a barrister practising at the Irish bar. She has appeared, *inter alia*, on behalf of Ireland and the European Commission before the EU courts and has published widely on EU law issues, with recent publications including the monograph *Greening EU Competition Law and Policy* (Cambridge University Press, 2012). She has been a visiting lecturer at Cambridge University, the University of Leiden, Queen's University, Belfast, and Osgoode Hall Law School, Toronto. She is a graduate of Oxford University (BA in Law) and the University of Leiden, the Netherlands (LLM in European Community Law, PhD). She served as a *référendaire* (legal adviser) in the cabinet of Advocate General Geelhoed at the European Court of Justice, Luxembourg from 2004–2006. Prior to this, she practised EU law at the Brussels office of the US law firm, Cleary Gottlieb Steen & Hamilton (2002–2004) and was a *stagiaire* at the European Commission.

Ludwig Krämer studied law and history in Kiel, München and Paris. He has been a judge at the Landgericht Kiel (1969–2004) and an official of the Commission of the European Community (1972–2004), and has now retired from both functions. He holds an LLD from the University of Hamburg and is an Honorary Professor at Bremen University and Visiting Professor at University College London. He has been a lecturer at the College of Europe, Bruges (2001–2010) and has published some 20 books and more than 200 articles on EU environmental law.

Owen McIntyre is a Senior Lecturer specialising in environmental law at the Faculty of Law, University College Cork. He serves on the editorial boards of a number of Irish and international journals and is currently involved in a number of research projects funded by the HEA and EPA, having recently completed research projects on behalf of the Heritage Council and the DoEHLG. He has co-authored a report for the Law Society of Ireland on

Environmental Enforcement: The Case for Reform (2008). He regularly acts as a consultant for the World Bank, UNDP, UNEP, EU, SIDA and GTZ in the areas of environmental law and water resources law. Since 2004, he has served as a member of the EBRD's Project Complaint Mechanism (PCM). In 2008 he was designated a member of the Scientific Committee of the European Environment Agency. He has published widely on environmental law issues and has published the monograph *Environmental Protection of International Watercourses under International Law* (Ashgate, 2007).

Joseph A. McMahon was appointed Professor of Commercial Law at University College Dublin in 2004 having previously been Professor of International Trade Law at Queen's University Belfast, and a lecturer at both the University of Leicester and Victoria University of Wellington, New Zealand. His research interests are primarily in the area of agricultural trade law in both the World Trade Organization and the EU and he has published on the WTO Agreement on Agriculture and the EU's Common Agricultural Policy.

Áine Ryall is a Senior Lecturer at the Faculty of Law, University College Cork (UCC), and a qualified barrister (called to the Irish Bar in 1995). At UCC, she teaches Environmental Law, Tort Law and the Law of the European Union. She is the author of *Effective Judicial Protection and the Environmental Impact Assessment Directive in Ireland* (Hart Publishing, 2009). She served as a member of the government-appointed Environmental Protection Agency Review Group which reported in May 2011. Her research focuses on implementation and enforcement of EU environmental law with particular reference to Ireland. Current projects include: implementation of Directive 2003/4/EC on public access to environmental information; the impact of the Aarhus Convention and EU obligations on access to justice in environmental matters at national level (including the impact on rules governing judicial review); and communicating EU environmental law rights to the public.

Foreword

I am honoured to have been invited to write a Foreword to this volume on European environmental law and governance. This book adds to the literature dealing with a rapidly evolving and critically important area. The book addresses a number of questions in relation to the legal and governance mechanisms required to achieve the sustainable management of natural resources and the protection of the natural environment from a European perspective.

The book has three sections. The first deals with the climate change challenge, offering commentary on the development of European Community climate change law and examining the international dimensions of climate change governance.

Climate change is one of the most critical issues of our time, not only from an environmental and economic perspective but also because of its impact on a whole range of basic human rights. Climate change has implications for national and international governance, for relations between states, for social justice, human rights and equality. Climate change also raises very challenging questions about the environmental ramifications of human activity and consumption, how these compare with the ecological limits and assimilative capacity of the biosphere, how these burdens should be shared more equitably and how they threaten the feasibility of sustainable development. I strongly believe that a climate justice approach is the best way to respond to these challenges.

In this regard, the decision by the UN Human Rights Council to appoint an Independent Expert on the issue of human rights obligations related to the enjoyment of a safe, clean, healthy and sustainable environment is an important development.

The application of law offers a potentially forceful weapon in the fight to tackle climate change, both in terms of how targets, policies and measures can be enshrined in supra-national and national law and also in the potential use of human rights litigation to enforce substantive and procedural rights. The commitment made at COP-17 in Durban to develop 'a new protocol, another legal instrument or an agreed outcome with legal force' by 2015, which would come into force by 2020, offers real hope that a legally binding agreement can be reached, one which will legally enshrine greenhouse gas emission reduction commitments. However, much work needs to be done to reach agreement on issues such as equity, the right to development, access to finance and common but differentiated responsibilities.

The second section of the book deals with what is termed 'the integration challenge': this examines how environmental policy can be integrated into other EU policies, for example trade, competition and agriculture, to strengthen and re-enforce the impact of sectoral policies through horizontal integration. The integration principle is an important aspect of EU law; integration of environmental concerns into other policies must be deepened if we are to move towards sustainable development.

The third section deals with the 'enforcement challenge', that is, how EU environmental law can be enforced at Member State level following transposition of EU Directives into national law. Enforcement may be required where the provisions of a Directive are not implemented, either in fact or in law. This is important because EU law which is incorrectly or inadequately implemented or not implemented at all will not achieve the desired effect. It is imperative that EU law is both adequately transposed and subsequently applied through consistent and harmonious interpretation in order to ensure the full protection of the earth's natural resources.

This book is a welcome contribution to the corpus of academic literature on European environmental law and governance and will be useful as a *vade mecum* both for academics and for policy-makers and practitioners. I commend the editor and authors for contributing to the volume and I wish them every success on its publication.

Mary Robinson
President, Mary Robinson Foundation – Climate Justice

Acknowledgements

This book arose out of a conference entitled 'Frontiers in European Environmental Law and Governance', which was held in Newman House, University College Dublin on 25 February 2011. Almost all contributions are based on papers presented at the conference, which have since been updated and edited in the light of the valuable discussions that took place on the day of the conference itself, and developments since.

Sincere thanks go to each of the contributors to the book, who gave so generously of their time on the day of the conference and subsequently, and to Dr Mary Robinson for speaking at the conference and kindly agreeing to write the Foreword. Thanks also go to UCD School of Law, which sponsored the conference, and especially Angela Ennis, UCD School of Law, and Donal Casey, PhD student at UCD School of Law, for excellent assistance in organising the conference. Finally, special thanks are due to Katie Carpenter and the team at Routledge for their support throughout the production process.

Editing this book has been an exciting venture, and a great pleasure, particularly given the outstanding calibre of the contributors. At a time when the need to focus on environmental protection has never been greater, it is hoped that the book will inspire further debate on the future of environmental law and governance within Europe and beyond.

Dr Suzanne Kingston BL
Dublin, 15 February 2012

1   Introduction

Suzanne Kingston

From small beginnings, when environmental law tended to be viewed as a rather minor sub-species of public international or tort law, the subject has grown to become a huge area within Europe, both in practice and in the academic literature. As the quantity and breadth of research in the field expands rapidly, and much of the literature becomes increasingly specialised, there remains a need to take a step back at frequent intervals, to attempt to identify some predominant cross-cutting trends, and to fit these trends into broader patterns emerging within European law and governance.

This book seeks to contribute to this process. The aim of the book is to provide a single-volume collection of views from some of the leading environmental academics and practitioners active in Europe today on three of the most serious cross-cutting contemporary challenges in environmental law, viewed from a European perspective. It is undoubtedly the case that there are many such challenges to choose from. At the conference giving rise to this book, held in Dublin in February 2011, the sense of urgency in the quest to improve the effectiveness of European environmental law was palpable among contributors and participants. Yet, at the same time, the magnitude of this task escaped no-one, particularly in the thick of one of the greatest financial crises that Europe and Ireland have ever witnessed. It is against this background that the present volume was produced.

1.1 Three critical challenges in environmental law and governance within Europe

The present book is split into three main themes, constituting some of the most pressing cross-cutting issues presently facing environmental law and governance within Europe. These are:

- the challenge posed by climate change for law and lawyers within Europe;
- the challenge of integrating environmental concerns into other fields of European law;
- the challenge of improving enforcement of European environmental law.

The business of selecting just three overarching themes for inclusion in the book is, by its nature, a thankless task. It is impossible to cover every important cross-cutting theme – or even all of the most important themes – presently emerging in environmental law within Europe in a single volume, at least in any useful depth; inevitably, therefore, this necessitates a process of selection. The three themes identified in the present book are those which, in the editor's view, pose perhaps the most considerable challenges to the structure and effectiveness of environmental law within Europe at present. They do so for differing reasons.

In the case of the first theme – *the legal challenges posed by climate change* – there can hardly be a better contemporary illustration of a challenge demanding a re-thinking of conventional approaches to environmental regulation, on a number of different levels. A fundamentally global problem requires effective concerted action at the international level, yet pending such action, state and non-state actors within Europe and beyond face difficult choices about how best to use law to promote their goals in this field. As the contributions in Part I of this volume highlight, this demands a careful reconsideration of some fundamental issues in how we view the relationship between law, human behaviour and the environment. How best should we construct regulation so as to incentivise the decarbonisation of economic activity, and the reduction of consumption, within a society whose very foundations seem to rest on carbon usage and increasing consumption?[1] In constructing this regulatory framework, how should the balance be struck between creating regulatory incentives for behaviour that is desirable in order to mitigate or adapt to climate change, and using law to prohibit certain behaviour outright? To what extent, for instance, are human rights approaches useful in building a body of law appropriate to deal with climate change, given that it will be the most vulnerable in society who will be hardest hit by the problem?[2]

In addition to being a stand-alone theme in its own right in this volume, in many ways the climate change challenge represents one – albeit critical – illustration of the second theme identified in this volume as a key overarching challenge in European environmental law at present – *the challenge of integrating environmental concerns into broader areas of law and policy*. Within the EU, the integration of environmental protection requirements into the 'definition and implementation' of all other EU policies has been a legal requirement since the entry into force of the Single European Act in 1987,[3] which obligation is now contained in Article 11 of the Treaty on the Functioning of the European Union (TFEU), as well as in Article 37 of the EU's Charter of Fundamental

---

1 See the contribution of Javier de Cendra de Larragán in Chapter 2 of this book.
2 See the contribution of Alan Boyle in Chapter 3 of this book.
3 A version of the duty was contained in the newly inserted environmental title at Article 130r of the Single European Act (requiring that environmental considerations be 'a component of the Community's other policies'). Its wording was later amended and it was promoted to Part One of the Treaty on the Principles of the Community by the Treaty of Amsterdam. See, further, the contribution of Owen McIntyre in Chapter 6 of this book.

Rights. The integration obligation carries enormous potential implications for a wide range of EU policy areas and, if taken seriously, could transform the way we think about environmental governance and the achievement of environmental (and other) goals.[4] Yet, despite this, the integration obligation's status and practical implications remain unclear, as the contributions in Part II of this volume demonstrate. In reality, in many EU policy areas, environmental requirements continue to receive scant attention. After so many years on the EU's law books,[5] does this show that the integration obligation is, at its heart, unworkable (and therefore of little practical use)? Or is there still potential for resurrecting the obligation to achieve real change in the way that EU law and policy is made and implemented?

If the book's first two themes constitute difficulties raised by the inherent interrelation between all areas of human activity and the environment, its third theme – *the challenge of improving the enforcement of European environmental law* – arises from the fact that the geographical scope of Europe's environment is vast, and the resources available for enforcement limited. Left unenforced, even the most carefully crafted environmental law is of little use, of course. Yet serious shortcomings persist in environmental enforcement across the EU,[6] not least in Ireland,[7] which ranks amongst the worst performers in terms of timely implementation of ECJ judgments finding a failure to comply with environmental obligations.[8] This unsatisfactory situation demands innovation and creativity in the way we look at traditional methods of enforcement of EU law and, in particular, requires that enforcement of EU environmental law by non-state actors be embraced and encouraged as a means of supplementing public (state) enforcement in this field.[9]

1.2 Beyond environmental law: the implications (and benefits) of a governance-focused approach

This volume emphasises not only trends in environmental *law*, but also trends in environmental *governance*. While much has been written about

---

4 See the contributions of Ludwig Krämer, Joe McMahon and Owen McIntyre to the present volume in Chapters 4, 5 and 6, respectively.
5 On the history of the integration principle, see the contributions of Ludwig Krämer and Owen McIntyre to the present volume in Chapters 4 and 6, respectively.
6 See the contributions of Suzanne Kingston and Áine Ryall to the present volume in Chapters 7 and 9, respectively. In 2010, environmental cases constituted 61 of the 619 cases (i.e. almost 10 per cent) lodged before the Court of Justice of the European Union based on causes of action flowing from the TFEU: see *Annual Report of the Court of Justice of the European Union* (Luxembourg: Publications Office of the European Union, 2011), at p. 85.
7 See the contribution of Liam Cashman to the present volume at chapter 8.
8 See, for instance, the Commission's 28th Annual Report on Monitoring the Application of EU Law COM (2011) 588 final, Annex V, which reports that environmental cases constituted eight of the eleven ECJ judgments not yet implemented by Ireland in the period up to 31 December 2010.
9 See the contribution of Joanne Blennerhassett to the present volume in Chapter 10.

European governance more broadly,[10] relatively little attention has been paid (with certain notable exceptions)[11] to European environmental governance as such, despite major changes in the way we conceive of environmental regulation and the nature of the actors involved therein. Given this, it is worth pausing for a moment to recall the ongoing debate about the direction of European governance more generally, and asking where environmental governance fits in to this debate. Can a governance-focused perspective add anything to our analysis of the three selected environmental themes?

1.2.1 *The European governance debate*

To begin, despite the fact that the concept of governance has a long history in the political science literature,[12] its meaning and definition remain contested[13] and often differ depending on the context in which they are discussed.[14] While this is not the place to revisit the debate on such meaning, efforts to define governance often focus on the distinction between law, on the one hand, and governance, on the other, with the former denoting a far narrower and more formal body of rules and norms than the latter.[15] This is exemplified by Keohane and Nye's classic definition of governance as:

---

10 See, for instance, I. Bache and M. Flinders (eds) *Multi-Level Governance* (Oxford: Oxford University Press, 2004); B. Kohler-Koch and B. Rittberger, 'The "Governance Turn" in EU Studies' (2006) 44(1) *Journal of Common Market Studies* 27; T. Börzel, 'European Governance: Negotiation and Competition in the Shadow of Hierarchy' (2010) 48 *Journal of Common Market Studies* 191.

11 See, for instance, A. Weale, G. Pridham, M. Cini, D. Konstadadkopulos, M. Porter and B. Flynn, *Environmental Governance in Europe: An Even Closer Ecological Union?* (Oxford: Oxford University Press, 2000); J. Scott, *Environmental Protection: European Law and Governance* (Oxford: Oxford University Press, 2009); G. Winter (ed.) *Multilevel Governance of Global Environmental Change: Perspectives from Science, Sociology and the Law* (Cambridge: Cambridge University Press, 2006); R. Macrory, *Regulation, Enforcement and Governance in Environmental Law* (Oxford: Hart Publishing, 2010); S. Kingston, 'Developments in EU Law: Environment' (2010) 59 *International & Comparative Law Quarterly* 1129.

12 See, for instance, M. Bevir, *Encyclopedia of Governance* (Thousand Oaks, CA: Sage, 2006).

13 D. Wincott, 'Looking Forward or Harking Back? The Commission and the Reform of Governance in the European Union' (2001) 39(5) *Journal of Common Market Studies* 897; D. Curtin and I. Dekker, 'Good Governance: The Concept and its Application by the European Union' in D. Curtin and R. Wessel (eds), *Good Governance and the European Union: Reflections on Concepts, Institutions and Substance* (Antwerp: Intersentia, 2005), at p. 3.

14 See, for instance, the illustrations given in United Nations Economic and Social Council, *Definition of Basic Concepts and Terminologies in Governance and Public Administration* (Committee of Experts on Public Administration, 2006, E/C.16/2006/4).

15 See the discussions in D. Osborne and T. Gaebler, *Reinventing Government* (Reading, Massachusetts: Addison-Wesley, 1993); J. Pierre and G. Peters, *Governance, Politics and the State* (New York: St. Martin's Press, 2000); J. Pierre, *Debating Governance* (Oxford: Oxford University Press, 2000); H.-P. Bang (ed.) *Governance as Social and Political Communication* (Manchester: Manchester University Press, 2003); C. Harlow, 'Deconstructing Government?' in T. Ginsburg and R. Rabin (eds), *Institutions and Public Law, Comparative Approaches* (New York: P. Lang, 2005).

the processes and institutions, both formal and informal, that guide and restrain the collective activities of a group. Government is the subset that acts with authority and creates formal obligations. Governance need not necessarily be conducted exclusively by governments and the international organizations to which they delegate authority. Private firms, associations of firms, non-governmental organizations (NGOs), associations of NGOs all engage in it ... to create governance.[16]

In this sense, while legal rules refer to rules emanating from formal (government) institutions, typically in a hierarchical context, governance refers to the way in which political, economic and administrative power or authority is exercised at all levels, going beyond the bureaucratic state.[17] An important advantage of employing a governance perspective, therefore, is to give a more complete picture of the actors, norms and processes influencing how power is exercised, whether within a nation-state context or beyond.[18] Thus, the scope of a governance perspective encompasses an appreciation of the influence of non-state actors from the private sector and civil society, in a hierarchical but also a non-hierarchical context. A further significant advantage in the European context, of course, is that a governance perspective is not confined to the nation-state, but may be employed within the context of a society or, indeed, at the regional or global level.[19]

This long-running global dialogue on the meaning and utility of the governance concept has been mirrored by a debate on the nature of European governance, which debate was revisited and revived in the run up to, and following the publication of, the Commission's 2001 White Paper on European Governance.[20]

16 R. Keohane and J. Nye, 'Governance in a Globalising World', reprinted in R. Keohane, *Power and Governance in a Partially Globalised World* (Abingdon: Routledge, 2002) 193, at p. 202.
17 See, for instance, the definition of governance adopted by the United Nations Development Programme, 'the exercise of economic, political and administrative authority to manage a country's affairs at all levels. It comprises the mechanisms, processes and institutions through which citizens and groups articulate their interests, exercise their legal rights, meet their obligations and mediate their differences' (United Nations Development Programme, *Governance for Sustainable Human Development*, New York: UNDP, 1997). See also, the World Bank's definition of governance as the method through which power is exercised in the management of a country's political, economic and social resources for development (*Governance*, Washington, DC: World Bank, 1993).
18 See generally, H.-P. Bang (ed.), *Governance as Social and Political Communication*.
19 For an illustration of the huge literature that has developed on global governance, see, for instance, M. Hewson and T. Sinclair (eds), *Approaches to Global Governance Theory* (Albany: SUNY Press, 1999); A. Ba and M. Hoffmann (eds), *Contending Perspectives on Global Governance: Coherence, Contestation and World Order* (Abingdon: Routledge, 2005).
20 White Paper on European Governance COM (2001) 428 final. See further, Wincott, 'Looking Forward or Harking Back?' and M. Jachtenfuchs, 'The Governance Approach to European Integration' (2001) 39(2) *Journal of Common Market Studies* 245, who defines governance as 'the intentional regulation of social relationships and the underlying conflicts by reliable and durable means and institutions, instead of the direct use of power and violence' or, more simply, 'the ability to make collectively binding decisions' (at p. 246).

The White Paper remains the principal policy document specifically setting out the Commission's vision of European governance. In it, the Commission defines governance in the EU context as 'rules, processes and behaviour that affect the way in which powers are exercised at European level, particularly as regards openness, participation, accountability, effectiveness and coherence'.[21] By focusing on the question of 'how the EU uses the powers given [to it] by its citizens', the White Paper placed the EU institutions at the heart of the European governance debate.[22] At that stage, the goal was to make policy-making more inclusive and accountable, thereby increasing the legitimacy of the EU's policies by reducing alienation between the EU and its citizens (increasing input legitimacy) and enhancing the quality of the output of EU policy-making (increasing output legitimacy),[23] so as to 'connect the EU more closely to its citizens and lead to more effective policies'.[24] In essence, the need to improve the EU's legitimacy may be traced back to the gradual broadening of the EU's aims far beyond the economic goal of achieving the internal market to encompass the fields of competence now covered in the EU Treaties, including social, employment, immigration and, of course, environmental policies. The need for increased legitimacy has become even more pressing since the defeat of the Constitutional Treaty and the reversion to the intergovernmental treaty-making method with the Lisbon Treaty.[25]

In the White Paper's vision, the key to improving governance within Europe centred around five principles: openness; participation; accountability; effectiveness; and coherence.[26] The Lisbon Treaty reaffirms the centrality of these principles by giving them – in some instances for the first time – a constitutional foundation. Thus, many of the Articles contained in the TEU's new title headed 'Provisions on Democratic Principles' reinforce the White Paper's approach,[27] including the Articles on the principles of openness and

---

21 White Paper on European Governance, at p. 8.
22 Contrast, for instance, the Report of the UN Commission on Global Governance, *Our Global Neighborhood* (Oxford: Oxford University Press, 1995), at p. 2.
23 White Paper, on European Governance, at pp. 21–22.
24 White Paper, on European Governance, at p. 8.
25 See M. Tsaktika, 'Claims to Legitimacy: The European Commission between Continuity and Change' (2005) 43 *Journal of Common Market Studies* 193.
26 This vision of good governance may be contrasted with other perspectives on governance, such as those adopted by the OECD, World Bank and the EU Council. See, for instance, the definitions provided by the OECD in *DAC Guidelines and Reference Series Applying Strategic Environmental Assessment: Good Practice Guidance for Development Co-operation* (Paris: OECD, 2006); by the World Bank in its World Governance Indicators project, which reported on six dimensions of governance during the period 1996–2009 (see http://info.worldbank.org/governance/wgi); and by the EU Council of Ministers' resolution on human rights, democracy and development of 28 November 1991 (Bulletin of the European Communities 11/1991; Council Press Release 9555/91).
27 These changes mirrored those that would have followed from the Constitutional Treaty. See Article III–115–122 of the Treaty Establishing a Constitution for Europe OJ 2004 C 310/1.

transparency;[28] the principle of participation;[29] and the principle of accountability.[30] Also notable is Article 7 TFEU, which elevated the principle of coherence and consistency between the EU's actions beyond a mere aim to an obligation ('the Union *shall* ensure consistency between its policies and activities, taking all of its objectives into account and in accordance with the principle of conferral of powers') (emphasis added).[31]

1.2.2 A European concept of environmental governance?

Against this background, a number of questions arise. Are there features distinctive to, or characteristic of, (good) *European* environmental governance and, if so, what can we say these are? And what can the use of an environmental governance perspective add to our analysis of the issues selected for coverage in this volume? At least three points should be made in response to these questions.

1.2.2.1 European environmental governance as multi-level, networked governance

First, governance perspectives have the potential to capture the increasingly *multi-level, networked* nature of decision-making affecting the environment, and the broad range of actors implicated in such decision-making. European governance has, of course, long been conceptualised as multi-level in nature in academic discourse. Very often, such discourse has focused on the variety of levels of formal public institutions and public administrations at play within the European polity – distinguishing, for instance, the supranational (EU) level of institutions and decision-making from the state level, and highlighting the growing role of the (sub-state) regions in EU policy-making.[32] It is evident that such a multi-level analysis is highly appropriate to describe the range of public institutions involved in European environmental governance – whether polities, bureaucracies, or courts. As with other areas of EU law, an appreciation

---

28 See Article 10(3) TEU on open decision-making, Article 11(2) TEU on open and transparent dialogue with representative associations and civil society, and Article 11(3) TEU on consultations with parties concerned.

29 See Article 10(3) TEU on the citizen's right to participate in the democratic life of the Union, Article 11(1) TEU on the expression of views by citizens and representative associations, Article 11(2) TEU on open and transparent dialogue with representative association and civil society, the citizens' initiative in Article 11(4) TEU, and Article 12 TEU enhancing participation of national parliaments.

30 See Article 10(2) TEU on democratic accountability of national Heads of State or government.

31 See also Article 11(3) TEU ('The European Commission shall carry out broad consultations with parties concerned in order to ensure that the Union's actions are coherent and transparent') and the six cross-cutting clauses which encourage or instruct the EU to have regard to particular aims in defining and implementing all of its policies. Of these, Article 11 TFEU (the environmental integration obligation) is worded most strongly. See generally, the contributions in Part II of this volume.

32 See, for instance, L. Hooghe and G. Marks, *Multilevel Governance and European Integration* (Lanham, MD, Rowman & Littlefield, 2001).

of which level (supranational, state, sub-state) should act in a particular instance is governed by the EU's fundamental constitutional principles of attribution of competences (Art. 5(2) TEU), proportionality (Art. 5(4) TEU) and, a principle long core to the EU's approach to environmental governance, subsidiarity (Art. 5(3) TEU).[33] A sensitivity to the multi-level nature of public environmental governance within Europe is evident in many of the contributions to this book, including the chapter by de Cendra de Larragán on climate change (and the application of the subsidiarity and proportionality principles to that issue); the chapters of Krämer, McMahon and McIntyre on the implications of the integration principle (as a principle applying to *all* those defining and implementing the EU's policies, whether at EU, national or sub-national level); and the chapters of Kingston, Cashman and Ryall on enforcement (with public enforcement responsibilities in relation to European environmental law split between the European and national courts, coupled with the European Commission, national authorities and, at international level, the Aarhus Convention Compliance Committee and the European Court of Human Rights).

The fact that international law and norms emanating from international sources are of vital importance in this field adds a further layer of complexity in mapping the multiple levels of European environmental governance. International norms also, of course, form part of (European) public environmental governance, in that they flow from the actions of states or international organisations created by states, as interpreted by (global, regional or national) courts. In part, the importance of such norms is a function of the proliferation of international environmental treaties, and the considerable increase in the volume of international environmental law, particularly in the past 40 years.[34] The EU is often a party to these treaties in its own right, meaning it is bound pursuant to the principle of *pacta sunt servanda*;[35] in other cases, the fact that all or most of its Member States have ratified a treaty may result in the principles contained in that treaty becoming part of EU law.[36] In still other cases, the EU may

---

33 Indeed, the principle of subsidiarity originated in the environmental title of the Single European Act (Art. 130r(4)), and was only subsequently elevated to become a generally applicable principle of Community law with the Treaty of Maastricht (Art. 3b). The principle was derived from German environmental law.

34 See generally, P. Birnie, A. Boyle and C. Redgwell, *International Law and the Environment* (Oxford: Oxford University Press, 2009), ch. 2.

35 See Article 216(2) TFEU. Whether the EU may become a party to a treaty depends: (1) as a matter of international law, on the provisions of the treaty itself, which may or may not allow for an international organisation to become a party; and (2) as a matter of EU law, on the treaty falling within the scope of the EU's external competences (whether exclusive or shared). As the environment constitutes a shared competence between the EU and its Member States (Art. 4(2)(e) TFEU), EU law generally holds that the EU and its Member States should be parties (unless, for instance, the treaty falls within the EU's exclusive competence as set out in Article 3 TFEU, e.g. deals with the conservation of marine biological resources under the common fisheries policy or falls within the *ERTA* doctrine summarised at Article 3(2) TFEU).

36 Insofar as such principles may be held to constitute general principles of EU law, as recognised by the Court of Justice of the EU.

voluntarily decide to implement a treaty into its legal order, despite the fact that it is not formally bound to do so in any sense.[37] In this sense, international environmental regimes flowing from treaties and conventions have become a vital part of the EU's own system of environmental governance, a point emphasised by Boyle's contribution to the present volume in the context of climate change governance. More broadly, the increasing body of non-treaty-based international environmental law, flowing from the gradual development of principles of international environmental law, has also played an important role in the development of European environmental governance.[38] At times, this has led to a fascinating inter-institutional dialogue between international and EU levels of environmental governance. The development of the precautionary principle forms a good example, with EU courts drawing inspiration from international sources in recognising the principle as forming part of EU law, even while it remains a contested principle at the international level.[39]

Aside from treaties with the principal aim of environmental protection, the influence of certain non-environmental sources of international law on the fabric of European environmental governance is undeniable. WTO law is an obvious and much-cited example,[40] and in particular the case-law of the WTO Appellate Body setting out the conditions in which a Contracting Party may validly take unilateral measures restrictive of trade on environmental grounds.[41] Perhaps less obvious, but increasingly important, in this regard is the law of the European Convention on Human Rights (ECHR), with the European Court of Human Rights holding human rights to have been breached in a variety of situations where regulation of environmental risk, enforcement of environmental laws, or access to environmental information has been inadequate.[42] In turn, ECHR law has long influenced the EU's own doctrine of

---

37 As was the case for the CITES convention, for instance.

38 For a discussion of non-treaty-based principles of international environmental law, see G. Winter, 'The Legal Nature of Environmental Principles' in Winter (ed.), *Multilevel Governance of Global Environmental Change*.

39 See, for instance, *ibid.*, at p. 588; N. de Sadeleer, *Environmental Principles: From Political Slogans to Legal Rules* (Oxford: Oxford University Press, 2005). The considerable implications of the difference in approach in relation to the precautionary principle between the EU and (certain) international levels of governance are evident in, for instance, the decision of the WTO Appellate Body in *Beef Growth Hormones* DS 26, DS 48 (finding the EU's ban on the import of US beef containing certain growth hormones to be contrary to WTO law) and of the Panel in *Biotech* DS 291, 292, 293 (finding that there had been undue delay and no adequate risk assessment on the part of the EU in relation to certain biotech products).

40 A rich literature exists on the interrelation between WTO law and the environment. See, for instance, E. Brown Weiss, J. Jackson and N. Bernasconi-Osterwalder (eds), *Reconciling Environment and Trade* (2nd edn, Leiden: Koninklijke Brill, 2008).

41 See, for instance, the well-known *Shrimp/Turtle*, *Beef Growth Hormones* and *Biotech* cases and, generally, C. Tietje, 'Process-related measures and global environmental governance' in Winter (ed.), *Multilevel Governance of Global Environmental Change*.

42 See, for instance, *Lopez Ostra v Spain* (1994) 20 EHRR 277 (breach of Article 8 ECHR); *Guerra v Italy* (1998) 26 EHRR 357 (breach of Article 8 ECHR); *Fadeyeva v Russia* [2005] ECHR 376 (breach of Article 8 ECHR); *Taskin v Turkey* [2006] 42 EHRR 50 (breach of Article 6(1) ECHR).

fundamental rights as developed by the EU courts, and as now reflected in the EU's Charter of Fundamental Rights.[43] More broadly, the ECHR's procedural standards of access to justice, as set out in Article 6 ECHR, have inspired not only EU law, but also the rapidly developing body of law flowing from the UNECE Convention on Access to Information, Public Participation in Decision-Making and Access to Justice in Environmental Matters (the Aarhus Convention).[44] The picture that develops of contemporary public environmental governance within Europe, therefore, is not only multi-level in the vertical sense of ranging from the local to the international, but also consists in parallel governance regimes (EU, ECHR, Aarhus) that co-exist. As Kingston notes in Chapter 7 of this volume, this increasingly results in inter-regime cross-fertilisation of a mutually reinforcing, and highly promising, nature.

As well as focusing on the multiple layers of governance through public institutions (courts, polities, bureaucracies), a multi-level conceptualisation of European environmental governance allows us to encompass broader spheres of governance: namely, governance through civil society and private actors. An initial question is what we mean by 'civil society' in this context. This is not the place for re-running the long-running debate on whether a distinctively *European* civil society can validly be said to exist, as opposed to an amalgamation of national (or indeed local) civil societies.[45] Leaving that discussion aside, if civil society is understood as all non-state actors, it extends not only to those acting otherwise than for profit (whether individuals or NGOs), but also those acting for profit in the marketplace (such as corporations).[46] In this sense, civil society is increasingly involved not only in agenda-setting in environmental matters, but also in norm creation and implementation in this field, whether at local, national, European, transnational or international levels.[47] In the European context, one sees this clearly with the emergence, for instance, of environmental NGOs based in Brussels and elsewhere, active not only in lobbying policy-makers, but also as partners in legislative consultations and as information sources on the level of enforcement of EU environmental law on the ground.[48] Conversely, the trend towards use of market-based instruments, explored further below, is evidence of the increasing importance of

---

43 The ECHR has long been a source of inspiration for the EU courts in establishing the scope of fundamental rights as general principles of EU law: see what is now Article 6(3) TEU.

44 On the link between the ECHR and the Aarhus Convention, see J. Ebbesson, *Access to Justice in Environmental Matters in the EU – Accès à la justice en matière d'environnement dans l'UE* (The Hague: Kluwer, 2002), at p. 15.

45 See, for instance, W. Maloney and J. van Deth, *Civil Society and Governance within Europe: From National to International Linkages* (Cheltenham: Elgar, 2008).

46 See, for instance, J. Keane, *Global Civil Society?* (Cambridge: Cambridge University Press, 2003), pp. 75–88.

47 See further, A. Alkolby, 'Globalising a Green Civil Society: In Search of Conceptual Clarity' in Winter (ed.), *Multilevel Governance of Global Environmental Change*.

48 See, for instance, the member organisations of the European Environmental Bureau, which promotes itself as Europe's largest coalition of grassroots environmental organisations (www.eeb.org).

profit-motivated actors (e.g. corporations) as players in European environmental governance.

This perspective taps into the strong movement towards *participatory* environmental governance in Europe, in contrast to the hierarchical approaches traditionally associated with governing through government.[49] This movement is now epitomised by the principles and techniques of environmental governance set out in the Aarhus Convention, inspired by Principle 10 of the Rio Declaration. As Ebbesson has noted, the Aarhus Convention reflects an 'expansive notion of democracy'[50] that goes beyond standard liberal conceptions whereby private parties should be afforded access to justice only to protect private interests, with public interests being protected primarily by public institutions.[51] In turn, the strong participatory trends in European environmental governance may be viewed as part of a broader trend of reflexive governance within Europe, which Scott defines as the establishment of institutions and processes which enable actors to learn 'not only about policy options, but also about their own interests and preferences'.[52] In the environmental sphere, governance principles such as openness and participation are evident in such long-established legislative instruments as environmental impact assessment and access to environmental information.[53] Yet, as Kingston, Ryall and Blennerhassett emphasise in Chapters 7, 9 and 10 of this volume, despite such rhetoric, this expansive concept of democracy has not yet been realised in environmental matters at EU level, in that access to justice for private parties in direct actions before the EU courts remains restrictive to the point of being almost non-existent where the interest being pursued is purely environmental.

---

49 See further, J.-P. Voss, D. Bauknecht and R. Kemp (eds), *Reflexive Governance for Sustainable Development* (Cheltenham: Elgar, 2006);

50 Ebbesson, *Access to Justice in Environmental Matters in the EU*, at p. 5.

51 Ibid., at p. 4, referencing M. Cappelletti, 'Vindicating the Public Interest through the Courts: A Comparativist's Contribution' in M. Cappelletti and B. Garth (eds) *Access to Justice Vol III: Emerging Issues and Perspectives* (Alphen aan den Rijn: Sijthoff and Noordhof, 1979).

52 See C. Scott, 'How Reflexive is the Governance of Regulation?', paper presented at the Annual Meeting of the Law and Society Association, Berlin, 2007 and O. de Schutter and J. Lenoble, 'Introduction: Institutions Equipped to Learn' in O. de Schutter and J. Lenoble, *Reflexive Governance: Redefining the Public Interest in a Pluralistic World* (Oxford: Hart, 2010). See also, U. Beck, 'The Reinvention of Politics: Towards a Theory of Reflexive Modernisation', in U. Beck, A. Giddens and S. Lash (eds), *Reflexive Modernisation* (Cambridge: Polity Press, 1994).

53 See the current codified version of the EIA Directive, Directive 2011/92/EU of the European Parliament and of the Council of 13 December 2011 on the assessment of the effects of certain public and private projects on the environment OJ 2012 L 26/1 and, in relation to access to environmental information, Directive 2003/4/EC of the European Parliament and of the Council of 28 January 2003 on public access to environmental information OJ 2003 L 41/26 and Regulation (EC) No 1367/2006 of the European Parliament and of the Council of 6 September 2006 on the application of the provisions of the Aarhus Convention on Access to Information, Public Participation in Decision-making and Access to Justice in Environmental Matters to Community institutions and bodies OJ 2006 L 264/13.

1.2.2.2 European environmental governance and novel regulatory techniques

In addition to highlighting the breadth of the range of actors implicated in European environmental decision-making, a governance approach also allows an appreciation of the increasing range of *policy instruments* employed to attain European environmental protection goals in recent years. Thus, a new generation of new environmental policy instruments have been developed to complement traditional techniques of direct, or command-and-control, regulation, which had relied primarily on hierarchical proscriptions by law-makers (such as the imposition of environmental standards, or the banning of environmental hazardous substances) to be enforced by public authorities (agencies or courts). An important element of the new generation of policy instruments is the use of market-based instruments, which use market mechanisms to achieve environmental aims.[54] These instruments reflect the ideological shift that had taken place under Reagan in the US, and Thatcher in the UK, towards neo-liberalism and a belief that free-market values should apply throughout not only economic, but also social, political and environmental life.[55] Such market- or incentive-based environmental regulatory instruments came into vogue in EU environmental policy in the 1990s sparked by a similar rise in interest in the US,[56] and are typically aimed at internalising negative environmental externalities into market actors' decision-making processes, thus bringing the environment 'into the boardroom.'[57] Consistently with the polluter pays principle,[58] this is normally achieved by placing a price on pollution – whether this price is decided upon by the state (in the case of environmental charges and taxes) or by market operators themselves (in the case of tradable permit systems). Other market-based instruments, such as eco-labels and eco-management certificates, work on the basis that voluntary environmentally friendly market activity should be incentivised and encouraged where possible.

While traditional direct regulation remains important within the EU, the use of market-based instruments is being considered in increasingly wide areas of

---

54 See generally, Kingston, *Greening EU Competition Law and Policy* (Cambridge: Cambridge University Press, 2011).
55 See generally, N. Gunningham, 'Environmental Law, Regulation and Governance: Shifting Architectures' (2009) 21(2) *Journal of Environmental Law* 179.
56 See generally, B. Ackerman and R. Stewart, 'Reforming Environmental Law' (1985) 37 *Stanford Law Review* 1333, R. Stewart, 'The Importance of Law and Economics for European Environmental Law' (2002) 2 *Yearbook of European Environmental Law* 1, P. Galizzi, 'Economic Instruments as Tools for the Protection of the International Environment' (1997) *European Environmental Law Review* 155, E. Rehbinder, *Environmental Agreements: A New Instrument of Environmental Policy* (European University Institute, Jean Monnet Chair Paper RSC No 97/45); G. Martin, 'Environnement et concurrence: approche en droit de l'environnement', *Ateliers de la concurrence, Droit de l'environnement et droit de la concurrence*, Direction Général de la Concurrence, de la Consommation de de la Répression des Fraudes (DGCCRF), 6 July 2005.
57 See J. Harman, 'Environmental Regulation in the 21st Century' (2004) 6 *Environmental Law Review* 141, at p. 147.
58 See Article 191(2) TFEU.

EU environmental policy, including areas such as habitat conservation where it was formerly thought inappropriate.[59] The popularity of such instruments is essentially due to their potential for providing an economically efficient, welfare-maximising way of achieving environmental goals, (in principle) allowing sustainable growth while maintaining competitiveness.[60] In contrast to command and control regulation, polluters who can reduce pollution more cheaply than other polluters have an incentive to do so, avoiding traditional problems of time lag and high enforcement costs associated with direct regulation.[61] As such, market-based instruments form an important part of the shift in the architecture of EU environmental governance, from a state-centred approach to a more pluralist harnessing of business and society in pursuit of the EU's environmental aims.[62] Despite certain successes in experiments with newer forms of market-based instruments (e.g. the EU's Emissions Trading Scheme),[63] important questions remain about the limits and capabilities of a market-based approach. De Cendra de Larragán's discussion of the possibility of implementing a Personal Carbon Trading scheme in Chapter 2 of this volume is illuminating in this regard.

1.2.2.3 Testing European environmental governance against the values of the White Paper

A final benefit of a governance-focused approach is that, from a normative perspective, the vision of *European good governance* set out in the White Paper, and to a certain extent constitutionalised by the Lisbon Treaty, can serve as a benchmark against which contemporary European environmental policy may be measured and – potentially – as a roadmap indicating its desired future directions. In the White Paper's vision, attention to, and an improvement in attainment of, the five principles of good governance identified by the Commission in this regard – openness, participation, accountability, effectiveness and coherence – can improve the 'credibility'[64] of the EU's policies, thereby contributing to the overall goal of reducing the sense of disconnect between the EU's work and its citizens and increasing the input and output

---

59 See EFTEC, *The Use of Market-Based Instruments for Biodiversity Protection – the Case of Habitat Banking*, Report of February 2010 for the European Commission, available at http://ec.europa.eu/environment; and the Commission's *Green Paper on Market-Based Instruments for Environment and Related Policy Purposes* COM/2007/0140 final.

60 Gunningham, 'Environmental Law, Regulation and Governance', at p. 185.

61 T. Tietenberg, 'Economic Instruments for Environmental Regulation' (1990) 6(1) *Oxford Review of Economic Policy* 17.

62 See further, A. Jordan, R. Wurzel and A. Zito, 'Policy Instrument Innovation in the European Union: A Realistic Model for International Environmental Governance?' in Winter (ed.), *Multilevel Governance of Global Environmental Change*.

63 See, e.g., D. Ellermann, F. Convery and C. de Perthuis, *Pricing Carbon: The European Union Emissions Trading Scheme* (Cambridge: Cambridge University Press, 2010).

64 White Paper on European Governance, at p. 9.

legitimacy of the EU's policies. While some may be cynical about the feasibility of attaining such a goal, a definite focus on each of these five principles is discernible in the EU's environmental policy in recent years (and indeed was discernible prior to the White Paper's publication).[65] In this sense, environmental policy forms an apt test case in considering the extent to which progress on the White Paper's principles has in fact been achieved.[66] The examples of the principles of openness and participation – both in the EU context and, more broadly, as represented by the Aarhus Convention and the case-law of the European Court of Human Rights – have already been discussed.

The emphasis on policy coherence is similarly immediately visible in the environmental sphere. Indeed, as already noted and as discussed in the contributions in Part II, the White Paper's coherence principle represents a general application of a movement which had been championed as regards environmental policy in the Community's Environmental Action Programmes since the 1970s, and which was subsequently incorporated into the EU treaties in the form of what is now Article 11 TFEU and the aim of sustainable development.[67] In one sense, the environmental policy integration movement can be viewed as a 'particularly ambitious' manifestation of network-based governance, aimed at eschewing the centralised governance previously the norm in EU environmental policy-making.[68] The movement is motivated not only by the inherent interconnectedness of environmental policy with economic and other policy areas, but also by the failure of traditional regulatory approaches to achieve the desired level of environmental protection (i.e. effectiveness concerns).[69] Such emphasis on *external* coherence between environmental and other policy areas has been coupled with an increased emphasis on *internal* coherence of approach within the environmental policy area itself, embodied, for instance, by the EU's Integrated Pollution Prevention and Control Directive, which moves

65 See generally, M. Heldeweg, 'Good Environmental Governance in the EU: Lessons from Work in Progress?' in Curtin and Wessel, *Good Governance*, and A. Jordan, 'The Implementation of EU Environmental Policy: A Policy Problem Without a Political Solution?' (1999) 17(1) *Environment and Planning* 69.

66 This was suggested in the White Paper itself in the case of certain of its principles. See, for instance, White Paper on European Governance, at p. 13.

67 See A. Lenschow, 'Greening the European Union' in A. Lenschow (ed.) *Environmental Policy Integration: Greening Sectoral Policies in Europe* (London: Earthscan Publications, 2002).

68 C. Joerges, 'The Law's Problems with the Governance of the European Market' in C. Joerges and R. Dehousse (eds), *Good Governance in Europe's Integrated Market* (Oxford: Oxford University Press, 2002). See also, S. Hix, 'The Study of the European Union II: The "New Governance" Agenda and Its Rival' (1998) 5(1) *Journal of European Public Policy* 38; A. Schout and A. Jordan, 'Co-ordinated European Governance: Self-Organizing or Centrally Steered?' (2005) 83(1) *Public Administration* 201; A. Schout, A. Jordan and M. Twena, 'From "Old" to "New" Governance in the EU: Explaining a Diagnostic Deficit' (2010) 33(1) *West European Politics* 154, at p. 156; C. Sabel and J. Zeitlin, *Experimentalist Governance in the European Union* (Oxford: Oxford University Press, 2010).

69 A. Jordan, 'The Implementation of EU Environmental Policy: A Policy Problem Without a Political Solution?' (1999) 17(1) *Environment and Planning* 69.

away from a sectoral approach to controlling pollution to a more horizontal, holistic one.[70]

If the White Paper's coherence principle has proven exceptionally difficult to achieve in the environmental sphere, so too has its principle of effectiveness, described in the White Paper as the ability to deliver 'what is needed on the basis of clear objectives, and evaluation of future impact and where available, of past experience'.[71] While many would view this element of good governance as the litmus test of the success (or otherwise) of an environmental policy, if delivering 'what is needed' is understood as achieving an improvement, or stabilisation, in the quality of the European environment, EU environmental policy continues to fail markedly. Thus, the European Commission's 2009 Annual Environmental Policy Review reports that, of the 33 environmental indicators it employs (broken down into the fields of: climate change and energy, nature and biodiversity; environment and health; and natural resources and waste), only four demonstrated a 'good performance', with performance in relation to the other 29 indicators being either average or poor.[72] Similarly, in the EEA's report *The European Environment: State and Outlook 2010*, the EU-27 was reported to be 'on track' for meeting its overall targets in only three of the 16 areas covered by the EU's environmental objectives.[73]

Ultimately, many if not all of the current environmental governance trends within the EU may be viewed as attempts to increase the effectiveness of environmental policy. This includes the increase in use of flexible, decentralised governance mechanisms such as the broadening in the range of policy instruments employed (as discussed above), the increased use of framework directives setting out the broad principles applicable in a particular area,[74] and the experimentation with co-regulatory techniques in some spheres (albeit not always successfully).[75] A desire to increase effectiveness clearly lies also at the heart of the movements to improve the enforcement of EU environmental

---

70 Directive 2008/1/EC of the European Parliament and of the Council of 15 January 2008 concerning integrated pollution prevention and control OJ 2008 L 24/8.

71 White Paper on European Governance, at p. 10.

72 As the most recent review available at the time of writing. Commission Staff Working Document, 2009 Environmental Policy Review (Part 2), SEC (2010) 975 final, at p. 10.

73 *The European Environment: State and Outlook 2010* (Copenhagen: EEA, 2010), at pp. 18–19.

74 See, for instance, Directive 2000/60/EC of the European Parliament and of the Council of 23 October 2000 establishing a framework for Community action in the field of water policy OJ 2000 L 327/1; Council Directive 96/62/EC of 27 September 1996 on ambient air quality assessment and management OJ 1996 L 296/55; Directive 2008/98/EC of the European Parliament and of the Council of 19 November 2008 on waste and repealing certain Directives OJ 2008 L 312/3.

75 Co-regulatory environmental governance is relatively common in certain Member States (for instance, the Netherlands, Belgium and Denmark), but is not at all common in others. At EU level, co-regulatory techniques have not been employed frequently, and have sometimes failed, e.g. in the case of regulation of passenger vehicle emissions, where a voluntary agreement between vehicle manufacturers was replaced by legislation in 2009. See generally, Kingston, *Greening EU Competition Law and Policy*.

law, discussed in Part III of this volume. Indeed, the EU's drive to be a global leader in environmental policy, whether by adopting a leadership role in negotiations for multilateral environmental agreements or by adopting the innovative regulatory techniques described above, may also be viewed as an attempt to increase the influence and effectiveness of its own environmental rules.[76]

In relation to the principle of accountability, however, environmental policy within Europe continues to exhibit major weaknesses, as Ryall and Kingston explore in their contributions to this volume. Ironically, in some cases such weaknesses have been exacerbated by efforts to achieve improvements in other areas of environmental governance. For instance, a shift towards the use of market-based, economic instruments in European environmental policy may mean that, without careful regulatory supervision, power to decide on the proper state of the European environment is shifted into the hands of unaccountable market actors lacking democratic legitimacy.[77] Similarly, the continued significant restrictions on access to justice in environmental matters at EU level and in many Member States, as discussed in each of the contributions in Part III of this volume, raise evident accountability concerns.

1.3 Contents of the book

The contributions to this volume highlight the extent to which the above-mentioned trends in European environmental governance may be observed, and the extent to which European good governance principles are respected, within three important themes of European environmental law at present.

Beginning with Part I, on the climate change challenge, de Cendra de Larragán's contribution, 'Linking Planetary Boundaries and Overconsumption by Individuals: a New Frontier for (EU Climate) Law?', considers the difficult question of the role that law can play in bringing about the changes in consumer behaviour now accepted to be necessary in order to combat climate change. In tackling this question, de Cendra de Larragán focuses particularly on the nature of overconsumption and the challenges it raises, viewed from normative, scientific and economic perspectives. Drawing on varied and interdisciplinary sources, he considers the arguments why law should be entitled to impose limits on human consumption, and arguments against that position, tackling in the process fundamental issues about the legitimacy of (environmental) law to impose limits on individual freedom. He concludes by considering the potential of personal carbon trading as a mechanism for imposing limits on consumption at EU or national levels.

---

76 See generally, E. Vanden Brande 'Green Civilian Power Europe?' in J. Orbie (ed.), *Europe's Global Role: External Policies of the European Union* (Farnham: Ashgate, 2008).

77 See, for instance, the example of the experiment with voluntary agreements and co-regulation in the field of emissions from passenger vehicles, discussed in Kingston, *Greening EU Competition Law and Policy*, at ch. 2.

Boyle's contribution, 'The Challenge of Climate Change: International Law Perspectives', critically analyses the potential of the current international legal framework to deal effectively with the problem of climate change. In so doing, Boyle discusses the methods and achievements of the regime established by the United Nations Framework Convention on Climate Change (UNFCCC), focusing particularly on the Kyoto Protocol's impact on greenhouse gas emissions and the changes brought about by the Copenhagen, Cancún and Durban agreements. He moves on to discuss the possibility of employing other instruments of international law – namely, international human rights law, the international law of the sea, and international trade law – to deal with the climate change issue. Ultimately, however, Boyle concludes that there is only limited scope for using such alternative legal instruments, which do not overall constitute a useful substitute for (political) negotiations.

Part II's contributions deal with the challenge of integrating environmental protection requirements into other policy areas, in implementation of the principle of coherence as a principle of European good governance.

In his contribution, 'Giving a Voice to the Environment by Challenging the Practice of Integrating Environmental Requirements into other EU Policies', Krämer takes a close look at the integration imperative contained in Article 11 TFEU, examining in detail its history, meaning and implications, as well as the implications of Article 37 of the EU Charter of Fundamental Rights in this area. Observing that the integration requirement is an objective and not a principle of EU law, he concludes, *inter alia*, that while Article 7 TFEU requires that all EU objectives be taken into account in the pursuance of EU policies, the Treaty demands that particular attention be given to the pursuit of a high level of protection of, and an improvement of the quality of, the environment. Further, Krämer notes, reading the fundamental right of the public of access to environmental information together with the obligation flowing from Article 37 of the Charter for the EU administration means that citizens have a right to be informed if and how the EU institutions ensure, in their policies and in their individual measures, that a high level of protection and an improvement of the quality of the environment is achieved, which right is fundamental if the integration imperative is (finally) to be operationalised in practice.

McMahon's contribution, 'The CAP in 2020: Vision or Hindsight?', focuses on what is a crucial element of the integration challenge in practice: the challenge of integrating environmental protection requirements into the EU's Common Agricultural Policy (CAP). With the future direction of the CAP largely uncertain at present, he offers a critical assessment of each of the three options for reform of the CAP in order to equip this policy for the period up to 2020, paying particular attention to the environmental implications of each of these options. In relation to the first option – limited adjustment of the current CAP – he concludes that the potential of the first option to achieve reform and refocus the CAP is doubtful. McMahon is more hopeful in relation to the second option, which would offer greater integration between the EU's agricultural and environmental policies by, *inter alia*, linking the single farm payment with the provision of environmental public goods (although the precise balance between environmental and other requirements will, he notes, be crucial). In contrast, the third option, which is the most radical under consideration, would involve the phasing-out of existing direct payments and the abolition of all market measures, with limited payments for the provision of environmental public goods and specific natural constraints. However, he concludes that this option is unlikely to be politically feasible, as application of the polluter pays principle 'would represent a sea-change in agriculture, which up to now has used the pay-the-polluter principle'.

In 'The Integration Challenge: Integrating Environmental Concerns into other EU Policies', McIntyre continues the debate about the meaning and implications of the integration principle, offering a thoughtful discussion of the contributions of Krämer and McMahon in this regard. While acknowledging that the proliferation of cross-cutting integration principles in the TFEU following the Lisbon Treaty has raised new uncertainties about the priority accorded to, and justiciability of, the principle of environmental integration, McIntyre recalls three distinct functions of Article 11 TFEU: an 'enabling function', whereby the provision extends the limits of the Union's legal competences as governed by the Treaties; a 'guidance function', requiring EU law to be interpreted in the light of the TFEU's environmental aims; and a (limited) function as a ground of judicial review of the validity of EU measures which fail to comply with, or at least take full account of, the essential environmental requirements of EU environmental policy. McIntyre concludes by welcoming Krämer's interpretation of Article 11 TFEU as requiring that information be provided to the public on the steps taken to ensure integration of environmental factors into decision-making in other related policy areas.

Part III's contributions move on to consider the challenge of improving the enforcement of European environmental law. Kingston's contribution, 'Mind the Gap: Difficulties in Enforcement and the Continuing Unfulfilled Promise of EU Environmental Law', highlights some persistent weaknesses of the increasingly network-based, multi-level system of enforcing EU environmental law, considering each of the three 'pillars' of environmental enforcement: the Commission, national authorities and private parties. As regards the Commission, she evaluates the impact of the recent emphasis within the Commission on prioritisation of certain types of (environmental) infringement cases, together with the institution of the EU Pilot scheme whereby Member State authorities may become involved at an early stage in responding to complaints made to the Commission. As regards national authorities, she considers the issue of harmonisation of environmental penalties and inspections, and the continued resistance in many Member States to harmonised environmental inspection standards in many fields. As regards private parties, she discusses the continued serious difficulties with accessing the EU courts in environmental cases and the significance of the Aarhus Convention in this regard, contrasting the EU courts' reluctance to countenance change in this respect with their innovative and pro-active approach to broadening access to environmental justice before national courts.

In his contribution, 'Commission Enforcement of EU Environmental Legislation in Ireland – a 20 Year Retrospective', Cashman examines the issue of enforcement of EU environmental law in the context of a Member State which has long been a laggard in this field: Ireland. In evaluating the history of EU environmental enforcement in this jurisdiction, Cashman analyses the Commission's efforts to address the particular difficulties underlying Ireland's enforcement failures, including the evolution from an *ad hoc* to a more strategic approach to enforcement. Ultimately, he observes, such failures may in part be attributed to embedded social phenomena – in Ireland's case, a 'utilitarian orthodoxy' meaning a 'perception of the landscape as a blank, a-historical canvas whose value could only be realised through development (i.e. building)'. Ireland's case, therefore, offers a good illustration of the reality that, in order to be effective, (Commission and civil) enforcement strategies must be tailored to the specific cultural difficulties at play in each Member State.

Ryall's contribution, 'Delivering the Rule of Environmental Law in Ireland: Where Do We Go From Here?', takes a sober look at the state of implementation and enforcement of environmental law in Ireland. Ryall observes that, notwithstanding significant developments in the law in recent years, a substantial implementation deficit persists and the quality of the environment remains under constant threat. This state of affairs is, she concludes, the result of a lack of political will to strengthen legal and other mechanisms to promote compliance, together with a parallel failure to resource the enforcement effort adequately. In discussing the particular challenges posed for the rule of environmental law in Ireland, Ryall considers the implications of the Aarhus Convention, Ireland's response to EU access to justice obligations, and current EU and international developments with the potential to improve matters into the future. While these developments provide cause for some optimism, Ryall emphasises that genuine improvement in environmental enforcement in Ireland demands stronger environmental leadership from government and a more proactive stance on the part of the judiciary.

Finally, Blennerhassett's contribution, 'Environmental Enforcement in Ireland – the Need to get a Piece of the Multi-Party Action', examines the prospects for environmental mass harm redress in Ireland, a common law jurisdiction that does not yet have an effective mechanism for multi-party litigation. This is despite recommendations by the Irish Law Reform Commission for the introduction of a new litigation procedure in the form of a multi-party action. She examines the alternative methods of litigation that have been used by courts in cases where a multi-party action mechanism would have had an obvious role. The implications of this approach for access to justice in Ireland are evaluated and discussed in light of the Law Reform Commission Report recommendations. In conclusion, Blennerhassett evaluates what the future may hold for multi-party litigation and access to environmental justice in light of domestic, European and international developments in this area.

Part I

The climate change challenge

2 Linking planetary boundaries and overconsumption by individuals

A new frontier for (EU climate) law?

Javier de Cendra de Larragán

2.1 Introduction

It is widely accepted that in order to avert dangerous climate change, both producers and consumers need to change their behaviour, and need to do it relatively fast.[1] What is much more controversial is what part law should, or could, play in bringing about such change in behaviour, particularly in relation to consumers, and the issue has not received sufficient attention in the literature.[2] This chapter seeks to add modestly to the discussion.

In the last 40 years or so, environmental law has mainly focused on producers of goods and services to encourage them to reduce pollution and waste.[3] But law has been more timid in dealing with the environmentally damaging behaviour of consumers, even if their contribution to environmental pollution and degradation has been increasing steadily.[4] The preferred approach has been to persuade consumers to adopt more environmentally friendly lifestyles. Lifestyles have been defined generally as 'the way in which a person lives'[5] or as 'a way of life or style of living that reflects the attitudes and values of a person or group'.[6] This goal has been pursued mainly through 'soft' measures that provide information, education and (economic) incentives to change behaviour and lifestyles. A particularly illuminating example is waste law and policy. Waste legislation is believed to have been extremely successful in

---

1 See, for instance, N. Stern, *The Economics of Climate Change: The Stern Review* (Cambridge: Cambridge University Press, 2007).

2 See most recently, K. F. Kuh, 'Capturing Individual Harms' (2011) 35 *Harvard Environmental Law Review* 156.

3 For a detailed description and analysis of EU waste law, see G. Van Calster, *Handbook of EU Waste Law* (Oxford: Oxford University Press, 2007).

4 K. F. Kuh, 'Capturing Individual Harms' (2011) 35 *Harvard Environmental Law Review* 156.

5 The Oxford Dictionary online defines lifestyle as 'the way in which a person lives'. Moreover, it notes that the term can be used as a modifier 'denoting advertising or products designed to appeal to a consumer by association with a desirable lifestyle'. See http://oxforddictionaries.com/definition/lifestyle.

6 www.thefreedictionary.com/lifestyle. The term has sometimes been criticized as voguish and superficial, perhaps because it appears to elevate habits of consumption, dress, and recreation to categories in a system of social classification.

achieving its goals across the EU. For instance, it seems that waste law in the UK has led to a decrease in the total volume of waste generated by households that goes to landfills, thanks to a combination of EU waste legislation and UK waste policies.[7] In Germany and the Netherlands, municipal waste generation fell during the 1990s. However, even waste law does not impose upon consumers any limits on the amount of waste they generate, and the fact is that the total volume of waste within the EU continues to increase.[8] EU waste policy has sought to reverse this trend by focusing on prevention and a shift to more sustainable consumption patterns, seemingly following the mantra that persuasion is superior to coercion.[9] The logical corollary is an increasing focus in the legal literature on the findings of social science research in human behaviour in order to help design more effective policies,[10] which has started to permeate legislation.[11]

These developments within environmental law need to be placed within the context of other non-legal literature exploring the scale and urgency of current environmental problems and their root (social, economic, political) causes. First, scientific literature exploring current environmental problems increasingly resorts to the idea of limits in the carrying capacity of the earth that, if surpassed, will negatively affect the capacity of societies to thrive.[12] Second, scholars studying the link between behavioural changes at individual level and the broader 'milieu' within which those changes take place often reach the conclusion that consumers are 'locked into' many environmentally damaging behaviours that they often cannot change, even if they really want to (though often they might not want to at all);[13] present societal structures in Western countries are committed to levels of production and consumption that are essentially unsustainable, and in the absence of sweeping structural changes, discrete changes in behaviour will be unable to revert current trends.[14] Third, although some legal literature has acknowledged the limits of persuasion, this insight has not been sufficiently pursued, often taking for

7 See Market & Business Development, 'UK Waste Management Market Development Report', February 2011.

8 See European Commission information at http://ec.europa.eu/environment/waste/index.htm.

9 M. Babcock, 'Assuming Personal Responsibility for Improving the Environment: Moving Toward a New Environmental Norm' (2009) 33(1) *Harvard Environmental Law Review* 117.

10 D. Rhode and L. Ross, 'Environmental Values and Behaviors: Strategies to Encourage Public Support for Initiatives to Combat Global Warming' (2008) 26 *Vanderbilt Environmental Law Journal* 161.

11 The case of the UK is well known, where a new cabinet office called Behavioral Insights Team (BIT) has been created by the current government to apply insights from behavioral sciences to public policies. www.cabinetoffice.gov.uk/resource-library/applying-behavioural-insight-health (last accessed 21 July 2011).

12 See, for instance, J. Rockström, W. Steffen, et al., 'Planetary Boundaries: Exploring the Safe Operating Space for Humanity' (2009) 14(2) *Ecology and Society* 32.

13 C. Sanne, 'Willing Consumers – or Locked-in? Policies for a Sustainable Consumption' (2002) 42 *Ecological Economics* 273.

14 T. Jackson, *Prosperity without Growth – Economics for a Finite Planet* (London: Earthscan, 2009).

granted that imposing restrictions upon consumers would be too intrusive and difficult to enforce.[15]

A consistent and coherent legal approach must consider all these literatures holistically if it is to yield insights into future regulatory frameworks for environmental protection. This chapter will attempt to do so by exploring the quintessentially modern notion of overconsumption and the perceived reluctance of law-makers to address it through legally binding means for the sake of environmental protection. The goal is to better understand both the notion of overconsumption and legislators' attitudes (in Western countries) towards it. The current state of affairs suggests a strong tension between, on the one hand, the duty of policy-makers to protect the (global) environment by imposing legally binding obligations upon consumers if necessary and, on the other hand, the perceived obligation of governments to respect the freedom of choice of consumers. This tension raises many interesting questions for the current dominant approach of (environmental) law towards consumers. These questions concern the origin of those tensions and the rationality of the current solutions, the sources and extent of law's potential legitimacy to limit consumer choice; the possible role and functions of (certain) legal principles in guiding legislative action; the extension, conditions and shape of legal interventions addressing consumers; and their relation with legislative measures on other sectors of the economy.

The chapter is structured as follows: the second section explores the nature of overconsumption and of its links with climate change. The third section explores in greater depth the different dimensions of overconsumption and the potential responsibility of consumers. The fourth section explores the nature of and justification for the responses that law has given to the problem of overconsumption of natural resources, and reflects on the justifiability of those responses. The fifth section briefly examines one possible instrument that law could make use of to address overconsumption, namely personal carbon trading. This tool is assessed against the findings obtained in the previous section regarding the conditions shaping the legitimacy of law in addressing overconsumption by individuals. The final section offers some conclusions.

2.2 The challenges arising from overconsumption: a portrait

The European Commissioner for the Environment, Mr Janez Potočnik, speaking in the context of the preparatory works of the Earth Summit 2012, expressed himself as follows:

---

15 An exception is K. F. Kuh, 'Capturing Individual Harms' (2011) 35 *Harvard Environmental Law Review* 156. This author explores the idea that legal mandates to reduce consumption might work better at local rather than at federal level.

The biggest challenge we are facing this century is essentially this: how can we live and prosper together in this planet – within the constraints of what one earth can provide? How, by the year 2050, do we ensure continued economic growth, eradicate poverty and feed 9 billion people without continuing and exacerbating current patterns of environmental degradation and resource depletion? We all know business as usual is not an option. But how do we move away from our usual business – and how do we do it quickly enough?[16]

One key idea hidden within the words of the Commissioner is that of overconsumption of natural resources. This can be best understood with an example: if in 1969 the entire world population had adopted the UK's consumption patterns prevailing at that time, one planet's worth of resources would have been required to satisfy global consumption. 40 years later, we would need 3.1 earth planets.[17] Put in another way, the world has, approximately from 1990 onwards, started a period of 'ecological debt'.[18] This term is often used to describe the consumption of resources from within an ecosystem that exceeds the system's regenerative capacity, where system can be understood as the entire earth.[19] It is closely related to that of 'biophysical environmental subsystems', otherwise termed 'planetary boundaries'.[20] These planetary boundaries collectively define a safe operating space for humanity where social and economic development does not create lasting and catastrophic environmental change. Some authors have suggested that, out of the nine planetary boundaries identified, three have already been exceeded, four are approaching their limit and for the remaining two there is not enough data to provide a clear diagnosis.[21] This could result, according to many natural scientists, in more ecological volatility and potentially disastrous consequences for humankind.

The European Commission has seemingly accepted these ideas, along the lines of Mr Potočnik's thinking:

16 Janez Potočnik, European Commissioner for the Environment, 26th UNEP Governing Council – Global Ministerial Environmental Forum, Nairobi, 22 February 2011.

17 New Economics Foundation, *The Consumption Explosion – The Third UK Interdependence Report* (London: New Economics Foundation, 2011), p. 60.

18 Ibid.

19 The ecological debt can be roughly calculated with a tool known as the ecological footprint, which estimates the rate at which human societies are depleting natural resources. Year by year, the day on which the world is starting to become in ecological debt arrives earlier, and the economic recession has not had any substantial impact on this (something like one day in 2010).

20 The concept of planetary boundaries derives from that of thresholds. While thresholds are non-linear transitions in the functioning of coupled human–environmental systems – e.g. the collapse of the termohaline ocean circulation – boundaries are human-determined values of the control variable set at a safe distance from dangerous levels or thresholds. See J. Rockström et al., 'Planetary Boundaries: Exploring the Safe Operating Space for Humanity' (2009) 14(2) *Ecology and Society* 32. See also J. Rockström et al., 'A Safe Operating Space for Humanity' (2009) 461 *Nature* 472.

21 Ibid.

Global demand for natural resources is growing fast, and will continue to increase due to the growth of population, which is expected to reach 9 billion people by 2050. Measured by the ecological footprint, it is estimated that this would be 30% more than the planet can sustain in the long term.[22]

Although this holistic approach to the exploitation of earth resources is important, this chapter will only focus on one boundary: that is, the capacity of the atmosphere to absorb greenhouse gas emissions. Canadell and colleagues have shown that 65 per cent of the rise in greenhouse gas emissions since 1970 is directly linked to the growth of the global economy.[23] Moreover, they note that many future scenarios used by policy-makers for the twenty-first century assume continued economic growth in at least one scenario. Indeed, as the Potočnik quote above suggests, a key dilemma facing society is whether continued economic growth is possible without exceeding planetary boundaries. Of course, this raises the question of how economic growth is understood, since the current models of economic growth are inevitably and directly linked to growth in carbon emissions.[24] Indeed, with current patterns of economic growth, the explosion of energy consumption in developed countries has meant that the average ecological footprint per person in high-income countries is almost six times larger on average than in low-income countries. From this overview we can conclude that not only is science increasingly able to locate planetary boundaries, but also that there is a deeply normative component embedded in the framing of, and the response to, the project of transitioning towards a human society that lives within the planetary boundaries. Steffen, Rockström and Costanza have suggested that while the concept of planetary boundaries suggests a threshold that humanity should not trespass, it does not say anything about how societies should respond to it:

> The planetary boundaries approach doesn't say anything explicit about resource use, affluence, or human population size. These are part of the trade-offs that allow humanity to continue to pursue increased well-being. The boundaries simply define the regions of global environment space that, if human activities push the Earth system into that space, would lead to unacceptably deleterious consequences for humanity as a whole. Because the planetary boundaries approach says nothing about the distribution of affluence and technologies among the human population, a "fortress world," in which there are huge differences in the distribution of wealth,

22 Communication from the Commission, 'Mainstreaming Sustainable Development into EU Policies: 2009 Review of the European Union Strategy for Sustainable Development' COM (2009) 400 Final, at p. 7.

23 Canadell et al., 'Contributions to Accelerating Atmospheric CO2 Growth from Economic Activity, Carbon Intensity, and Efficiency of Natural Sinks' (2007) *PNAS* 104(47) 18866, at p. 18868.

24 Some have suggested that indefinite growth is not only impossible but is also conceptually defective in the face of finite natural resources. See A. Simms, V. Johnson, et al., *Growth Isn't Possible: Why We Need a New Economic Direction* (London: New Economics Foundation, 2010), p. 148.

and a much more egalitarian world, with more equitable socioeconomic systems, could equally well satisfy the boundary conditions. These two socioeconomic states, however, would deliver vastly different outcomes for human well-being. Thus, remaining within the planetary boundaries is a necessary – but not sufficient – condition for a bright future for humanity.[25]

Accordingly, it is not only the position of the boundary which is a normative judgment, but also the distribution of the remaining ecological space. The ethical and moral challenges are inescapable.[26] The question is what these challenges mean for law's approach to citizens as consumers. The next section focuses therefore on overconsumption as individual behaviour.

2.3 A brief exploration of the notion of overconsumption by individuals

2.3.1 *What is overconsumption? Different approaches to the concept*

While the previous section has addressed the problem of overconsumption of natural resources by way of overview, this section focuses on overconsumption as an *excessive* consumption of goods and services by individual human beings.

2.3.1.1 *A normative approach*

The normative approach to overconsumption is understood as referring to types and quantities of goods and services that exceed some level perceived by the speaker as constituting 'enough'.[27] From this perspective, overconsumption is considered to be an immoral behaviour, a particular manifestation of greed or gluttony, with negative consequences for the individual and for society. This approach has been particularly explored from religious and philosophical perspectives and links directly with understandings of what constitutes a good life.[28] As Pieper explains, the virtue of temperance is that which allows us to cherish and enjoy the good things of life while respecting natural limits. Temperance in fact does not diminish but actually heightens the pleasure we

---

25 W. Steffen, J. Rockström and R. Costanza, 'How Defining Planetary Boundaries Can Transform Our Approach to Growth' (2011) 2(3) *Solutions*, available at www.thesolutionsjournal.com/node/935.

26 But this is not all. As these authors point out, there are, in addition, massive challenges for global governance that challenge the core of the concept of national sovereignty in the exploitation of natural resources. However, this chapter will not focus on the governance challenges.

27 See, for instance, J. Swearengen and E. Woodhouse, 'Overconsumption: An Ethical Dilemma for Christian Engineers' (2002) 54(2) *Perspectives on Science and Christian Faith* 80.

28 See, for instance, C. Murphy, 'The Good Life from a Catholic Perspective: The Challenge of Consumption', at www.usccb.org/issues-and-action/human-life-and-dignity/global-issues/the-good-life-from-a-catholic-perspective-challenge-of-consumption.cfm (United States Conference of Catholic Bishops).

take in living by freeing us from a joyless compulsiveness and dependence.[29] As it should become clear, this normative approach is, however, very controversial because determining when enough is 'enough' is widely seen as a highly subjective exercise.[30]

Another, related attempt to draw the line between a sufficient and an excessive level of consumption has been made by seeking empirically to probe the assumed links between consumption levels and happiness within Western societies[31] by linking data on consumption levels with reported levels of quality of life and happiness.[32] A general finding is that while there is a direct correlation between quality of life and energy consumption at low levels of consumption, such correlation quickly breaks down as energy consumption levels rise. On this approach, the view that the main goal of public policy is to promote happiness measures to limit overconsumption, e.g. through taxation and labour policies, would appear to be justified.[33]

2.3.1.2 A scientific approach

As seen above, the scientific approach tries to estimate the aggregate level of consumption of natural resources that exceeds planetary boundaries. Accordingly, 'enough' can be defined as a level of (aggregate) consumption that ensures that the carrying capacity of the earth (or the planetary boundaries) is not exceeded. The possibility to estimate individual shares of use of remaining ecological space provides a robust starting point for an ethical discussion on how to share the remaining ecological space. However, it is almost impossible, in our highly complex and globalised economy, to disaggregate and attribute the consumption of natural resources to individual consumers. Moreover, concepts such as ecological footprint are still loaded with uncertainty and therefore should be handled with care when seeking to determine the precise contribution of each citizen to the global problem. Thus notwithstanding, by shifting the

---

29 J. Pieper, *The Four Cardinal Virtues: Prudence, Justice, Fortitude, Temperance* (Notre Dame, IN: Harcourt, Brace & World, 1966).

30 And, moreover, one often associated with a religious mindset. E.F. Schumacher, in his most influential book, *Small is Beautiful: Economics as if People Mattered* (London: Blond & Briggs, 1973), contrasts the consumerist way of life which multiplies human wants with the simple life whose aim is to achieve maximum well-being with the minimum use of the earth's resources. The 'logic of production' that demands more and more growth in consumption is a formula for disaster, he argues. 'Out of the whole Christian tradition,' Schumacher concludes, 'there is perhaps no body of teaching which is more relevant and appropriate to the modern predicament than the marvelously subtle and realistic doctrines of the Four Cardinal Virtues' and in particular temperance that means knowing when 'enough is enough'.

31 P. Brown and L. Cameron, 'What Can be Done to Reduce Overconsumption?' (2000) 32 *Ecological Economics* 27.

32 New Economics Foundation, *The Consumption Explosion*, p. 60.

33 See, for instance, B. Gruzalski, 'Mitigating the Consumption of the US Living Standard' in W. Aikin and J. Haldane (eds), *Philosophy and Its Public Role: Essays in Ethics, Politics, Society and Culture* (Exeter: Imprint Academic, 2004), p. 135.

discussion from consumption of products and services to natural resources, and by linking natural resources to planetary boundaries, the scientific approach adds a new crucial dimension to the concept of overconsumption. Indeed, a veneer of objectivity is added to the normatively loaded concept. The implications of this for legal purposes can be profound, as will be argued below. This objectivity may not ease the ethical discussion on burden sharing; on the contrary, it can make it more controversial, since by providing factual data on the contributions and therefore responsibilities of states and individuals to the problem it sharpens the object of the dispute. It also provides an aura of legitimacy to scientists to derive normative implications from scientific findings. For instance, Jacqueline McGlade has noted that, in order to achieve global sustainability not only deep changes in production and consumption processes are required, but also absolute reductions in levels of per capita consumption, and all of this in a more equitable context. Otherwise it is simply not possible to ensure that all human beings have 'enough' with the resources provided by 'one earth'.[34] Clearly, these are moral and ethical questions that, due to their relevance for the common good, demand a legal response.

2.3.1.3 An economic approach

The traditional approach to the notion of overconsumption springs from the Hardinean 'tragedy of the commons'. According to Hardin, many consumers, each one of them acting in its own rational interest, will consume from the common pool resource to the point where that resource is depleted. Overconsumption could be defined as any level of consumption that does not maximise social welfare, i.e. because negative externalities have not been sufficiently internalised. Traditional regulatory solutions proposed by economists include allocating property rights or putting in place Pigouvian taxes. The difficulty in this model lies in determining the 'optimal' level of pollution or consumption, and a critical issue is the degree of perceived substitutability between natural and man-made capital. Neoclassical economics tends to assume a high level of substitutability, but other schools such as ecological economics consider that the level has to be much lower. For ecological economists, the economy is a subset of human activity, itself limited by the available ecological space.[35] The economy cannot carry on indefinitely while ignoring these restraints, because it will eventually reach its physical limits and will collapse. This starting point allows the problematisation of the central concept of neoclassical economics: growth. If current global growth trends are unsustainable,

---

34 J. McGlade, 'How Many Earths?' available at www.unep.org/ourplanet/imgversn/154/mcglade.html (last accessed 20 May 2011).

35 For one of the founding documents of this movement, see H. Daly and J. Cobb, *For the Common Good: Redirecting the Economy Toward Community, the Environment, and a Sustainable Future* (Boston: Beacon Press, 1989).

then reversing them requires redefining growth,[36] which necessarily requires 'deep' behavioural changes – as opposed to the 'soft' changes in lifestyle mentioned above. This view acknowledges the profound challenges that arise for governments, producers and consumers stemming from the need to revise entirely their understandings of human flourishing, the rights of future generations and the relationship of humans with the natural world.[37] It is to these changes that the words of Mr. Potočnik quoted above seem to allude, which bring to the fore the ethical and normative implications of policy responses.

2.3.2 Potential causes of overconsumption by individuals

It has been suggested that overconsumption is a syndrome of a deeper problem, partly caused by the very makings of our economies. By this view, it is a problem characteristic of capitalist economies, and therefore a relatively recent one.[38] Some of the reasons include the fact that economies of scale need consumers that can consume all production, and advertising businesses work hard to create new (consumer) needs that can be fulfilled with new goods and services.[39] Also, the very design of many of our cities forces us to drive long distances to go to work, do our shopping and seek leisure.[40] Global trade, while having many benefits, also leads to a huge waste of natural resources. For instance, critics of prevailing models of economic growth point out some of the 'bizarre' phenomena that these models lead to. One is termed 'ecologically wasteful trade', exemplified by UK trade patterns (to give a few examples, the UK exports annually 27,000 tonnes of potatoes while importing 22,000 tonnes, and exports 4,000 tonnes of toilet paper only to import back 5,000 tonnes).[41] Further, the structure of the global food chain can account for much of the food waste currently generated. For instance, a report prepared for the Food and Agricultural Organization (FAO) suggests that roughly one-third of food produced for human consumption is lost or wasted globally.[42] Huge amounts of the resources used in food production are used in vain, and huge amounts of waste (i.e. in the form of greenhouse gas emissions) are generated. Food is lost or wasted throughout the entire supply chain, from initial agricultural production

---

36 This notion of redefining growth has been taken up by many government sponsored research programmes and initiatives, and is at the basis of attempts to redefine economic concepts such as GDP.

37 T. Jackson, *Prosperity without Growth – Economics for a Finite Planet* (London: Earthscan, 2009).

38 It is usually considered that overconsumption as currently understood is a phenomenon that arose after the end of the Second World War: ibid.

39 A. Simms, V. Johnson, et al., *Growth Isn't Possible*, p. 148; J. Swearengen and E. Woodhouse, 'Overconsumption: An Ethical Dilemma for Christian Engineers' (2002) 54(2) *Perspectives on Science and Christian Faith* 80.

40 New Economics Foundation, *The Consumption Explosion – The Third UK Interdependence Report* (London: New Economics Foundation, 2011), p. 60.

41 Ibid.

42 J. Gustavsson, C. Cederberg, et al., *Global Food Losses and Food Waste – Extent, Losses and Prevention* (Rome: FAO, 2011), p. 38.

down to final household consumption. In industrialised countries, food can get lost due to 'overproduction' by farmers, demands from supermarkets for high-quality standards (including appearance related), trimming of sub-standard items in the production line to ensure quality, large quantities on display in supermarkets that lead to products reaching the sell-by date before being sold, and consumer attitudes that lead to high food waste. However, while waste exists across the entire chain, the abovementioned FAO report shows that consumer attitudes are the single most important cause.[43] There would seem to be two underlying reasons: first, the system itself encourages waste. The amount of available food per person in retail stores and restaurants has increased during the last decades in both the USA and the EU. A lot of restaurants serve buffets at fixed prices, which encourages people to fill their plates with more food than they can actually eat. Retail stores offer large packages and 'get one free' bargains. Likewise, food manufacturers produce oversized ready to eat meals. Second, consumers 'simply can afford to waste food'.[44] There are many other examples of wasteful overconsumption of this sort. Babcock has gathered evidence showing, for instance, that households in the US discharge as much mercury to wastewater as do all large industrial facilities combined. They also release one-third of the chemicals that form ozone or smog, generate approximately one-third of US greenhouse gas emissions, and consume one-third of total energy consumption.[45] Babcock notes that 'both resource depletion and industrial pollution are ultimately traceable to the individual'.[46]

2.3.3 Exploring the responsibility of consumers for overconsumption

The first reason behind food waste offered in the FAO report has to do with structural considerations: in highly complex and globalised economies, individuals as consumers may, to a substantial extent, lack control over the consumption of natural resources associated with their daily actions. But if consumers cannot avoid performing activities that are highly resource intensive (consuming high greenhouse gas emitting electricity for an individual living in an isolated place where the only source of electricity is an old and inefficient coal power plant, driving to work when there is no other less carbon intensive alternative, etc.), they are not responsible for the deleterious impacts on the environment. By this view, environmental problems are 'structural' problems demanding technocratic solutions.

The second reason looks more particularly at consumer behaviour, but presents some problems. Saying that consumers waste food simply because they can

43 Ibid, p. 4.
44 Ibid, p. 14.
45 M. Babcock, 'Assuming Personal Responsibility for Improving the Environment: Moving Toward a New Environmental Norm' (2009) 33(1) *Harvard Environmental Law Review* 117.
46 *Ibid.*

afford to do it might well be true, but reveals a highly mechanistic approach to human choice. Humans are essentially moral agents so it follows that all human decisions are necessarily backed up at least partially by moral reasons, whether articulated or not. One can then look for different moral theories to justify those choices. For instance, from a utilitarian perspective, people might decide that since food is cheap and abundant, the loss of utility generated by the search for ways to save is not compensated by the utility gained by reduced consumption. Consumers might think that there is something wrong with wasting food, but consider, adopting a consequentialist framework, that their efforts will amount to nothing if others do not do the same. It is also possible that, due to the existence of cognitive barriers, consumers fail to realise the consequences of their acts, hence they do not see anything morally wrong with it. Or it could be that some consumers waste food because even if they try to reduce waste, they fail time and again because of lack of commitment, force of habit, lack of time, or lack of (knowledge of) adequate alternatives. In short, the gamut of possible justifications for food waste is very large indeed. The conclusion could be easily reached that there are as many possible justifications as individuals, and a relativistic and pragmatic attitude is inescapable. In this view, a moral debate about waste is essentially fruitless and should be avoided by policy-makers, which could instead rely upon sophisticated accounts of human behaviour developed within the social sciences to set up strategies that lead to less waste. (For more on this, see below.)

Taken together, these two explanations seem to point to the futility of engaging in moral discussions of individual behaviour within policy and law-making processes. A focus on solutions exclusively based on behavioural science and technology seems to be the only justifiable one. But such a conclusion, as will be discussed more fully below, risks weakening an important claim that law can make: to demand compliance from individuals based on justice.

However, an alternative arises if we focus on another crucial finding of the FAO report. The report concludes that citizens are, by means of their choices as consumers, responsible for at least (a rather large) part of the phenomenon of food waste. After discounting issues such as the structure of the food chain, the behaviour of food businesses, including their marketing and pricing strategies, and even issues having to do with access to shopping malls or food markets, we find that consumers still must make choices as to what and how much to consume. These choices involve moral considerations, and hence demonstrate the inescapability of moral reflection in understanding consumer choice. This finding is not surprising, but the crucial question is in considering the legal implications (if any). Should law engage with the moral dimension of consumer choices, particularly when they cause damage to other people (including future generations) and the environment?[47] Law as an institution is

---

47 J. Nolt, 'How Harmful Are the Average American's Greenhouse Gas Emissions' (2011) 14(1) *Ethics, Policy & Environment* 3. See also the very interesting responses to this article within the same journal issue.

inescapably moral, for instance insofar as it seeks means of redressing injustice such as systems of checks and balances in the law-making process, legislation, adjudication, administrative procedures, recognition of rights, etc. One question is whether new legal mechanisms are needed to redress the injustices arising from consumer choices, particularly when they affect the environment and future generations.[48]

2.4 Some thoughts on the contribution of law to tackling overconsumption

2.4.1 *Traditional legal responses to overconsumption of natural resources*

Traditionally, environmental law has been used as a conveyor belt for policies aiming at influencing the behaviour of consumers.[49] The limited effectiveness of these approaches has led scholars and policy-makers to turn their attention to the insights generated by behavioural sciences.[50] There it is often pointed out that the challenges of achieving even apparently trivial behavioural changes are massive and have not yet been adequately overcome through policy interventions.[51] The contribution of technological innovations to assist behavioural change is often emphasised.[52] Whether technology alone will lead to a reduction in energy consumption is, however, not clear in the absence of conscious decisions to change behaviour.[53]

Current laws and legal literature do not generally consider in detail the potential legitimacy and effectiveness of law in changing consumption behaviour by doing what law is uniquely placed to do: imposing legally binding restrictions

---

48 The representation of future generations in law-making processes is a topic that is receiving increasing attention in the literature. The issue of the legal standing of natural objects can be traced at least to the seminal book of Christopher Stone, *Should Trees Have Standing* (3rd edn, Oxford: Oxford University Press, 2010). In both cases, it is obvious that standing strictly speaking is not possible. However, it is possible to grant standing to representatives of those collective bodies, both in the law-making process and in adjudicative procedures.

49 For an analysis of the approach of EU climate change law to consumers, see J. de Cendra de Larragán, 'EU Climate Change Law and Consumers' (2011) 1 *European Journal of Consumer Law* 149.

50 This is particularly the case in US law journals, where there is a growing literature on the subject starting more or less with M. Vandenbergh, 'From Smokestack to SUV: The Individual as Regulated Entity in the New Era of Environmental Law' (2004) 57 *Vanderbilt Law Review* 515.

51 H. Babcock, 'Responsible Environmental Behavior, Energy Conservation and Compact Fluorescent Bulbs: You Can Lead a Horse to Water, But Can You Make it Drink?' (2009) 37 *Hofstra Law Review* 943.

52 S. Stern, 'Smart-Grid: Technology and the Psychology of Environmental Behavior Change' (2011) 86(1) *Chi.-Kent L. Rev* 139.

53 The well-known phenomenon known as rebound effect attests to this. See A. Druckman, M. Chitnis, et al., 'Missing Carbon Reductions? Exploring Rebound and Backfire Effects in UK Households' (2011) 39 *Energy Policy* 3572.

on individual behaviour.[54] Very often the assumption is that legally binding restrictions are at the end of a regulatory ladder often called the 'Nuffield Ladder of Interventions', which classifies public policies according to their degree of intervention in the personal life of individuals.[55] Only when less intrusive interventions are proven ineffective would one climb up the ladder, one step at a time. Though this might be reasonable, it can be challenged on two grounds. First, it assumes that imposing legally binding requirements is more intrusive than not doing so. However, whether that is the case depends on the nature and details of the interventions considered, rather than on whether they are legally binding or not. For instance, it could be argued that a measure that seeks to manipulate the behaviour of a consumer without him realising it is more intrusive than a well publicised legal limit on his volume of consumption expressed, e.g. in terms of associated greenhouse gases, while respecting the freedom to choose how to allocate that volume among different products and services. Second and more fundamentally, the Nuffield Ladder takes as the central value that of 'freedom of choice'; however, if it focused on the value of freedom as the capacity to strive for excellent behaviour, the order of the steps in the ladder would be reversed, and legal obligations would come first as a necessary step in enabling citizens to make excellent choices for themselves. Before accepting the charge that this would amount to paternalism, it should be noted that the law imposes certain behaviour all the time – for instance when it imposes limits on driving speed, parking places and hours, smoking places, noise limits, etc. All these prohibitions seek to imbue citizens of civic virtues that enable societies to flourish. Even if not everyone accepts the adequacy or convenience of those measures, most recognise their legitimacy and obey them. But before concluding that limits on consumption are akin to these measures, and therefore that law should impose them, we need to consider the issue more closely. Accordingly, the argument will proceed by considering: (1) why law may be entitled to impose such limits, and what the conditions are for that legitimacy to hold; (2) counterarguments; (3) possible challenges to the ability of law to actually impose such limitations.

2.4.2 *Why law may be entitled to impose limits on individual consumption*

A very old definition of law – developed from Aristotle by Aquinas – is that law is a rational ordinance, for the common good, enacted by the legitimate

---

54 The obvious starting point here is the trite distinction between law and policy. Essentially, law imposes obligations, and is backed by the use of legitimate force to ensure that they are fulfilled, whereas policies are not, or at least not in the same way. So here we are concerned not with 'soft' interventions to 'nudge' consumers to adopt more environmentally friendly behaviors, but with hard interventions that force upon them limits on the types of products they can consume and/or on overall consumption levels of natural resources.

55 The Nuffield Ladder of Interventions is an analysis of interventions developed by the Nuffield Council of Bioethics in a report on ethical issues in public health published in 2007. It classifies categories of public policies according to degree of intervention in the personal life of individuals. See *Public Health: the Ethical Issues* (London: Nuffield Council of Bioethics, 2007).

legislator, and made publicly accessible (which includes some requirements of internal morality such as clarity, stability, accessibility, etc.)[56] From this perspective, a law that seeks to promote the common good can introduce limits to personal freedom as long as those limits are necessary to achieve its aims, there is adequacy between means and ends and the fundamental rights of citizens are respected (proportionality *stricto sensu*). However, this definition of law is by no means universally accepted, and is moreover open to multiple and conflicting interpretations regarding what is adequate and proportionate and what counts as fundamental rights and how to interpret those rights. A second goal of law under the abovementioned definition is to promote among citizens the basic civic virtues that are necessary to enhance and sustain the common good. In this, law is similar to public policy.[57] However, there is a basic difference: while policies seek to encourage those virtues, laws generally seek to enforce them, if necessary with recourse to force. Serious questions that arise in this regard include whether promoting civic virtues among the citizenry can be a proper goal of law, whether civic virtues can be imposed and enforced upon citizens through law, and whether law is an effective way of creating virtuous citizens.

2.4.3 Why law might not be entitled to impose limits on individual consumption levels

2.4.3.1 Challenges arising from different understandings of what law is and what the law does

To start with, the definition of law proposed above is by no means universally accepted. The most fundamental challenge comes from instrumental conceptions of law that deny that it is possible to define the common good, and therefore law cannot be concerned with it; instead, law is at best an instrument to balance conflicting interests (which is different to promoting the common good), and at worst an instrument to promote particular ends, which often coincide with those of the most powerful in society to the detriment of others and the environment.[58]

A second challenge arising from persisting disagreements about the notion of the common good is the relativistic view of law as a tool for the protection

---

56 These are some of the requirements that Fuller considered to form the internal morality of law.

57 Clearly, one legitimate aim of (environmental) policies is to help people become 'better' persons, for instance by promoting 'green virtues'. Indeed, environmental policies cannot work in the absence of virtuous citizens that take it upon themselves to reduce their levels of consumption, to reuse, and to recycle. Policy in liberal democracies is (or should be) therefore in part the art of promoting those civic virtues that are essential for the political system to work and for the public good to be achieved. W. Kymlicka, *Contemporary Political Philosophy* (2nd edn, Oxford: Oxford University Press, 2002).

58 See the analysis in B. Tamanaha, *Law as a Means to an End: Threat to the Rule of Law* (Cambridge: Cambridge University Press, 2006).

of individual freedom primarily understood as freedom of choice. The only limit to that freedom comes from the rights of other citizens. To achieve this goal, civil and political rights need to be granted that can in turn be used to protect oneself against the state. The welfare state has added to those rights social, economic and cultural rights. These rights are vertical (they apply between individuals and the state, not among individuals), individual rights (as opposed to community rights), they can always be increased with new rights or expansions of existing rights, and crucially, they are not matched by corresponding obligations.[59] Some authors have argued that potential consequences of this trend include: (1) a decline in the moral responsibility of the citizenry, which is now used to make claims against the state, but not to acknowledge their moral and social obligations towards other members of society; (2) a focus on present generations *vis-à-vis* future ones; (3) passivity in the relations that build thriving democracies; and (4) a depoliticisation of social questions. One of the consequences is that legislative welfare projects based on reciprocity and solidarity are rejected as being either unrealistic or unacceptable; another consequence is that debates about the good society or the common good are either absent and/or largely incomprehensible. The law-making process suffers from this mindset, because it cannot set goals that are not liberal, i.e. communitarian. Against this background, legislators seem to be barred from using laws to foster a society of solidarity, reciprocity and equality, and instead will be locked in processes that generate laws that foster individualism and conflicts of interests.

A third challenge comes from disagreement about what the central function of law is. Paraphrasing Gabriel Marcel, law is not primarily concerned with the world of being, but with the world of having.[60] In other words, law, as opposed to policy, deals primarily with facts, not with the internal dispositions of actual people. At the same time, it is clear that, in order to achieve its ends, law needs to forbid certain behaviour that is considered to be socially unacceptable and morally wrong, e.g. killing or stealing. But this alone does not show that law is concerned with promoting civic virtues, rather that it seeks to prevent seriously asocial behaviour that undermines the polity and makes the peaceful existence of societies impossible. Assuming for a moment that law is legitimised to impose civic virtues, the next question is whether it constitutes an effective means to do so. There seems to be a contradiction between, on the one hand, practising virtues, which is a voluntary act, and, on the other hand, complying with the law, which would seem on the surface to be an involuntary act stemming from coercion. It has been argued that this contradiction is only apparent, and that compliance with legally binding obligations has the potential to generate civic virtues in those that comply

---

59 L. Eriksson, 'Making Society Through Legislation' in L.J. Wintgens (ed.), *Legisprudence: A New Theoretical Approach to Legislation* (Oxford: Hart, 2002), at pp. 43–44.

60 M. Villey, *Compendio de Filosofía del Derecho* (Pamplona: EUNSA, 1979–81), p. 340.

with them. The key issue to note here is that citizens always have a choice in complying with the law. They can comply out of the exercise of a civic virtue consisting in complying with (just) laws, they can comply out of a calculation of interests, or they can comply out of fear of being detected and punished. In any case, the decision to comply in each specific instance is one in which the will of the subject is always at play. So it follows that in choosing to comply, even if it is out of fear, the subject is performing a good act. And performing a good act out of free will – even if mediated by other considerations – has the capacity to generate the associated civic virtue that naturally leads to further compliance with the law.

So it follows that compliance with the law can either flow from the exercise of a civic virtue or could lead to the formation of civic virtues in those that previously lacked them. Another challenge is more fundamental. Where does the capacity of law to encourage civic virtues among citizens come from? In other words, on which factors does the normative legitimacy of the law rest?[61] While this is an issue that falls beyond this chapter, it must nevertheless be noted. Suffice it here to point out that the mere choice to comply with a law, provided that law is not clearly against morality – however defined – is in itself a virtuous act that can therefore lead someone to become a virtuous person. To say that a law is not clearly against morality implies, at a minimum, that it complies with the minimum requirements of the internal morality of law as famously spelled out by Fuller.[62] One of those principles relates to the rationality of law. In adopting laws that impose restrictions on individual behaviour to protect and promote the public good, the legislator is bound to follow principles of practical rationality, so that citizens can understand the reasons why they are being ordered to do or not to do something, and ideally share these reasons. For those that accept these reasons as correct ones, compliance is not an issue and in fact arises out of pre-existing civic virtues. For those that do not accept the reasons as valid, compliance will not be forthcoming out of civic virtues, but might come instead out of fear of being punished. In the latter case and as shown above, the fear of being punished leads to behaviour in accordance with the rational law, and in that way it has the capacity to develop the civic virtues of that citizen. So it can be shown that law, by mandating certain behaviour backed with sanctions, can not only promote the solution of environmental problems, but can also promote civic virtues. Of course law's ability to promote civic virtues does not only depend on its rationality (including its justice), but also on other requirements of internal morality such as feasibility (not asking too much too fast), accessibility (that citizens indeed have the chance to know the law and to understand what

61 See, for instance, S. Delacroix, 'You'd Better Be Committed: Legal Norms and Normativity' (2009) 54(1) *American Journal of Jurisprudence* 117.
62 L. Fuller, *The Internal Morality of Law* (New Haven, CT: Yale University Press, 1964).

it is that is required from them) and stability (that the law is not changed so often that the meaning of civic virtues becomes blurred).

2.4.3.2 Challenges arising from prevailing assumptions within environmental law

To the challenges mentioned in the previous section, it is possible to add others that seem to apply more specifically to environmental law.

2.4.3.2.1 CONCEPTUAL CHALLENGES

While traditional environmental law has been effective in solving many discrete environmental problems (mainly deriving from source pollution), current environmental problems have reached a scale and pervasiveness that sets them apart from the old ones, in that they have more to do with resource depletion rather than with pollution, as the first section showed. Moreover, while in the past it was relatively easy to distinguish between polluters and victims, this is becoming increasingly difficult, because all of us contribute (to different extents) to the degradation of the environment. Thus environmental laws increasingly are faced with the need to address individual consumer behaviour directly if they are to be effective and fair.[63] But doing this raises a number of challenges, normative, psychological and empirical.

2.4.3.2.2 NORMATIVE CHALLENGES

This challenge arises from the observation that there are a number of reasons why most of us may not be ready to accept legally imposed restrictions on our freedom as consumers for the sake of environmental protection.

First, a dominant view among consumers is that environmental problems arise primarily from the smokestack, while individual actions are largely irrelevant. Flowing from this view is a resistance to attempts by law to restrict personal freedoms for the sake of environmental protection.

Second, even if consumer responsibility were to be accepted, there are further difficulties. To start with, society is so wedded to the idea of an unfettered right to consume that it is not likely that such notion of responsibility will have serious practical consequences for consumer behaviour. This value attached to consumer freedom (and consumer protection) does not apply equally to

---

63 The fairness element comes from the fact that an equitable sharing of the burden depends on incorporating criteria of contributive justice, so that those responsible for the damage and capable of reducing it actually contribute to do so. If the behaviour of citizens is tackled by the law to a much lower extent than the behaviour of industries and businesses, then it is possible to argue that a basic tenet of contributive justice is not being fulfilled. This is as much a requirement of justice as one of rationality. Laws that do not tackle all sources of emissions are in principle less likely to achieve their mitigation goals than those that are comprehensive.

producer freedom, which is often subject to restrictive regulations.[64] However, even weaker in this context than both the producer and the consumer is the environment, which is damaged by both. But consumer law has not yet embraced the environmental rationale.[65] To continue, it can be argued that the predominant moral outlook within Western societies has not yet accepted that engaging in behaviour that leads to the exhaustion of natural resources is morally comparable to engaging in behaviour that leads to the destruction of particular portions of the surrounding environment (such as killing a particular member of a species). While killing a member of an endangered species meets with general repulsion, driving an SUV does not (yet) give rise to the same reaction. The dominant moral outlook has probably not (yet) accepted that individuals can be morally responsible for normal daily activities that cause environmental damage. In this state of affairs, imposing 'green virtues' among citizens can easily be seen as akin to imposing upon them a certain view of morality, opposed to the dominant one based on values cherished by neoliberal capitalism. Last but not least, while many citizens may accept their share of responsibility for environmental degradation, they can also consider that it is so small compared with the enormity of the problem, and their capacity to make a change so limited, that it does not make sense for law to regulate it.

In view of these reflections, it does not come as a surprise to learn that, in the UK (but this conclusion can be extended to many other countries), while a clear majority of citizens (70 per cent) consider that reducing household energy use is a virtuous thing to do for the environment, a similar majority rejects policy measures aimed at reducing household energy use. For instance, only 34 per cent would accept green taxes, only 30 per cent would accept road pricing and only 28 per cent would accept carbon rationing. Likewise, there is very little enthusiasm for changing lifestyles in order to protect the environment. In this regard, while 65 per cent of people tend to agree that they are prepared to greatly reduce their energy use to help tackle climate change, only 44 per cent are prepared to pay significantly more money for energy-efficient products.[66]

Third, there is a difficulty more closely related to law's nature. Law, as a social institution, employs dominant moral outlooks and works at least in part to reinforce them. Accordingly, contemporary law-making processes are shaped

---

64 One rationale could be the dominant focus of consumer law on protecting the consumer, who is perceived to be the weakest actor in market exchanges within market-based economies. Another possible explanation is that liberal societies recognise that respect for the freedom of rational individuals is a fundamental value of society, but this recognition does not extend to commercial organisations in so far as they are not rational agents of that kind.

65 L. Krämer, 'On the Interrelation Between Consumer and Environmental Policies in the European Community' (1993) 16(3–4) *Journal of Consumer Policy* 455.

66 L. Whitmarsh, P. Upham, et al., *Public Attitudes, Understanding and Engagement in relation to Low-Carbon Energy: A Selective Review of Academic and Non-Academic Literatures* (London: RCUK Energy Programme, 2011), at p. 10.

by prevailing values such as open markets, efficiency, consumer choice, and individual autonomy. Markets orientate personal freedom towards increased consumption, in order to ensure their long-term growth and thus their viability. So law itself might be promoting levels of consumption that are excessive from the perspective of the resources that the planet can provide. Indeed a dominant trend within environmental law is to promote market-based instruments to protect the environment. But, more insidiously, many areas of law work directly to fuel growth of the traditional kind and the virtues that promote it, chiefly freedom of consumption.

All these factors sketch a very complex landscape, which probably explains in part why it is so difficult to change dominant paradigms and therefore why so far the principal approach followed in environmental law has been largely limited to persuasion.[67]

2.4.3.2.3 PSYCHOLOGICAL CHALLENGES

If environmental law is to tackle effectively the environmentally damaging behaviour of consumers, it needs to be based on an accurate understanding of human behaviour. At least two strands of literature exist, one focusing on understanding consumer behaviour and the other focusing on understanding public attitudes to environmental or energy policies.

The first strand of the literature is prompted by the realisation that consumers do not appear to behave as rational actors, as traditional economists would predict.[68] Rather than seeking always to maximise their utility, consumers are strongly influenced by emotional factors, by the behaviour of other people, by habits and by the use of mental short-cuts, often used to speed up decision-making processes in the face of multiple and conflicting options. Moreover, consumer preferences are inconsistent, changing over time and according to the situation and the way in which information is presented. Consumers rarely weigh up all the costs and benefits of choices; they respond more to losses than gains, value products much more once they own them, place a greater value on the immediate future, are easily overwhelmed by too much choice, are heavily influenced by other people and use products to make a statement about themselves. On the basis of these facts, researchers have sought to derive policy recommendations, including a focus on:[69]

- the effectiveness of pricing as a policy tool;
- the importance of helping consumers to consider long-term costs;

---

67 This is certainly the case within EU environmental law. See J. de Cendra, 'EU Environmental Law and Consumers' (2011) *European Journal of Consumer Law* 149.

68 For a recent review of that literature, see Policy Studies Institute, *Designing Policy to Influence Consumers: Consumer Behavior Relating to the Purchasing of Environmentally Preferable Goods* (London, Policy Studies Institute, 2009).

69 Ibid.

- the importance of brand recognition;
- the importance and structure of information provision;
- the facilitation of environmentally friendly choices;
- realising that fines are less acceptable to the public than incentives;
- ensuring that standard products or services (those chosen by consumers 'by default') are the environmentally preferable ones;
- allowing consumers to change their mind through 'cool-off' periods;
- keeping in mind that all consumers are different.

The underlying message is the importance of helping consumers to behave in environmentally friendly ways. But the methodologies used in these studies makes them blind to relevant questions. For instance, by seeking to understand how consumers behave, they do not engage with the deep motivations underlying the dynamics of human action. Another, perhaps more serious, problem stems from the limitations of this literature when seeking to inform policies. By focusing on 'nudging' consumers to change their consumption choices, they neglect the more fundamental question whether law and policy can be used to present to consumers substantially different ways of living, less consumption-oriented and yet arguably more rewarding. Critics point out that achieving sustainability requires a deep rethinking of what it means for human societies to flourish, and what the consumption of products and services does to reach that goal. Jackson has suggested that a new moral imagination is needed that creates new visions of human flourishing,[70] based on a renewed understanding of the common good, more accessible and attractive to all members of society. This project is a very profound one requiring, as it does, engaging seriously with the deepest needs and desires of human beings, but it does not seem possible to address it with the mainstream tools used in the literature.

I would argue that it is in this light that the second strand of the literature, on public attitudes to environmental policies, should be considered. In essence, this literature tries to understand public attitudes to environmental and energy policies.[71] How do people react to policy proposals that attempt to change their lifestyles in order to make them more environmentally friendly? The issue of public acceptability is of the essence. The literature tends to regard people as citizens who have an interest and a right to participate in important societal decisions, and who may be willing to contribute (to differing extents) to the success of societal goals. Hence, the focus is on better

---

70 T. Jackson, *Prosperity Without Growth – Economics for a Finite Planet* (London: Earthscan, 2009), at p. 189.
71 For a good review of this literature, see L. Whitmarsh, P. Upham, et al., *Public Attitudes, Understanding and Engagement in Relation to Low-Carbon Energy: A Selective Review of Academic and Non-Academic Literatures* (London: RCUK Energy Programme, 2011).

understanding how citizens perceive their responsibilities towards society and how the exercise of those responsibilities is shaped by policy initiatives, social, economic, political and technological contexts, habits and routines. It is impossible to synthesise this literature here, but there seem to be at least two key messages: first, the degree of virtuosity of citizens is rather modest; citizens are more willing to support public policies as long as they do not have to shoulder (a considerable part of) the burden and are assisted in doing it; second, citizens do appear to demand more participatory rights in policy-making processes. This seems to resonate with literature mentioned above in the section 'Challenges arising from different understandings of what law is and what the law does', regarding the increasing recognition of rights within welfare states, but could also be related to a genuine desire to be constructively involved in policy-making processes.

In the light of these literatures, a number of interesting questions arise.

First, how do 'nudges' relate to the scale and urgency of current natural resource challenges such as climate change? The House of Lords has concluded, on the basis of evidence collected over a year, that the recent choice of the English government to rely more on nudge theory in public policy has three main limitations. First, there is a dearth of evidence about how effectively to translate theoretical knowledge about (individual) human behaviour into actual behavioural changes at a collective level through public policy. Second, there is a lack of evidence about the cost-effectiveness of policy interventions aimed at behavioural change. Third, there are almost no long-term data against which the effectiveness of interventions over sustained periods can be measured.[72] Moreover, assessing the extent of the rebound effect following energy efficiency interventions in households, Druckman et al. have noted that the money saved is often spent on carbon intensive activities that can, in extreme cases, more than counter the original savings.[73] Hence, they conclude that it is not really useful to put all the focus on single behavioural changes without engaging with people at a deeper level, focusing on values and social identities. In short, while people can be nudged into making a specific change in order to adopt low carbon or low environmental impact lifestyles, they need to make that decision in full awareness and with a full commitment to live by it.[74] Interestingly, Druckman et al. do not stop here, but fully acknowledge that policy-makers not only require information on unintended consequences of policies such as the abovementioned rebound effect, but also practical solutions. They mention – but do not elaborate upon – two possibilities: first, enacting regulatory measures that encourage shifts to less carbon intensive

---

72 House of Lords Science and Technology Select Committee, *Behaviour Change* (London: House of Lords Science and Technology Select Committee, 2011), at p. 18.

73 For instance, if a family used the money saved on the energy bill to pay for a holiday to Thailand.

74 A. Druckman, M. Chitnis, et al., 'Missing Carbon Reductions? Exploring Rebound and Backfire Effects in UK Households' (2011) 39 *Energy Policy* 3572.

categories (examples of such measures are obvious enough: taxes, domestic emissions trading schemes, publicity campaigns, etc.); second, encouraging households not to spend savings but rather to invest them in low carbon investments (such as green saving accounts).

Second, how does the human behaviour literature engage with moral theories of individual responsibility? Can it overcome the tendency to an ever-increasing fragmentation in the study of public attitudes, by focusing on particular technologies and sub-technologies? And if not, how do we engage with people at a deeper level, focusing not only on values and social identities but going even deeper into the core of human motivations, as suggested, for instance, by Jackson?

From this perspective, the key questions are as follows. Is law able to make a contribution, and if so which one? What are the limitations of law in doing so? And how could law make its contribution in practice? The short answer is that law can make a contribution by deploying its potential to generate green virtues among citizens. But what does this mean and how can it be done?

2.4.4 A possible response to the challenges posed

2.4.4.1 The problem of law's legitimacy

The three challenges considered above, namely the lack of agreement on the meaning of the common good, the increasing instrumentality of law, and the pre-eminence of a rights culture in Western societies, are certainly formidable. They are further empowered by the other challenges identified, which portray a culture where imposing legal limits on personal freedom for the sake of protecting the environment and future generations appears not to resonate with the majority of members of society. Together they would seem to render implausible a defence of the legitimacy of law to impose any sort of limits on personal consumption.

At the same time, we can point to numerous instances where laws have been passed to regulate, or directly ban, certain individual behaviour, including restrictions or prohibitions on drug and alcohol use, smoking, speed limits, use of seat belts when driving, parking rules, noise limits, etc. All these rules are based on considerations of public policy: in other words, the prevalence of the public good over individual freedom. So what is it that makes these interventions different from imposing limits on general consumption for the sake of environmental protection?

It seems from the above discussion that the legitimacy of all these restrictions (and their reach) may come from a number of factors:

- the legitimacy of the end itself, which can be judged, for instance, by its relevance and urgency;

- the legitimacy of the legislator to pass laws restricting personal freedoms for the common good;
- the rationality of those restrictions, in the sense that they must be necessary to promote a legitimate end, and must not impose restrictions that are out of proportion to the end sought;
- the fact that the laws adopted take into account the real situations of real people, thus avoiding the imposition of requirements that are beyond their capacity or that would put them in a dire situation;
- the fact that those restrictions resonate with societal convictions as formed over relatively extended periods of time.

Inevitably, the question of law's legitimacy to impose restrictions on consumer behaviour involves so many considerations that a single dimensional answer is not possible. Arguments can be provided for very different and even opposing responses. Even if the basic authority of the legislator is presumed, much will hinge on the procedures it uses to reach its decisions. And even then, it is not guaranteed that the decisions reached will remain valid for long, that they will be adequately implemented at lower levels of governance, and that they will be complied with and adequately enforced.

In addition to the issue of law's legitimacy, there is also that of law's opportunity. In the absence of widespread public enthusiasm for, or at a minimum, acceptance of the need for introducing personal limits on consumption, it is highly unlikely that policy-makers will take the risk of passing them through legislation. This is the greatest challenge faced by law, and points to the nature of law as a social institution. This reality of law's nature suggests that technocratic approaches that perceive law as a tool for achieving goals of public policy will not be successful.[75] This arguably illustrates the key difference between tobacco related prohibitions and climate change. While the former resonate with societal convictions, arguably the latter do not yet share the same degree of public support. This explains why they are widely regarded as unrealistic, at least for the time being.

2.4.4.2 The problem of law's effectiveness in reducing personal consumption

To put it starkly, legitimate laws can be utterly ineffective. Laws imposing limits on consumption on the basis of consumers' responsibility for the problem might be just, but at the same time totally ineffective.[76] Of course, law needs to reflect the fact that different consumers will have very different degrees of responsibility and capacity. A blanket approach to all consumers might, with

---

75 E. Claes and B. Keirsbilck, 'Facing the Limits of the Law' in E. Claes, W. Devroe and B. Keirsbilck (eds), *Facing the Limits of the Law* (Berlin: Springer, 2011).

76 Such ineffectiveness could also raise the question whether the law is actually just in the first place.

good reason, be considered illegitimate and resisted.[77] Achieving the right balance is obviously crucial for law's legitimacy but is not sufficient to guarantee effectiveness. In considering the effectiveness of potential instruments, it is necessary, as suggested above, to consider carefully existing theoretical knowledge and empirical data.

It is also necessary to consider the role that existing societal structures and cultural norms play in locking consumers into current behaviour. More generally, it is necessary to recognise that the (regulatory) status quo within Western societies is still largely tilted against sustainability (due in part to the reasons described above).

Law has a proper role to play here beyond channelling knowledge from psychological studies. It can be a tool to open up the societal space to alternative cultural, behavioural, ethical and philosophical responses to the challenges posed by environmental problems. In doing this, it is, however, important to be aware of the fact that law is resistant to being used as a purely instrumental tool to achieve certain goals. Very often law is seen in this context as a tool to overcome barriers, yet this view overlooks the real nature of law and its power to achieve societal change. Law is a reflection of past, present and future mores; it is a conservative yet dynamic institution, filled with contradictions, ambiguities and limitations. Thus, it is a very imperfect tool to 'engineer' societal changes. In contrast, law can powerfully channel new sentiments within society, new ideologies, hopes, goals, fears and angers. This does not suggest that law should be used as a tool to manipulate consumer behaviour, but rather suggests that law is effective in capturing new thoughts and ideas and in translating them into legal rights and responsibilities. In this way, law can break existing conceptions of the world, expand horizons, and open up new avenues for the development of society. In short, law can help to crystallise visions of sustainability. These changes will be slow, and will come up in piece-meal ways. There will be many failures, many dead-ends; when law is used as an instrument of social engineering it always, sooner or later, ends up failing, because even if the human condition can be to an extent shaped, human nature remains immutable.[78] Nonetheless, law can help bring about and normalise new ways of life that are more sustainable than those of hitherto. Laws that work to overcome structural barriers make it easier, more legitimate and more attractive for consumers to reduce their consumption levels and eventually to change their lifestyles permanently. A wide range of measures have been proposed, including:

---

77 On the other hand, a too finely grained approach is also unrealistic and would be a bureaucratic nightmare. Fortunately, states are used to making regulatory distinctions among different types of consumers, and tax rules reflect precisely that, though the tendency to over-complexity is in-built in the process.

78 For a detailed analysis of the concepts of human nature and human condition and differences therein, see H. Arendt, *The Human Condition* (Chicago: University of Chicago Press, 1998 reprint).

- providing education about the environmental consequences of consumers' consumption choices;
- providing more and better information about consumers' (energy) consumption levels;
- enabling use of technologies such as smart meters that are consumer friendly;[79]
- obliging energy service companies to provide energy services that effectively enable consumers to engage in energy demand management;
- enabling consumers to self-generate their own electricity and to send the excess to the grid;
- developing electric or hydrogen cars accompanied by a well developed charging infrastructure;
- developing well conditioned cycle lanes in cities;
- developing good, attractive and affordable public-sector transportation;
- making changes to labour rules that allow and incentivise part-time working;
- creating incentives to put savings into low carbon investments.

Lawyers may worry about the potential (in)compatibility of some of these measures, and might want to ensure consistency and coherence. I think it is unlikely that the goal of consistency will be achieved at all. The problem of scarcity of natural resources is too large, too urgent and too complex to permit elegant solutions. Clearly there is a need to ensure that regulatory regimes do not become so complex that they are self-defeating, but complexity is unavoidable in a learning-by-doing process (which seems the only feasible approach).

To conclude this section, the crucial role of law is to make explicit through regulation the link between green virtues and global sustainability. The remainder of this chapter will look at the potential of one particular instrument that has recently received much attention in environmental law and policy, though it has never been applied to consumers – emissions trading. Emissions trading for consumers could be one part of the regulatory approach that links the need to ensure that planetary boundaries are not exceeded – the cap – with the measures needed to overcome structural barriers that reduce the capacity of consumers to alter their lifestyles.

---

79 Consumer friendly smart meters are those that help consumers to improve control over their energy use while providing them with tools to reduce it and making sure that their pre-existing rights and expectations are protected. This means that smart meters do not represent high additional costs for consumers, that they do not allow for remote switching and disconnection, that data protection and security issues are well addressed, and that smart meters are coupled with new services such as automated and demand-side control, energy saving tariffs, load-management devices, energy efficiency and insulation measures, micro-generation, etc. See for instance G. Owen and J. Ward, *The Consumer Implications of Smart Meters* (London: National Consumer Council, 2007).

2.5 How should a legally binding limit on consumption be designed and how would it relate to the wider body of environmental regulation?

2.5.1 One possible regulatory tool to address overconsumption by individuals: personal carbon trading

Personal carbon trading (PCT) is a generic term used to refer to emission trading schemes whereby individuals are allocated emission credits broadly on an equal *per capita* basis, under a total cap defined, for instance, at national level. Individuals surrender these credits when buying goods covered by the scheme. If they go over their quota they can buy more; if not they can sell them to others.

2.5.1.1 PCT is in line with the concept of law developed above

Because there would be a cap that could be reduced over time, PCT could account for the issues of scale and urgency. In addition, it might also be able to incorporate the relevant findings of psychology and behavioural economics outlined above.[80] At the same time, it presents some limitations: it focuses only on one planetary boundary; it can look like a radical measure thereby risking being seen as not acceptable; it can quickly get very complex and expensive; and its implementation through law – which would certainly be needed if the scheme were to be binding – would be in the context of the already crowded and rather messy regulatory frameworks in place (certainly in the EU and its Member States). A lot of early work on PCT focused on its acceptability, by looking at technical complexity and economic costs. The UK's Department for the Environment, Food and Rural Affairs (DEFRA) for instance concluded that, although PCT was in principle very attractive, it faced extreme challenges on both counts, and dismissed the idea as being potentially powerful but ahead of its time.[81] Although more recent work has sought to challenge the assumptions used by DEFRA and to carry out small-scale studies that could throw new light on its acceptability,[82] the key challenge seems to be fitting PCT within the paradigm of individual freedom in neoliberal market economies.

---

80 For an analysis of personal carbon trading from the perspective of behavioral economics, see E. Woerdman and J. Bolderdijk, *Emissions Trading for Households? A Behavioral Law and Economics Perspective* (Groningen: University of Groningen, 2010). PCT could potentially acknowledge the lessons derived from behavioural economics by incorporating findings that can help to increase its acceptability among policy makers and the public, and by actually encouraging individuals to change their behaviour, as they realise that doing so will provide them with a number of previously unrealised benefits both personally and for the environment.

81 DEFRA, *Synthesis Report on the Findings from Defra's Pre-Feasibility Study into Personal Carbon Trading* (London: DEFRA, 2006).

82 J. Bird and M. Lockwood, *Plan B? The Prospects for Personal Carbon Trading* (London: Institute for Public Policy Research, 2009).

Faced with this challenge, it is notable that the key advantage of PCT is that it does not force consumers into making particular choices; rather, consumers are free to make choices as long as they remain within the cap. The crucial issue is to ensure that consumers are presented with new and attractive choices while respecting that limitation. PCT cannot, therefore, exist without measures addressing the structural barriers outlined above. In other words, PCT will not be seen as a legitimate regulatory tool unless smart meters that are consumer friendly are in place, convenient alternatives to combustion engine cars are available at affordable prices, etc.

Another (possibly complementary) route is to use PCT to open up space for reflection on what the role of consumption is in the pursuit of a good life. Faced with a new, carbon constrained reality, the consumer can be encouraged to reconsider the value of consumption in bringing about happiness. Whilst this is not the primary role of law, law could serve to create space for that reflection.

2.5.1.2 *Some early trials and attempts*

Despite the fundamental challenges noted above, some small-scale experiments of PCT are currently taking place. On Norfolk Island, the Norfolk Island Carbon/Health Evaluation Study has just been implemented.[83] It is the world's first PCT. One goal is to test the links between carbon intensive lifestyles and health. Another is to deliver a model that could inspire applications elsewhere. It is a voluntary scheme, whereby citizens get allowances for free and have to surrender them when purchasing electricity, fuels, and certain foodstuffs. While the Norfolk scheme is certainly interesting in testing issues of acceptability and capacity to change behaviour, the very characteristics of Norfolk Island and of its environmentally conscious citizens – which determined its selection in the first place – may make its replication elsewhere challenging, to say the least.

There are also signs of change within the UK. The 2008 Climate Change Act would allow the Government to introduce PCT without further primary legislation. DEFRA, as mentioned above, has rejected the idea for the time being. However, the Parliament's Environmental Audit Committee rebuked DEFRA for being too quick in doing so and recommended more publicly funded research on the matter. The UK All Parliamentary Group on Peak Oil has returned to the idea and has linked it to the perhaps more powerful notion of energy security.[84] In the words of John Hemming, the chairman of the Group:

'[Tradable Energy Quotas] provide the fairest and most productive way to deal with the oil crisis and to simultaneously guarantee reductions

83 www.niche.nlk.nf/ (last accessed 5 August 2011).
84 D. Fleming and S. Chamberlain, *Tradable Energy Quotas: A Policy Framework for Peak Oil and Climate Change* (London: House of Commons, 2010).

in fossil fuel use to meet climate change targets. The challenge is urgent and TEQs are among the best tools we have at our disposal to meet it.'

The scheme proposed by the UK All Parliamentary Group would focus on electricity and fuels, whereby the credits would cover their entire lifecycle. Each energy source would carry a carbon rating set by the government. The entire society would be covered – not just individuals but also firms and the government. Allowances would be given for free to individuals and through auctions to the rest. There would be a national cap that would be reduced annually. Nevertheless, the UK All Parliamentary Group on Peak Oil report is short on legal detail. For instance it does not explain how such a scheme would fit with existing instruments such as the EU Emissions Trading Scheme (ETS), but this would clearly be relevant to judge its practical feasibility *vis-à-vis* EU law.

2.5.2 PCT as an instrument of EU climate law? Some considerations of positive law

2.5.2.1 *Would the EU have competence to introduce PCT?*

An important threshold question is whether the EU would constitute the right level to introduce PCT. Here a number of very basic observations can be made, beginning with the need to respect the principles of attribution of powers, subsidiarity and proportionality. The EU shares competence in environmental policy with Member States.[85] It was on the basis of that competence that it introduced the EU ETS, after a few Member States had introduced their own domestic schemes. In terms of respect for the principle of attribution of powers, introducing a PCT would largely follow the same logic, as a PCT is merely an emissions trading system introduced at the farthest possible point downstream. So the important question is not whether the introduction of a PCT would respect the principle of attribution of powers, but whether doing so would be in compliance with the principles of subsidiarity and proportionality.

2.5.2.2 *Would an EU PCT be in compliance with the principles of subsidiarity and proportionality?*

Article 1 TEU and Article 5(3) TEU introduces a clear presumption in favour of taking legal action at Member State level rather than at EU level whenever possible. The principle of subsidiarity[86] means that:

---

85 Article 4(2)(e) TFEU.
86 According to the principle of subsidiarity, the Union shall act only if and insofar as the objectives of the proposed action cannot be sufficiently achieved by the Member States, either at central level or at regional and local level, but can rather, by reason of the scale or effects of the proposed action, be better achieved at Union level (Art. 5(3) TEU).

- the Union should only act when Member States cannot sufficiently achieve the desired goals by themselves;
- the Union should only act when it can better achieve the desired goals in comparison to the Member States, and;
- the Union's actions should be limited to the extent necessary to achieve those goals.

A set of criteria has been developed in legal and economic literature to assist in the application of the principle of subsidiarity to specific cases.[87] Arguments in favour of decentralisation include:

1 when legislators compete with each other in the market of laws *à la* Tiebout;
2 when there are informational asymmetries, and hence local governments would seem to be in a better position than central regulators to monitor the behaviour of industries;
3 when competition between regulators may serve as a learning process to achieve better solutions in terms of welfare.

Arguments in favour of (a higher degree of) centralisation are:

4 the existence of transboundary externalities;
5 the existence of economies of scale and of transaction costs;
6 the existence of a collective action problem whose unilateral regulation could lead to a race to the bottom.

Clearly, while some of these reasons would appear to argue in favour of introducing PCT at EU level (particularly 4 and 5), others would appear to counsel against it (particularly 2 and 3), and others are either inapplicable or not very illuminating (1 and 6). So there is additional work needed to further clarify the meaning of some of these reasons for PCT (1 and 6) and to examine which reasons seem to carry more weight, (2+3 or 4+5) while acknowledging that in practice competence for an EU-wide PCT would be distributed across many levels of governance (EU, national, sub-national). In any case, the most daunting political problem regarding PCT is its political acceptability. Given the perceived 'radical' nature of PCT, a crucial issue would be the perceived legitimacy of the public institutions introducing it. Since the EU's social legitimacy cannot be compared to that of

---

87 See for instance R. Van den Bergh and M. Faure, 'The Subsidiarity Principle in European Environmental Law: An Economic Analysis', in E. Eide, R. Van den Bergh, *Law and Economics of the Environment* (Oslo: Jurdisk Forlag, 1996), pp. 128–41.

national governments,[88] it would be for the latter to decide whether to implement PCT.

2.5.2.3 How would PCT fit into the broader regulatory picture of EU climate law?

The EU has put in place a very complex and comprehensive legal framework for climate protection, which moreover is developing in a way that suggests a progressive Europeanisation of climate change law.[89] Decision 406/2009/EC, setting emission reduction targets for Member States that cover sectors not included in the EU ETS, is very much a framework allowing Member States substantial leeway to decide which specific policies to put in place for these sectors. From this perspective, a PCT would be just one option among many, and if one or more Member States were to introduce it, important lessons would be learnt that eventually could feed into a EU-wide scheme. One option for Member States would be to explore the possibility of expanding the EU ETS to bring in consumers, or to create a domestic PCT and link it to the EU ETS. This would of course risk making the EU ETS even more complex to administer. Indeed, the Commission's proposal for a Directive establishing a scheme for greenhouse gas emission allowance trading discussed the possibility of including chemical installations in the scheme, and rejected it due to the imbalance between the added administrative complexity that such a decision would bring and its limited additional environmental benefits.[90] Arguably bringing in end-users would be even more cumbersome. Some studies on PCT have argued that there are ways to reduce administrative complexity, for instance if consumers surrender credits upon payment for fuels and if monitoring, reporting and surrendering obligations fall upon producers and importers.[91] However, the complexities brought by such a link would have to be considered.

Aside from technical considerations, PCT would probably only become a realistic regulatory tool once other key measures facilitating changes in consumer behaviour have been implemented (including for instance consumer friendly smart meters, zero carbon buildings, low carbon transport infrastructure, etc.). It is not therefore realistic or even advisable to include such an instrument until all those structural measures are effectively working.

---

88 See, for instance, S. Dierckxsens, 'Legitimacy in the European Union and the Limits of the Law' in E. Claes and B. Keirsbilck (eds), *Facing the Limits of the Law* (Berlin: Springer, 2009).

89 See, for instance, S. Oberthür and C. Roche Kelly, 'EU Leadership in International Climate Policy: Achievements and Challenges' (2008) 43(3) *The International Spectator* 35.

90 European Commission, Proposal for a directive establishing a scheme for greenhouse gas allowance trading within the Community and amending Council Directive 96/61/EC, COM (2001) 581 final, p. 10.

91 M. Johnson, H. Pollitt, M. Harfoot et al., *A Study in Personal Carbon Allocation: Cap and Share* (Dublin: Sustainable Development Council, 2008).

2.5.3 PCT at Member State level: some considerations of EU and international law

Whilst comprehensive consideration of the potential EU and international law issues that could arise in introducing a PCT system is beyond the scope of this chapter, a few very basic remarks can be made. First, as a purely domestic measure, a PCT system would first of all have to comply with EU primary law (for instance with the law of free movement of persons and goods, and with state aid rules)[92] and with EU secondary law (for instance, with the EU ETS). As a PCT can be designed in many different ways, it would be necessary to assess each option individually for compliance with the requirements of EU law, and generalisations are not possible. Important issues could arise, for instance, in relation to the scope of the PCT system (e.g. whether it applies only to residents or also to visitors; whether it applies to all citizens or only to adults; its treatment of foreign companies, etc.). In addition, the Member State would need to make sure that it is in compliance with obligations under international law, in particular certain WTO agreements. WTO law could come into play because a PCT scheme, if mandatory, would have to be accompanied by mandatory labelling, which would have to be assessed under the GATT and the TBT agreements. Moreover, a Member State could seek to set up its PCT scheme as an extension of the EU ETS, and in that case the relevant provisions of Directive 2003/87/EC would be applicable.[93] The point made here is simply that the requirements of EU and international law would need to be taken into account when deciding upon the possible introduction of a domestic PCT.

2.6 Concluding remarks

This chapter has argued that, if overconsumption is seen as a serious and urgent problem at the root of the current environmental crises, it ought to receive more attention by law-makers the world over. In fact, this is what we are starting to detect. While addressing the behaviour of consumers is not sufficient to solve problems such as climate change – large structural and institutional changes are also certainly needed – it is a necessary element of the equation, and a more important one than has been conceded so far. Further, this chapter does not argue that law is the most adequate tool to effectuate moral changes; what it has argued is that law can provide a link between the protection of public goods such as environmental protection and necessary changes in individual and social behaviour. Law can in particular play a role in setting up structures that open up new avenues for citizens to fulfil their

---

92 For an analysis of the fit of PCT or similar schemes with EU State aid rules, see M. Johnson, H. Pollitt, M. Harfoot et al., *A Study in Personal Carbon Allocation*, pp. 66 *et seq.*
93 In particular, Article 24.

civic obligations. Failure to use legal tools leaves a gap that cannot be filled by other types of interventions.

In that vein, PCT has been examined as one possible legal solution. The chapter suggests that more work, including by legal scholars, is required to determine whether PCT would be acceptable and effective. What seems clear is that PCT would be just one tool within the regulatory mix, along with structural measures empowering citizens to make real behavioural changes.

3 The challenge of climate change

International law perspectives

*Alan Boyle**

3.1 Introduction

Climate change represents one of the greatest challenges to international cooperation the UN and the EU have ever faced. Few topics provide a better illustration of the importance of a globally inclusive regulatory regime focused on preventive and precautionary approaches to environmental harm – or of the problems of negotiating one on such a complex subject.[1] It is *par excellence* a global problem, potentially affecting all states, and for which global solutions are essential. That was the reason for negotiating the two principal multilateral environmental agreements (MEAs) on the subject – the UN Framework Convention on Climate Change (UNFCCC) and the Kyoto Protocol. It was the reason for trying to negotiate a further global agreement at Copenhagen in 2009. Often referred to as 'international regimes', MEAs with their related protocols and soft law have been employed by states and international institutions to provide a regulatory system capable of dynamic evolution. The UNFCCC and Kyoto Protocol have thus become complex regulatory regimes, with regular meetings of the parties developing policies, principles and rules.

The process of elaborating these regimes has been characterised as one of 'interactional dialogue',[2] but its essential feature is negotiation and bargaining leading to adoption of a text agreed by consensus. Negotiations on climate change have always been difficult because of the complexity of the issues and the diversity of the interests at stake. This is not because the science is difficult or uncertain: it is not. We know that greenhouse gas emissions have already raised average global temperatures by some $0.7\,°C$, and that whatever measures are

* I am grateful to Darragh Conway, LLM Edinburgh 2010, for research assistance, and to my colleague Navraj Singh Ghaleigh for various insights, but any errors or oversights are all my own.
1 See *inter alia* L. Rajamani, 'Addressing the Post-Kyoto Stress Disorder' (2009) 58 *ICLQ* 803; A. Proelss, 'International Environmental Law and the Challenge of Climate Change' (2010) 53 *German YbIL* 65.
2 J. Brunnée, 'COPing with Consent: Law-making under MEAs' (2002) 15 *Leiden JIL* 1. See also J. Brunnée and S. Toope, 'International Law and Constructivism: Elements of an Interactional Theory of International Law' (2000) 39 *Columbia JTL* 19.

taken now can at best limit future increases to around 2°C.[3] That will inevitably cause damage on a significant scale, especially to countries that are already low-lying or arid. But whatever the scientists may say, the politicians have a shorter-term perspective. Developed states want to keep the costs of adaptation down and the timescales long. Many have serious problems convincing electorates and legislatures that more needs to be done, although in this respect Europe is arguably further advanced than its main competitors. It has certainly been more willing to make commitments on greenhouse gas (GHG) emissions reductions[4] than the US, Canada or Japan, but the attempt by the European Union to provide international leadership on climate change has plainly not succeeded. European diplomacy has failed to move the US or the major developing states, partly because Europe has much less leverage on climate change than on trade. But opposition to new measures on GHG emissions or fossil fuel consumption is so strong in the US that it must be doubtful whether greater leverage would achieve anything. The newly industrialised economies such as China, India and Brazil want the developed states to show that they will live up to their commitment to shoulder most of the burden of change. Only then is it realistic to expect them to agree to take measures to contain their own GHG emissions. Many of the states most likely to be seriously affected by climate change are poorly resourced developing countries, and they rely heavily on developed states, the UN and the World Bank to come up with the money and resources they need to mitigate the worst effects. They have little or no leverage over the main players.

International agreement on further measures nevertheless remains essential for future progress – reducing GHG emissions and sustaining carbon sinks can no more be left to national policies and measures than could the promotion of free trade. In both cases international regulation provides the indispensable basis for collective action based on agreed objectives and common standards. But it does not follow that the existing structure of global climate regulation created by the 1992 UNFCCC and the Kyoto Protocol is the right one for the future or that it can succeed without support from other international regimes and institutions. The purpose of this chapter is to explore some of those questions.

The UNFCCC is a 'framework convention', i.e. it does not itself regulate climate change but only creates a basis for doing so. The strength of this framework is the opportunity it offers for negotiating multilateral solutions to environmental problems and the development of policies and measures, including binding regulations and non-binding guidelines, based on the best

3 IPCC, *Climate Change 2007: Synthesis Report* (Bangkok: IPCC, 2007); UNEP, *The Emissions Gap Report: Are the Copenhagen Accord Pledges Sufficient to Limit Global Warming to 2° C or 1.5° C? A Preliminary Assessment* (Nairobi: UNEP, 2010). For a good general study see E. Zedillo (ed.), *Global Warming: Looking Beyond Kyoto* (Washington, DC: Brooking Institution Press, 2008).
4 In 2009 the EU Council agreed a unilateral emissions reduction target of 20 per cent by 2020, calculated from a 1990 baseline.

science available. It has legitimacy: no other model of international governance offers such an inclusive and transparent basis for regulating phenomena of global character, such as global warning or ozone depletion, where no single state's acts are responsible and where the interests of all are at stake.

The model's most fundamental weakness, evidenced by the Kyoto Protocol and the Copenhagen negotiations in 2009, is that it depends on the ability of the parties to reach the necessary agreement on further measures that are strong enough to have an impact within the necessary timescale. This cannot be taken for granted. While the Kyoto Protocol certainly dictates reductions in GHG emissions for some developed states based on 1990 levels, even if met in full these targets fall well short of what will be needed to achieve a meaningful effect on atmospheric concentrations of GHGs. The protocol represents at best only a first step in the development of a stronger regime. Nor can the participation of all the important players be guaranteed, as the continuing opposition of the United States to participation in the protocol or a successor shows only too well.

Just as importantly, the concept of common but differentiated responsibility, as conceived in the UNFCCC and replicated by Kyoto, has so far relieved developing states of any obligation to constrain GHG emissions, however significant they may become. The rapidly rising CO_2 emissions generated by China and India are thus currently unregulated by Kyoto. At the same time, the globalisation of industrial output brought about by the World Trade Organization (WTO) free trade regime has in effect outsourced production from developed states covered by Kyoto's emissions reduction targets to developing states that have no such obligation. Changing this element of the trade bargain would also entail challenging the principle of common but differentiated responsibility, which is one of the cornerstones of the UNFCCC and Kyoto Protocol. Thus a key issue in the climate negotiations remains whether to preserve the architecture of historic responsibility agreed at Kyoto, or to start again with a new set of basic assumptions about who must take responsibility for reducing GHG emissions in future.

Here we can see that the climate regime established by the UNFCCC is not the whole picture. If climate change is to be tackled successfully then not just the US but also the industrialised developing states – especially China, India and Brazil – have to be brought into the GHG emissions and carbon management control regime. If trade is part of the problem, then alterations to the WTO trade regime may also have to be part of the answer. That cannot be achieved through the UNFCCC. Similarly, carbon capture and storage requires sub-seabed depositories and must be compatible with the Law of the Sea Convention and the London Dumping Convention. That requires cooperation by the parties to those treaties. Climate change policy cannot be implemented through the UNFCCC alone but requires co-ordination of policies and measures by a range of international institutions inside and outside the UN system.

The remaining sections of this chapter will focus on six sets of issues: the impact of Kyoto on GHG emissions; the Copenhagen, Cancun and Durban agreements; alternative negotiating frameworks; human rights perspectives; law of the sea perspectives; trade law perspectives.

3.2 The impact of the Kyoto Protocol on Greenhouse Gas (GHG) emissions

By the end of 2010 GHG emissions from the EU had fallen by more than 17 per cent since 1990. It seems very likely that the EU will not merely meet its Kyoto obligations, but also its own voluntary commitment to achieve a 20 per cent reduction by 2020.[5] However, this is a somewhat illusory achievement, since it is more than offset by increased GHG emissions in those developing countries from which the EU now imports manufactured goods, most of all China. On that basis EU and US consumption emissions are estimated to have risen by over 40 per cent since 1990, corresponding to the rapid acceleration in Chinese production.[6] Since Kyoto targets are focused on GHG emissions rather than on consumption, most parties to Kyoto appear likely to meet their targets, except Canada (which has given notice to terminate its participation in the protocol). The data shows that global CO_2 emissions have stabilised, but they have not reduced, nor have they stabilised global temperatures.[7] Overall world emissions are down by just 0.1 per cent in 2009 compared to the previous year, but the detailed picture is more varied. CO_2 emissions derived from energy use have fallen 6.9 per cent in Europe and North America over the previous year, but this may owe more to the economic recession in these states than to measures taken to reduce emissions. In Africa emissions over the same period have fallen by 3.1 per cent, and in Eurasia by 9.2 per cent, while in Asia and Oceania they have risen by 7.5 per cent. In South America they are up by 3.6 per cent, and in the Middle East by 3.3 per cent. While US emissions are down 7.0 per cent compared to the previous year (to 5425 m tonnes), China's have risen 13.3 per cent in a year (to 7711 m tonnes) and it is now the world's largest emitter of CO_2. India's emissions have risen by 8.7 per cent (to 1602 mt) but Brazil's emissions have stabilised, while Russia and South Africa have lower emissions. At 4310 mt European emissions are now well below those of China and the US, but still ahead of South America, Africa and the Middle East combined.

On this data China and the US hold the key to controlling future anthropogenic emissions. China is not only the biggest emitter, but has by far the fastest growth in emissions. Its CO_2 emissions from energy use are up 340 per cent on 1990 levels. However, on a *per capita* basis Chinese emissions are still less

5 EEA Technical Report No 2/2011, *European Union Greenhouse Gas Inventory 1990–2009 and Inventory Report 2011: Submission to the UNFCCC Secretariat* (Copenhagen: EEA, 2011).

6 A. Brinkley and S. Less, *Carbon Omissions – Consumption-based Accounting for International Carbon Emissions* (London: Policy Exchange, 2010).

7 US Energy Information Administration 2011, available at www.guardian.co.uk/data. The data referred to in this section are all from this report.

than one-third of the US, while European and Japanese per capita emissions are just under half those of the US. To that extent the US remains easily the least efficient user of energy on the planet. Moreover, even in the midst of a recession, US energy-derived CO_2 emissions are still some 7.6 per cent higher than 1990 levels, while Europe's are down about 5.1 per cent compared to 1990. These figures suggest that the US would not have complied with Kyoto had it become a party, but they also suggest that it could have done so with relatively little effort through more efficient use of energy. However, these calculations take no account of other GHGs or of forestry or land-use changes.

Most importantly, there has been no overall reduction in the rate of increase in atmospheric CO_2 or global mean temperature. Limiting global temperature increase to $1.5\,°C$ is not achievable on this record and even $2\,°C$ is doubtful. Given the conclusions of the 4th IPCC Assessment Report we can see that Kyoto alone cannot meet the 'ultimate objective' of stabilising GHG concentrations 'at a level that would prevent dangerous anthropogenic interference with the climate system'.[8] Much more is needed, and would be, even if the US were a party and everyone complies fully with their existing Kyoto emissions reduction requirements. Even with US participation, the developed economies cannot by themselves do all that would be necessary to contain the global temperature rise to 2°C. The developing economies – and above all China – will have to carry some of the burden. From this perspective common but differentiated responsibility as represented in the Kyoto Protocol is not a viable basis for saving the climate.

A United Nations Environment Programme (UNEP) report in 2010 concluded that steep emission reductions are needed post-2020 in order to have any chance of limiting global warming to 2°C. The report explains:

—That emission levels of approximately 44 gigatonnes of carbon dioxide equivalent (GtCO2e) (range: 39–44 GtCO2e) in 2020 would be consistent with a "likely" chance of limiting global warming to 2° C.
—Under business-as-usual projections, global emissions could reach 56 GtCO2e (range: 54–60GtCO2e) in 2020, leaving a gap of 12 GtCO2e.
—If the lowest-ambition pledges were implemented in a "lenient" fashion, emissions could be lowered slightly to 53 GtCO2e (range: 52–57 GtCO2e), leaving a significant gap of 9 GtCO2e.
—The gap could be reduced substantially by policy options being discussed in the negotiations.[9]

3.3 Copenhagen, Cancun and Durban negotiations

The Copenhagen Conference in 2010 was supposed to agree, *inter alia*, GHG emissions reduction targets to come into effect after the expiry of the 2012

---

8 UNFCCC, Article 2.
9 UNEP, *The Emissions Gap Report: A Preliminary Assessment* (Nairobi: UNEP, 2010), p. 4.

Kyoto commitment period. It failed to do so. There were serious divisions and a negotiating breakdown. No binding agreement was concluded to replace or extend Kyoto. Only a non-binding 'accord' was adopted, but not as a decision of the Conference of the Parties (COP), and not by consensus of all the states participating. In contrast the subsequent meetings at Cancun and Durban have restored trust in the UNFCCC process and produced concrete results: they reflect far better diplomacy and the absence of high-profile politicians. Consensus was achieved, albeit with Bolivian opposition.

The Copenhagen Accords – essentially voluntary commitments to reduce carbon emissions and undertake other measures – have now been adopted as COP decisions at Cancun. Draft decision-/CP.16 defines, for the first time, a timetable and a precise objective. The parties agree ' … in the context of the long-term goal and the ultimate objective of the Convention and the Bali Action Plan, to work towards identifying a global goal for substantially reducing global emissions by 2050'. Further negotiations are thus required, but they will remain within the framework of the UNFCCC. Moreover there is also agreement:

> that deep cuts in global greenhouse gas emissions are required according to science, and as documented in the Fourth Assessment Report of the Inter-governmental Panel on Climate Change, with a view to reducing global greenhouse gas emissions so as to hold the increase in global average temperature below 2°C above pre-industrial levels, and that Parties should take urgent action to meet this long-term goal, consistent with science and on the basis of equity. …

Here we can see that holding global temperature increase to 2°C has now become the agreed long-term target. This is still 0.5°C higher than the small island states had sought, and it will not prevent harmful effects, but it is – potentially – achievable, albeit not easily.

Cancun does not repudiate the principle of common but differentiated responsibility, but it subtly and significantly changes the terms of the engagement between developed and developing economies. First, all states agree that:

> Parties should cooperate in achieving the peaking of global and national greenhouse gas emissions as soon as possible, recognizing that the time frame for peaking will be longer in developing countries, and bearing in mind that social and economic development and poverty eradication are the first and overriding priorities of developing countries and that a low-carbon development strategy is indispensable to sustainable development.

There is a longer timescale for developing states, but both developed and developing states have now made commitments to do more, albeit in different terms. For Annex I parties the commitment is to make 'quantified economy-wide emission reduction targets to be implemented by Parties included in Annex I to the Convention as communicated by them and contained in document FCCC/SB/2010/INF.X4'. Translated into plain English the developed states have undertaken to reduce GHG emissions by the amount indicated by them as part of the Copenhagen Accord. These are not multilaterally agreed targets, unlike Kyoto; instead, each party has determined the level of its own reductions.[10]

Second, the more important departure from Kyoto is that developing state parties, including China, for the first time accept a commitment to reduce their own emissions: 'developing country Parties will take nationally appropriate mitigation actions in the context of sustainable development, supported and enabled by technology, financing and capacity-building, aimed at achieving a deviation in emissions relative to business as usual emissions in 2020'. This is less precise than the commitments made by Annex I parties, but it is more than non-Annex I parties are required to do by Kyoto. To that extent common but differentiated responsibility no longer means no emissions reductions by developing states: it means a commitment to different levels of reduction at different speeds.[11] The agreement on REDD (Reducing Emissions from Deforestation and Forest Degradation in Developing Countries) is also significant for the same reason.

Third, and equally importantly, the parties agreed:

> to establish a process for international assessment of emissions and removals related to quantified, economy-wide emissions reductions targets in the Subsidiary Body for Implementation, taking into account national circumstances, in a rigorous, robust and transparent manner, with a view to promoting comparability and building confidence.

Put simply, there will now be international monitoring and verification of national commitments to reduce GHG emissions. This is perhaps the most important achievement at Cancun since it will provide some mechanism for ensuring that all parties comply with what has been agreed.

The Durban conference finally moved the negotiating process back to the question of what happens after the current Kyoto Protocol emissions reduction period expires later this year. There are three important decisions. First, the

---

10 Among the more important but heavily conditional GHG emissions reduction 'commitments' are the following: Australia: 5 per cent unconditionally or 25 per cent by 2020 if further agreement; Belarus: 5–10 per cent if access to technology etc; Canada: 17 per cent aligned with US if legislation enacted; EU: 20 per cent unconditionally or 30 per cent conditionally; Japan: 25 per cent if comprehensive agreement; Russia: No specific target – range of reductions 'will depend on' various conditions; Ukraine: 20 per cent, if agreement among Annex I parties; USA: 'In the range of' 17 per cent against a base year of 2005, subject to legislation (which has not been passed).

11 Commitments include: China: 40–50 per cent per unit of GDP by 2020, and an increase in forests and non-fossil fuels; Brazil: 36–38 per cent by 2020 through reduced deforestation, new farming practices, energy efficiency and alternative fuels; India: 20–25 per cent voluntary reduction by 2020 (base year 2005); South Africa: 34 per cent reduction by 2020 and 42 per cent by 2025, depending on financial support/technology transfer etc., and the conclusion of a binding agreement.

parties agreed to a second Kyoto commitment period which will last either five (2013–17) or eight (2013–20) years, but without Japan, Russia and Canada. Second, they initiated the negotiation of a 'protocol, another legal instrument or an agreed outcome with legal force' applicable to all Parties to the Convention. The new protocol will enter into force in 2020 and address, *inter alia*, mitigation, adaptation, finance, technology transfer, transparency and capacity-building. Third, the gap between commitments made and commitments needed to meet the 2°C target would be addressed by further negotiations in the years before the new agreement comes into force. There are significant ambiguities here, and further negotiations are still required to finalise the new protocol and agree on additional commitments. But this does move the process beyond Cancun.

It nevertheless remains true that we are still a long way from doing enough to stabilise the situation at a 2°C increase. The key question continues to be whether China and the US will do more domestically to drive down global emissions much faster than at present. The US Congress has shown no interest in doing so, but China appears more serious about the commitments it has made. An economic boom would rapidly negate the current modest progress, however.

3.4 Institutional problems: the negotiating framework

The UNFCCC and the Kyoto Protocol are simply treaties – legally binding agreements between participating states that create what is in effect a free-standing international regulatory regime. The key institutional element of that regime is the Conference or Meeting of the Parties (MOP) which provides a political forum for negotiating more detailed rules and commitments. The most important of these is obviously the Kyoto Protocol, which itself follows the same institutional arrangements. These bodies operate outside the formal structure of the UN system or any other international organisation. They are neither UN specialised agencies like the International Maritime Organization (IMO) nor UN programmes like UNEP. Rather, they operate as autonomous intergovernmental structures whose competence is neither exclusive nor comprehensive, but is limited to regulating climate change.

The UNFCCC negotiating model involves universal participation and negotiation by consensus, rather than voting on the text. The benefit of this model is that it allows complex, comprehensive and inclusive agreements to be negotiated, relying on the 'politics of interdependence' that characterises regulation of world trade, the oceans, or the global environment. This model was successful at Rio and Kyoto, but it is does not always work, and it has not worked smoothly in the current phase of negotiations on climate change.

Participation in the UNFCCC regulatory process is open to all members of the UN system (UNFCCC, Art. 20). In theory any state can stay outside the regime: there is no compulsion to become a party. In practice participation is nearly universal. At the time of writing there were 192 parties to the

UNFCCC[12] and only three UN Member States were not parties but participated as observers: Andorra, Somalia and Iraq. Taiwan was the only significant non-UN non-party.[13] Diversity of political interests among the participants is a prominent feature of the UNFCCC/Kyoto process. This is not a regime that can be understood in terms of a simple split into developed (Annex I) and developing states (non-Annex I). While the major developed states are nearly all members of the Organisation for Economic Cooperation and Development (OECD), they disagree over climate policy. Many developing state parties have little in common. Notable examples are the small islands states which may disappear with sea-level rise and the Arabian oil producers with a vested interest in pumping more fossil fuels. The main groupings within the system include the Association of Small Island States (AOSIS) (43 states), least developed countries (49 states), the EU (27 states), the group of 77 (developing countries plus China), the Umbrella Group of non-EU developed states (which includes Canada, Australia, Japan, Russia, Ukraine and US), the 'environmental integrity group' (Mexico, Korea, Switzerland, Liechtenstein, Monaco) and 13 OPEC states. Membership of groups is important because only group representatives have access to many of the informal consultations and to the final phase of the negotiations.

The inclusivity of the regime is strengthened by a consensus/package deal negotiating procedure which generates a greater need to engage in diplomacy, to listen, and to bargain than would be the case when decisions are taken by majority vote. A consensus agreement usually entails an interlocking whole or 'package deal' whose integrity is protected by a prohibition on reservations – in effect an all-or-nothing bargain. In essence this means that there is normally no voting and a text is adopted only when states no longer object to the deal as a whole. Bringing the negotiations to that stage requires delicate diplomacy which balances the vital interests of all the main groups in the negotiations. Every group of states has to be accommodated in this process – none can be ignored. Powerful states or groups of states cannot simply dictate what should be in an agreement without risking ultimate breakdown. The concerns of small or otherwise insignificant states have to be accommodated. This explains the influence of AOSIS during the original UNFCCC negotiations, but also the need to keep the United States on board during the current negotiations.

Processes of the kind just described tend to enhance the legitimacy of what has been agreed and make it more likely that states will comply, but they also make it harder to reach agreement. The failure of the Copenhagen negotiations in 2009 shows that consensus requires compromises that may be unobtainable, or may result in a text that is weaker or more ambiguous than some states are prepared to accept. Negotiations can only proceed at the pace of the slowest learner. There is little doubt that it is quicker and easier to negotiate a new

12 This includes the EU and two non-UN members (Niue and Cook Islands).
13 The Holy See participates as an observer.

text by majority vote, but also little point. If global problems require global solutions then the process must be capable of delivering globally. Even two-thirds majorities are not enough for that purpose if some key states are in the minority, and that is why the climate regime is not in principle a process of majority decision-making. But if the compromises necessary to engineer con-sensus cannot be reached then nothing will be agreed, and some way must be found to overcome that outcome. For that reason the option of adopting a text by majority vote is normally retained as a fallback if all else fails. Much will then depend on how many states are in the minority and how important their participation may be.

Whether to join in a consensus is thus a potentially delicate decision. A state that refuses to do so may find itself ignored, as Bolivia was eventually ignored at Cancun, or it may simply be part of a tiny minority if it forces matters to a vote, a position in which the US regularly finds itself. But if the participation of a state is essential to the deal under discussion then other states may have no option but to keep negotiating if stalemate is to be avoided. Thus, to stand any chance of success, a deal on climate change will have to enjoy the support of the EU, the US, China, India, Brazil, Canada, Australia, Japan, the major oil-producing states, AOSIS and the G77 grouping of developing states. A simple majority of votes will not be sufficient to produce a globally inclusive outcome.

Are there alternatives to a global consensus deal? Possibly, but they all have serious drawbacks. The easiest alternative is a coalition of the willing within the OECD – in effect an agreement among the Kyoto Annex I parties. The obvious problem is that the OECD does not include China, India, or Brazil. A G20 agreement is possibly a better model because it includes these states. Nevertheless, even that would probably remain useful only in tandem with UNFCCC negotiations, but the G20 could supply the necessary political input for a broader agreement if it could agree on one.

A more contentious alternative is the creation of an international environ-mental organisation, based on turning UNEP into something more like the WTO. The fragmented structure of international environmental governance is obvious when viewed from a climate perspective, and it might be thought that regulation of climate change and the co-ordination of international environmental law-making should therefore be the responsibility of a dedicated international environmental organisation. Proposals to create such a body or to turn UNEP into a UN specialised agency have not so far found the necessary support, but the idea has not gone away and it remains strongly supported by some states, most notably France and Germany. The main argu-ments in favour are essentially bureaucratic. First, it is said that UNEP's standing, funding and political influence would be enhanced. Second, co-ordination and policy coherence would be improved if it hosted the secretariats of the major environmental treaties. This could reduce overlaps and duplication, while improving effectiveness. Protagonists rightly point to fragmentation of existing structures, the relative weakness of UNEP as the principal UN body with general environmental competence and the powerful focus the International Monetary Fund (IMF), the World Bank and the WTO bring to economic development. Several models are canvassed by those in favour. The most radical would merge existing bodies into a powerful new intergovernmental environmental organisation with decision-making and enforcement powers. A less radical vision would merge existing environmental institutions and treaties into a new organisation similar to the WTO. The least radical choice would simply upgrade UNEP into a UN specialised agency rather like the IMO.

Sceptics remain unconvinced by some of these arguments. To them a new environmental organisation is politically unrealistic and would not be any better at securing the necessary decisions. Insofar as reform is necessary to enhance the efficiency of the present eclectic system, they favour a simple clustering of MEAs within UNEP and greater efforts to co-ordinate international action.[14] A UN environment agency could not monopolise the field. It could not take over the environmental responsibilities of other specialised agencies, such as the Food and Agriculture Organization or the IMO: the work of these bodies has an important climate change dimension which cannot be separated from their general responsibilities. Nor is it evident how co-ordination of environmental treaty regimes would be any easier under a specialised agency. States are no more likely to negotiate or revise climate agreements under a new agency than they are at present, and the agency could not impose change unless given unusual powers. There may well be efficiencies to be gained from a 'clustering' of secretariat services and non-compliance procedures within UNEP. Certainly, there is a need for a system that can ensure the integration of environmental and development objectives in a more balanced and efficient manner,[15] but a more centralised, bureaucratic and entrenched institution may be less likely to influence the system as a whole, or to facilitate the cross-sectoral integration that the UN's Agenda 21 seeks to promote.

It is thus far from obvious that this idea represents a viable alternative to the present system, whether for regulation of climate change or in respect of any other environmental topic. The WTO has not succeeded in negotiating a deal in the current Doha trade round. It is hardly a good model for regulating an even more contentious subject. A new environmental organisation could work if given sufficient power and resources, but that is most unlikely to happen.

That leaves the UN as the only existing body with the potential to influence the UNFCCC negotiating process effectively. The main asset of the UN General Assembly (UNGA) is its universality, but if consensus cannot be achieved

---

14 All of these are arguments are comprehensively addressed in F. Biermann and S. Bauer, *A World Environment Organization* (Aldershot: Ashgate, 2005). On clustering see K. Von Moltke, 'On Clustering International Environmental Agreements', in G. Winter (ed.), *Multilevel Governance of Global Environmental Change* (Cambridge: Cambridge University Press, 2006), pp. 409–29.

15 J. Ayling (1997) 9 *JEL* 243, at p. 268; W. Chambers (ed.), 'Serving Many Voices: Progressing Calls for an International Environmental Organisation', in *Reforming International Environmental Governance* (New York: United Nations University Press, 2005), pp. 13–39.

through the UNFCCC process it seems unlikely that the UNGA will be any more successful. It would face exactly the same political obstacles. Only the UN Security Council (UNSC) has the necessary status and legal authority to change the mould and legislate for climate change without the consensus agreement of other states. Could the UNSC become an alternative international legislature in order to fill the vacuum left by any failure in the UNFCCC law-making process? Some authors have used the concept of 'environmental security' to envisage a greater role for the UNSC in dealing with environmental threats and emergencies.[16] Measures to promote environmental protection may in some circumstances be necessary for the maintenance of international peace and security, thus giving the UNSC power to take mandatory action under Chapter VII, but 'the language of the Charter, not to speak of the clear record of the original meaning, does not easily lend itself to such an interpretation'.[17] The UNSC has acted cautiously in this respect, using its Chapter VII powers only once in relation to an environmental matter, to hold Iraq responsible in international law for environmental damage inflicted on Kuwait during the 1991 Gulf war.[18] In 2007 it also held its first ever debate on climate change.

Moreover, although the UNSC is not formally a law-making body, since 9/11 it has started to use its mandatory powers to adopt a small number of binding resolutions on anti-terrorism measures laying down general rules for all states.[19] There are some obvious advantages to UNSC law-making rather than the more formal processes of negotiation through the UNGA or a treaty conference. First, all UN Member States are bound to comply with Chapter VII resolutions – there is no room for opt-outs or reservations. Second, such resolutions prevail over other international agreements and they do not have to conform to existing general international law.[20] UNSC law-making could thus enhance the coherence of international law if used appropriately. To that extent the UNSC could become an instrument of law reform, overcoming the problem of the 'persistent objector' in customary law and the 'free-rider' in multilateral treaties.

Nevertheless, to give the UNSC an enhanced role as an international legislator in areas such as climate change would be a tenable option only if the

---

16 A. Timoshenko, 'Ecological Security: Response to Global Challenges', in E. Brown Weiss (ed.), *Environmental Change and International Law* (New York: United Nations University Press, 1992), ch. 13; L. Elliott, 'Expanding the Mandate of the United Nations Security Council', in Chambers (ed.), *Reforming International Environmental Governance*, but for contrary views see P. Szasz, 'International Norm-making', in E. Brown Weiss (ed.), *Environmental Change and International Law*, pp. 359–61; C. Tinker (1992) 59 *Tennessee LR* 787.

17 Szasz, 'International Norm-making', p. 359.

18 UNSC Res 687.

19 Two striking and unprecedented examples are SC resolutions 1373 (2001) and 1540 (2005) both Chapter VII resolutions passed in the aftermath of the 11 September 2001 attacks in New York and Washington and later atrocities.

20 'The Charter does not provide that decisions ... in order to be enforceable must be in conformity with the law which exists at the time they are adopted.' Kelsen, *The Law of the United Nations* (New York: United Nations University Press, 1950), pp. 294–95.

process can be legitimised and made generally acceptable to states. At present it is questionable whether the unreformed UNSC can be said to have the right process to make itself legitimate as a law-making body. Whether viewed in terms of accountability, participation, procedural fairness, or transparency of decision-making, it remains a seriously deficient vehicle for the exercise of legislative competence. It presents a stark contrast to consensus-based treaty negotiations like the UN Convention on the Law of the Sea (UNCLOS) or the UNFCCC, or to the adoption of resolutions by the UNGA. The vast majority of UNGA Member States would in effect be excluded from the law-making process. This may be justifiable in cases where urgent action is required to maintain or restore peace and security, but should the UNGA be excluded even when less urgent law-making is undertaken? Further resort to Chapter VII law-making would also evade national control over the process of treaty ratification and may on that basis be regarded as undemocratic. It has already encountered problems of acceptability before national courts.[21] For all these reasons expansive use of Chapter VII powers by an unreformed UNSC is more likely to be resisted by some states regardless of the binding character of these resolutions.[22]

The problems are obvious if we consider current UNSC membership from the perspective of major GHG emissions: the US, China, Russia are already on the UNSC, but India and Brazil are not permanent members. The EU is fully represented only if Britain, France and the one other EU Member State on the UNSC can present a co-ordinated European position. Most of the other GHG emitters and oil-producing states are only represented in the UNGA: a UNSC law-making process would have to involve UNGA participation to be inclusive.

But if we get the process right then the UNSC could be seen as one way of breaking any deadlock in UNFCCC negotiations. In this context legitimacy, constitutionality and process are intimately connected. The most effective way to engage in UNSC law-making would be to ensure that such resolutions are debated and adopted in UNGA first – before giving them binding force in UNSC. It would also be necessary to maintain and enhance deliberative and transparent processes in both the UNGA and UNSC when such resolutions are under discussion, but there is no reason why observers and accredited NGOs should not be involved at this stage as they are in the UNGA and in the UNFCCC.

Law-making by 15 states for the rest of the world is not attractive or likely to work without broader support. In any event, it would be no use unless the US, Russia, China and Europe could agree on what to do, since they all have a veto over the UNSC. But if they can agree then it is probably unnecessary to

---

21 Joined Cases C-402/05 P and 415/05 P *Yassin Abdullah Kadi and Al Barakaat International Foundation v Council of the European Union and Commission of the European Communities* [2008] ECR I-6351.

22 See India's opposition to UNSC 1540: Letter from the Permanent Representative of India to the United Nations, addressed to the President of the Security Council, dated 27 April 2004.

resort to the UNSC in the first place. Thus there seems little practical alternative to the present UN negotiating framework, however slow it may be. Cancun and Durban thus offer at least the illusion of progress while holding open the possibility of a future pregnant with possibility.

3.5 Human rights perspectives

The growing environmental caseload of human rights courts – over 20 cases since 2002 – indicates the importance of the topic. In effect a greening of human rights law has taken place. So extensive is the environmental jurisprudence of the European Court of Human Rights (ECtHR)[23] that proposals for the adoption of an environmental protocol to the European Convention on Human Rights (ECHR) have not been pursued.[24] Instead, a *Manual on Human Rights and the Environment* adopted by the Council of Europe in 2005 recapitulates the ECtHR's decisions on this subject and sets out some general principles. It would be wrong to assume that this is simply a European phenomenon, however. The greening of human rights law extends to the Inter-American and African human rights systems, as well as the 1966 UN Covenant on Civil and Political Rights.[25]

Despite their evolutionary character, human rights treaties still fall short of guaranteeing a right to a decent or satisfactory environment if that concept is understood in broader, essentially qualitative, terms unrelated to impacts on specific humans. It remains true, as the ECtHR re-iterated in Kyrtatos, that 'neither Article 8 nor any of the other articles of the Convention are specifically designed to provide general protection of the environment as such'.[26] This case involved the illegal draining of a wetland. Although the applicants were successful insofar as the state's non-enforcement of a court judgment was concerned, the ECtHR could find no violation of their right to private life or enjoyment of property arising out of the destruction of the area in question. Although they lived nearby, the applicants' rights were not affected. They were not entitled to live in any particular environment, or to have the surrounding environment indefinitely preserved.

---

23 See in particular *Lopez Ostra v Spain* (1994) 20 EHRR 277; *Guerra v Italy* (1998) 26 EHRR 357; *Hatton v UK* [2003] ECHR (Grand Chamber); *Fadeyeva v Russia* [2005] ECHR 376; *Öneryildiz v Turkey* [2004] ECHR 657; *Taskin v Turkey* [2004] ECHR, paras. 113–19; *Tatar v Romania* [2009] ECHR, para 88; *Budayeva v Russia* [2008] ECHR.

24 See Council of Europe: Committee of Experts for the Development of Human Rights, *Final Activity Report on Human Rights and the Environment*, DH-DEV(2005)006rev, Strasbourg, 10 November 2005, pp. 2–3.

25 *Maya indigenous community of the Toledo District v Belize*, Case 12.053, Report No. 40/04, Inter-Am. C.H.R., OEA/Ser.L/V/II.122 Doc. 5 rev. 1 at 727 (2004), para. 150; *Ilmari Lansman et al. v Finland* (1996) ICCPR Communication No. 511/1992, para. 9.4; *Lubicon Lake Band v Canada* (1990) ICCPR Communication No. 167/1984, para. 32.2; *The Social and Economic Rights Action Center and the Center for Economic and Social Rights v Nigeria* (2002) ACHPR Communication 155/96, paras. 52–53.

26 *Kyrtatos v Greece* [2003] ECHR 242, para. 52.

The Inter-American Commission on Human Rights has taken a similar view, rejecting as inadmissible a claim on behalf of all the citizens of Panama to protect a nature reserve from development.[27] In a comparable case concerning objections to the growing of genetically modified crops the UN Human Rights Committee likewise held that 'no person may, in theoretical terms and by *actio popularis*, object to a law or practice which he holds to be at variance with the Covenant'.[28] These cases demonstrate the limitations of civil and political rights as a basis for advancing the general public interest in environmental protection.

Economic and social rights may potentially have somewhat broader environmental implications that could help guarantee some of the indispensable attributes of a decent environment. A 2009 report for the Office of the High Commissioner on Human Rights (OHCHR) emphasises the key point that, 'While the universal human rights treaties do not refer to a specific right to a safe and healthy environment, the United Nations human rights treaty bodies all recognise the intrinsic link between the environment and the realization of a range of human rights, such as the right to life, to health, to food, to water, and to housing.'[29] The UN Human Rights Committee has adopted various General Comments relevant to environmental protection and sustainable development, notably General Comments 14 and 15, which interpret Articles 11 and 12 of the International Covenant on Economic, Social and Cultural Rights (ICESCR) to include access to sufficient, safe and affordable water for domestic uses and sanitation, the prevention and reduction of exposure to harmful substances including radiation and chemicals, or other detrimental environmental conditions that directly or indirectly impact upon human health.

Would human rights law help us to address climate change or ensure justice for those most affected? Certainly the connection has been noted.[30] In 2009 the UN Human Rights Council adopted Resolution 10/4 (2009) on human rights and climate change:

> Noting that climate change-related impacts have a range of implications, both direct and indirect, for the effective enjoyment of human rights including, *inter alia*, the right to life, the right to adequate food, the right to the highest attainable standard of health, the right to adequate housing, the right to self-determination and human rights obligations related to access to safe drinking water and sanitation, and recalling that in no case may a people be deprived of its own means of subsistence.

27 *Metropolitan Nature Reserve v Panama*, Case 11.533, Report No. 88/03, Inter-Am. C.H.R., OEA/Ser.L/V/
II.118 Doc. 70 rev. 2 at 524 (2003), para. 34.
28 *Brun v France* (2006) ICCPR Communication No. 1453/2006, para.6.3.
29 UN HRC, *Report of the OHCHR on the Relationship Between Climate Change and Human Rights*, UN Doc.
A/HRC/10/61, 15 January 2009, para. 18.
30 See generally S. Humphreys (ed.), *Human Rights and Climate Change* (Cambridge: Cambridge University
Press, 2009).

However, before concluding that human rights law may provide answers to the problem of climate change, two cautionary observations in the OHCHR Report[31] are worth highlighting:

> [w]hile climate change has obvious implications for the enjoyment of human rights, it is less obvious whether, and to what extent, such effects can be qualified as human rights violations in a strict legal sense.
>
> (para. 70)

> (...)human rights litigation is not well-suited to promote precautionary measures based on risk assessments, unless such risks pose an imminent threat to the human rights of specific individuals. Yet, by drawing attention to the broader human rights implications of climate change risks, the human rights perspective, in line with the precautionary principle, emphasizes the need to avoid unnecessary delay in taking action to contain the threat of global warming.
>
> (para. 91)

On the view set out here, a human rights perspective on climate change essentially serves to reinforce political pressure coming from the more vulnerable developing states. Its utility is rhetorical rather than juridical. Governments obviously have a legal responsibility towards their own population at least to help them adapt to or mitigate harmful impacts of climate change. But this essentially domestic, internally focused perspective does not address the larger global issue of preventing climate change – it merely assists with amelioration of harm to particular individuals and communities within a state's own borders.

The more difficult question is whether GHG emitters have a legal responsibility to protect people in *other* states from the harmful impacts of those emissions on the global climate. Human rights treaties generally require a state party to secure the relevant rights and freedoms for everyone within its own territory or subject to its jurisdiction.[32] The question whether these treaties can have extra-territorial application is for that reason a difficult one. There are some precedents in favour but mainly where a state is in control of territory or there is a 'common legal space'.[33] Even if this reasoning is correct in cases of transboundary pollution affecting a neighbouring state,[34] it does not follow

---

31 UN HRC, *Report of the OHCHR on the Relationship between Climate Change and Human Rights.*

32 1950 European Convention on Human Rights, Article 1; 1966 UN Covenant on Civil and Political Rights, Article 2.

33 See, e.g., *Legal Consequences of the Construction of a Wall in the Occupied Palestinian Territory, Advisory Opinion,* ICJ Reports 2004, para. 109; *Ecuador v. Colombia (Admissibility)* [2010] IACHR Report No.112/10, paras. 89–100; *Cyprus v Turkey* [2001] ECHR No.25781/94; *Loizidou v Turkey (Preliminary Objections)* [1995] ECHR Sers. A/310, para. 87; *Loizidou v Turkey (Merits)* [1996-VI] ECHR, para. 52. Contrast *Bankovic v Belgium and ors.* [2001] ECHR No. 52207/99.

34 The question arises in the *Aerial Spraying Case (Ecuador v Colombia)* currently (2011) awaiting a hearing in the ICJ.

that it will be equally valid in cases of global environmental harm, such as climate change. Here the obvious problem is the multiplicity of causes and states contributing to the problem, and the difficulty of showing any direct connection to the victims. The inhabitants of sinking islands in the South Seas may justifiably complain of human rights violations, but who is responsible? Those states like the UK, US and Germany whose historic emissions have unforeseeably caused the problem? China and India whose current emissions have foreseeably made matters worse? The US or Canada, which have failed to agree to, or to take adequate measures to, limit further emissions, or to stabilise global temperatures at 1990 levels? At this point it may be better to accept, as the OHCHR appears to have done, that human rights law is not the right medium for addressing a shared global problem of this kind and that further negotiations through the UNFCCC process are the only answer.

3.6 Law of the Sea perspectives

For low-lying states and small islands, sea-level rise and changes in the marine ecosystem are the most immediate threats posed by climate change. The 1982 UNCLOS provides a fairly comprehensive regime for the protection and preservation of the marine environment and the prevention, reduction and control of marine pollution damage to other states. Its provisions are increasingly relevant to climate change insofar as GHG emissions cause marine pollution and harm the marine environment. In particular, Article 192 provides that 'States have the obligation to protect and preserve the marine environment'. The 'marine environment' for this purpose includes 'rare and fragile ecosystems as well as the habitat of depleted, threatened or endangered species and other forms of marine life'.[35] In addition, states parties to UNCLOS also have an obligation under Article 117 to conserve 'the living resources of the high seas'. The latter phrase certainly covers fish and marine mammals.[36] Later treaties, such as the 1992 Convention on Biological Diversity, suggest that, consistently with the objects and purposes of UNCLOS,[37] Part XII can readily be interpreted to cover protection of marine biodiversity in general, and conservation of coral reefs in particular.[38] The obligation of states is thus not confined to the protection of economic interests, private property or the human use of

---

35 Article 194(5).

36 See references to fisheries organizations, fishing patterns, and marine mammals in Articles 118–20.

37 See in particular the preambular paragraphs: 'Recognizing the desirability of establishing through this Convention, with due regard for the sovereignty of all States, a legal order for the seas and oceans which will facilitate international communication, and will promote the peaceful uses of the seas and oceans, the equitable and efficient utilization of their resources, the conservation of their living resources, and the study, protection and preservation of the marine environment ... '

38 In *Import Prohibition of Certain Shrimp and Shrimp Products*, WTO Appellate Body (1998) WT/DS58/AB/R, at paras. 130–31, the WTO Appellate Body interpreted the phrase *'exhaustible natural resources'* in the GATT Agreement by reference *inter alia* to the 1992 Convention on Biological Diversity.

the sea implied in the Convention's definition of 'pollution'.[39] Part XV provides for compulsory settlement of UNCLOS disputes by a variety of international courts and tribunals, and this may give weaker states with limited influence in negotiations the opportunity to exert greater pressure on GHG emitters through litigation.

Atmospheric deposition of CO_2 into the marine environment arguably falls within the terms of Article 192 and the subsequent provisions of Part XII. It may be that other greenhouse gases are also relevant, but CO_2 appears to be the most important and to have the greatest impact on the health of the oceans. Article 194 requires states to take measures necessary to prevent marine pollution 'from any source'. There is an indicative list of sources in Article 194(3) which covers, *inter alia*, 'the release of toxic, harmful or noxious substances, especially those which are persistent, from land-based sources, from or through the atmosphere or by dumping'. While anthropogenic GHG emissions are not specifically listed here, it is entirely plausible to read Article 194(3) as covering atmospheric depositions of CO_2 resulting in marine pollution. A significant proportion of marine pollution already comes from airborne depositions, and it has never been suggested that this is excluded from UNCLOS. If there were any doubt about this, reference could also be made to Article 207 on land-based sources of marine pollution. Article 212 would cover CO_2 emissions from ships or aircraft, although it might be argued that it goes no further than that. Taken together, Articles 194 and 212 appear to cover all airborne sources of marine pollution comprehensively, including GHGs.

These CO_2 emissions have caused marine pollution. Article 1(1)(4) of UNCLOS defines 'pollution of the marine environment' to include the introduction of *substances* or *energy* resulting in harm to the marine environment. CO_2 emissions appear to have resulted in the deposition of excess anthropogenic carbon into the oceans, altering their chemistry, and making them more acidic.[40] They also appear to have added 'energy' to the oceans, either directly by causing ocean temperatures to rise, or indirectly by melting ice caps and glaciers, resulting in sea-level rise. Evidence evaluated in reports from various UN specialised agencies has shown that these depositions have caused or are likely

---

39 Article 1(1)(4), on which see below.
40 The surface ocean absorbs around one quarter of the carbon dioxide emitted to the atmosphere. 'As more ... anthropogenic CO2 has been emitted into the atmosphere, the ocean has absorbed greater amounts at increasingly rapid rates' (CBD, *Scientific Synthesis of the Impacts of Ocean Acidification on Marine Biodiversity*, CBD Technical Series no. 46, p. 9). 'Ocean uptake of CO2 ... from increasing atmospheric CO2 concentrations, reduces surface ocean pH and carbonate ion concentrations. ... ' As a result, ' ... the oceans are becoming increasingly acidic, jeopardizing marine biodiversity and even entire ecosystems (e.g. coral reefs)' (IOC/UNESCO, *Building Stewardship for the Ocean: The Contribution of UNESCO to Responsible Ocean Governance, Our Changing Oceans: Conclusions of the First International Symposium on the Effects of Climate Change on the World's Oceans (Gijon, 2008), ICES Journal of Marine Science Advance* Access (4 June 2009) pp. 1–4, at p. 1.). See generally, M. Allsopp *et al.*, *State of the World's Oceans* (Dordrecht: Springer, 2009), ch. 5.

to cause the kind of harmful effects listed in Article 1(1)(4).[41] Typical damage that has been identified includes sea-water intrusion affecting freshwater aquifers and inundating coastal areas, causing disruption of family life for those who live on affected coastlines. There is also economic loss to coastal communities resulting from depleted fish stocks, coral bleaching and loss of marine bio-diversity resulting from higher temperatures and acidification. Sea-level rise may in extreme cases result in internal displacement of populations or even wholesale abandonment of islands or territory. Low-lying countries such as Bangladesh are particularly vulnerable.

Article 194(2) of UNCLOS is directed at protecting *other states* from marine pollution damage. It is particularly pertinent to climate change insofar as states are required to take measures to control and regulate polluting 'activities' within their jurisdiction. Examples of such activities would include industrial installations which generate CO_2, power generators that use oil or coal, oil extraction industries, coal-mining, or possibly deforestation. This does not mean that corporate polluters would be responsible under the Convention, or that the contribution of each plant would have to be quantified. The Convention does not address private parties directly. But it does make state parties responsible under Article 194 for regulating and controlling the risk of marine pollution damage to other states resulting from the activities of the private sector. Fundamentally this is an obligation of due diligence – states must take the measures necessary to prevent or minimise harmful pollution, including environmental impact assessment, regulation and use of best available technology, application of the precautionary principle and enforcement.[42] On that basis states have an obligation to control and reduce CO_2 emissions from any source likely to pollute the marine environment and cause harm to other states.

The standard of conduct set by Articles 194 and 212 is very general – 'prevent, reduce and control' – and it does not imply that all pollution must be prevented, nor that anthropogenic CO_2 emissions must cease immediately, or even eventually. Measures that gradually reduce pollution and that result in meaningful lowering of carbon emissions over a period of time would be sufficient. The UNFCCC would be relevant when interpreting and applying both articles.[43] In particular, Article 2 talks about *stabilising* GHG concentrations at a level that would prevent 'dangerous anthropogenic interference with the climate system'. It does not talk about eliminating or reducing them. It envisages a timescale 'sufficient to allow ecosystems to adapt naturally to climate change, to ensure

41 CBD, *Scientific Synthesis of the Impacts of Ocean Acidification on Marine Biodiversity*; FAO, *Fisheries Report No. 870: Report of the FAO Expert Workshop on Climate Change Implications for Fisheries and Aquaculture* (Rome: FAO, 2008); IPCC, *Climate Change 2007: Synthesis Report* (Geneva: IPCC, 2008).

42 ILC, 2001 Articles on Prevention of Transboundary Harm, Article 3 and commentary, *ILC Report* (2001) GAOR A/56/10, 391–95, paras. (7) – (17); *Pulp Mills on the River Uruguay*, 2010 ICJ Reports, paras. 197 and 223; *Advisory Opinion on Responsibilities and Obligations of States Sponsoring Persons and Entities with Respect to Activities in the Area*, 2011 ITLOS Seabed Disputes Chamber, paras. 115–20.

43 In accordance with Article 31(3)(c) of the 1969 Vienna Convention on the Law of Treaties.

that food production is not threatened and to enable economic development to proceed in a sustainable manner'. It does not talk about immediate results. At the same time, given the scientific uncertainty and the risk of serious and irreversible harm to the marine environment posed by climate change, the measures taken must be adequately precautionary. Article 3(3) of the UNFCCC says that parties 'should' take precautionary measures to anticipate, prevent or minimise climate change and mitigate its effects. Plainly, if there is evidence of a risk of serious or irreversible harm to the marine environment, application of the precautionary principle would strengthen the argument for saying that more should be done to reduce CO_2 emissions.

The most obvious way of showing a failure to take the measures required by Articles 192 and 194 is to argue that the Kyoto Protocol sets a standard for giving effect to these provisions – that, in other words, UNCLOS developed state parties must comply with their emissions reduction targets under the Kyoto Protocol. This argument thus presents a very clear pathway through which compliance with Kyoto's CO_2 emissions reduction standards could be litigated in UNCLOS proceedings. Of course it would have to be shown that Kyoto parties have not complied with their emissions reduction commitments. It is quite likely that most of the Annex I states will meet their Kyoto emissions targets by 2012: only Canada currently stands out as likely to be in breach.

Kyoto does not set specific standards for CO_2 emissions by the aviation or shipping industries. Article 2(2) provides:

> The Parties included in Annex I shall pursue limitation or reduction of emissions of greenhouse gases not controlled by the Montreal Protocol from aviation and marine bunker fuels, working through the International Civil Aviation Organization and the International Maritime Organization, respectively.

As noted earlier, Article 212 requires states to control atmospheric pollution from ships and aircraft and it provides a basis for reducing CO_2 emissions from these industries. The interaction of this provision with Kyoto Article 2(2) is problematic. On the one hand, Article 2(2) does not exempt aviation and shipping from controls on CO_2 emissions. On the other, it envisages negotiations and further measures within the relevant international organisations. A resolution on reduction of aviation emissions of CO_2 was adopted by the International Civil Aviation Organization (ICAO) in 2010.[44] Regulations on CO_2 emissions from ships were adopted by the IMO in 2011.[45]

The argument that Kyoto sets a standard for giving effect to UNCLOS Part XII is even less useful against developing states, or against developed states that are not parties to Kyoto. Developing states parties to Kyoto have no obligation to

---

44 ICAO resolution A37–19 (2010). The EU has extended its emissions trading scheme to aviation.
45 The Marine Environment Protection Committee of the IMO adopted amendments to MARPOL Annex VI, with entry into force on 1 January 2013, making the Energy Efficiency Design Index (EEDI) and the Ship Energy Efficiency Management Plan (SEEMP) mandatory subject to certain conditions.

reduce GHG emissions, even if like India and China they are large emitters of CO_2. They will still be in compliance with Kyoto even if their CO_2 emissions have greatly increased since 1997. They would not be in breach of UNCLOS Articles 192 and 194 if Kyoto defines the content of those articles. With regard to the US, which is not a party to Kyoto or UNCLOS, it might be argued that it is bound by customary law to apply internationally agreed standards on CO_2 reductions in order to give effect to their obligation to protect the marine environment and other states from pollution.[46] But the obvious difficulty is that developed state parties to Kyoto have different percentage reductions targets, and in some cases they are permitted to increase emissions. Taking Kyoto as a standard of diligence for non-parties simply begs the question – what standard and for whom?

An additional argument is that compliance with Kyoto is not enough to satisfy the requirements of UNCLOS Part XII – that the two agreements are wholly unrelated, and that UNCLOS is the more demanding, especially if interpreted by reference to the precautionary approach and the duty of due diligence referred to earlier. This is an attractive argument precisely because it would set a common higher standard for CO_2 emissions reductions for all developed states and would address the obvious inadequacy of the Kyoto emissions reduction commitments. Marine pollution will worsen even if every party complies with Kyoto in full, since GHG emissions overall will still continue to rise – they will simply do so less quickly. If the evidence of serious or irreversible harm to the marine environment is good enough then surely we could say that stronger precautionary measures must not be postponed?

Attractive though this may be as an argument, the counter-arguments are considerably easier to make. There is first the *lex specialis* problem. Can it plausibly be claimed that UNCLOS regulates climate change impacts on the oceans in splendid isolation from Kyoto? Other marine pollution agreements are directly relevant to the interpretation and application of Part XII obligations, including the 1973/78 International Convention for the Prevention of Pollution from Ships (MARPOL Convention) and the London Dumping Convention. Why should Kyoto be different? The argument that compliance with agreed standards of pollution control (such as Kyoto) is not enough to satisfy the more general duty of due diligence has been tried and, so far, it has not been successful. Ireland made precisely that argument, based on UNCLOS, in the *Mox Plant Case*. The point was never decided for jurisdictional reasons, but Ireland's case received no support from the European Commission whose job it is to enforce European treaties against Member States.[47] More recently, Argentina made the same argument unsuccessfully before the ICJ in the *Pulp Mills*

46 In other contexts the US has accepted that UNCLOS reflects the customary international law of the sea, by which it is bound.

47 As the ECJ subsequently made clear, that court has exclusive jurisdiction over a dispute involving two EU Member States and a treaty to which what was then the EC is a party and in respect of which it has competence: Ireland had thus violated the duty of co-operation under EU law by bringing Annex VII proceedings. See Case C-459/03 *Commission of the European Communities v. Ireland* [2006] ECR I-4635.

Case.[48] Both developed and developing state parties would undoubtedly point to Article 193 of UNCLOS, which refers to their 'sovereign right to exploit their natural resources pursuant to their environmental policies and in accordance with their duty to protect and preserve the marine environment.' This would be interpreted as a reference to the right to sustainable development, in accordance with the case law of the ICJ.[49] Fundamental to the ICJ's case law is the balancing of interests that must take place when environmental matters are involved. Taking these decisions into account, and the two previous points, it seems very likely that any tribunal would view reduction of GHG emissions as an exercise in balancing continued economic development against environmental protection, and that it would be reluctant to require more of states than they have agreed to under Kyoto, or under Article 2 of the UNFCCC, which refers to enabling 'economic development to proceed in a sustainable manner.' This approach would not be helpful to states trying to argue that compliance with Kyoto is not enough in order to fulfil UNCLOS obligations.

The final point to consider is whether the decisions reached at Copenhagen, Cancun and Durban, summarised in the third section of this chapter, change the position under UNCLOS. It seems unlikely that they do. None of the 'commitments' made in any of these venues is binding on states, and they are lacking in the kind of precision that would normally be necessary in order to show that new international standards for preventing marine pollution have been agreed. The most that might be said is that there is now consensus on holding the global temperature increase to 2°C as the agreed long-term target, and that measures must be taken under UNCLOS to meet that target in respect of the marine environment. Much will depend at this point on how far – and whether – states set about implementing the Copenhagen/Cancun/Durban Accords. The more they do so the stronger an argument based on UNCLOS becomes.

The relationship between UNCLOS and climate change is not clear-cut, despite its obvious importance. Nevertheless, it is doubtful whether viewing climate change through the law of the marine environment greatly alters the overall picture. At best it provides a vehicle for compulsory dispute settlement notably lacking in the UNFCCC regime. Realistically, while UNCLOS may import any newly agreed standards for the control of GHGs, it is not a substitute for further agreement.

3.7 Trade law perspectives

The WTO has no specific mandate to protect the environment, but the preamble to the 1994 Marrakesh Agreement establishing the WTO acknowledges that expansion of trade must allow for 'the optimal use of the World's resources in

---

48 ICJ Reports (2010).
49 *Gabčíkovo-Nagymaros Dam Case* (1997) ICJ Reports 7, para. 140; *Iron Rhine Railway Arbitration* (2005) PCA, paras. 58–59; *Pulp Mills Case (Provisional Measures)(Argentina v Uruguay)* (2006) ICJ Reports, para. 80; *Pulp Mills Case (Merits)* (2010) ICJ Reports, para. 177.

accordance with the objective of sustainable development, seeking both to protect and preserve the environment and to enhance the means for doing so in a manner consistent with their respective needs and concerns at different levels of economic development'. To that extent protecting the world from climate change is a legitimate concern of those charged with developing and applying WTO law. Nevertheless, the problem of entrenched and competing institutional values is well illustrated by the interaction of WTO law and the UNFCCC regime. Reflecting the objectives of the WTO, a commitment to an 'open international economic system' is expressed in Article 3 of the UNFCCC. Yet it is the lack of GHG emissions controls on developing states that has in effect enabled developed states to export GHG production to China, India, Brazil and other developing states.[50] By doing so they have neatly evaded the emissions constraints placed on Annex I developed states by the Kyoto Protocol. Those constraints focus on emissions of GHGs within the country concerned; they ignore emissions generated by goods produced elsewhere that are then imported.[51] As we saw earlier, the EU's consumption of GHGs has in fact increased since 1990, because of imports from China and other developing countries. In that sense free trade and the globalisation of production and transport have exacerbated the difficulty of regulating GHG emissions. It is an obvious question whether a post-Kyoto accord can sustain this bargain unaltered – doing nothing about trade will certainly make climate change harder to solve. At the very least it may be necessary to factor imports from non-Annex I countries into Annex I GHG reduction commitments, but it also raises larger questions about whether WTO rules on free trade can survive if we want to get serious about oil and coal consumption or deforestation.[52]

Article XX of the GATT allows for national exceptions from the principle of free trade. There is no reference to the environment as such, but two provisions are broad enough to cover certain environmental problems: Article XX (b), which allows for measures 'necessary to protect human, animal or plant life or health', and Article XX (g), which allows for measures 'relating to conservation of exhaustible natural resources'. Both exceptions are subject to the requirement that the measures taken must neither be 'arbitrary or unjustifiable discrimination', nor 'a disguised restriction on international trade'.[53] Article XX(b) was relevant in the Asbestos Case, where the Appellate Body held that a measure is 'necessary' for the protection of public health if no

---

50 Brinkley and Less, *Carbon*.
51 Contrast the Montreal Protocol to the Ozone Convention, which regulates both production and consumption of ozone-depleting substances across all of its parties. This effectively prevented the outsourcing of production. The Kyoto negotiators could not reach agreement on a similar approach.
52 See S. Barrett, *Climate Change and International Trade: Lessons on their Linkage from International Environmental Agreements* (Geneva: CTEI, 2010); UNEP/WTO, *Trade and Climate Change* (Geneva: UNEP/WTO, 2009).
53 Article XX, *chapeau*.

GATT-consistent alternative is reasonably available and provided it entails the least degree of inconsistency with other GATT provisions.[54] However, it is for each Member State to determine what level of protection it wishes to require, provided it can demonstrate a risk to health: 'we note that it is undisputed that WTO Members have the right to determine the level of protection of health that they consider appropriate in a given situation'.[55] It seems clear that climate change is or will become a risk to human health, as evidenced by the following extract from the above-mentioned 2009 OHCHR Report on the relationship between climate change and human rights:

> 32. Climate change is projected to affect the health status of millions of people, including through increases in malnutrition, increased diseases and injury due to extreme weather events, and an increased burden of diarrhoeal, cardiorespiratory and infectious diseases. Global warming may also affect the spread of malaria and other vector borne diseases in some parts of the world. Overall, the negative health effects will disproportionately be felt in sub-Saharan Africa, South Asia and the Middle East. Poor health and malnutrition increases vulnerability and reduces the capacity of individuals and groups to adapt to climate change.[56]

Climate change is equally obviously a threat to exhaustible natural resources.[57] Article XX (g) has been considered in several cases, most notably the *Shrimp–Turtle* decision of the Appellate Body. Its significance for the climate change appears to be as follows. First, 'exhaustible natural resources' may be living or non-living, and need not be either rare or endangered. Thus the term potentially covers, *inter alia*, forests, biodiversity, terrestrial and marine living resources, and the quality of air and water.[58] Second, national measures will be accepted under Article XX if they are reasonably related to the purpose of protecting exhaustible natural resources. Third, the measures in question may relate to natural resources located intra- or extra-territorially, i.e. in the oceans. Fourth, in the case of resources which are shared or common property and where there is therefore a duty under general international law to cooperate in conservation and management, unilateral trade restrictions are more likely to be regarded

---

54 See *European Communities – Measures Affecting Asbestos and Asbestos-Containing Products*, WT/DS135/AB/R (2001), at paras 155–75.

55 *Ibid.*, para 168.

56 UN HRC, *Report of the Office of the United Nations High Commissioner for Human Rights on the Relationship Between Climate Change and Human Rights*, GAOR A/HRC/10/61, 15 January 2009, citing IPCC, *Climate Change 2007: Synthesis Report* (Geneva: IPPC, 2008) p. 48. Footnotes omitted.

57 CBD, *Scientific Synthesis of the Impacts of Ocean Acidification on Marine Biodiversity*, CBD Technical Series no. 46; FAO, *Fisheries Report No. 870: Report of the FAO Expert Workshop on Climate Change Implications for Fisheries and Aquaculture* (Rome: FAO, 2008); IPCC, *Climate Change 2007: Synthesis Report* (Geneva: IPCC, 2008).

58 In *Standards for Reformulated Gasoline*, WT/DS2/AB/R (1996), the WTO Appellate Body found that clean air is 'an exhaustible natural resource'.

as arbitrary or discriminatory for the purposes of Article XX if the state concerned has not first sought a cooperative solution through negotiation with other affected states. This requirement can be observed in Principle 12 of the 1992 Rio Declaration and in the *Shrimp–Turtle* decision, where the failure of the US to negotiate disabled it from relying on Article XX.[59] It seems probable that the same requirement of prior negotiation would apply to unilateral measures intended to prevent climate change causing harm to natural resources. Fifth, there was 'arbitrary discrimination' because US law required a 'rigid and unbending ... comprehensive regulatory program that is essentially the same as the US programme, without inquiring into the appropriateness of that program for the conditions prevailing in the exporting countries'.[60] Moreover, the Appellate Body found that the GATT requires 'rigorous compliance with the fundamental requirements of due process' with respect to exceptions to treaty obligations.[61]

Resort to unilateral measures is thus heavily circumscribed but the *Shrimp–Turtle* decision by implication suggests that they are permitted if the other party rejects good faith attempts at negotiation, provided the measures in question comply with the *chapeau* to Article XX. What is less clear is whether unilateral measures are also permitted where both sides have negotiated in good faith but have simply been unable to reach agreement, for example because they differ in their view of what tackling climate change requires. It is one thing to say that states must cooperate, but what constitutes a failure to cooperate?

This is a special problem in climate law. There are legitimate differences of opinion on what measures should be taken to address climate change, how soon they should begin to operate and whether they should be in a form binding on all states or only on developed states. The idea that Europe or any other party could resort to unilateral trade sanctions under GATT Article XX if climate negotiations fail is tenable only if it can be shown that the other party has failed in its obligation to cooperate. Assuming a challenge to the legality of unilateral measures the decision must, in such a case, be made by the WTO Dispute Settlement Body. In its *Shrimp–Turtle Art 21.5* decision the Appellate Body held that:

> The conclusion of a multilateral agreement requires the cooperation and commitment of many countries. In our view, the United States cannot be held to have engaged in 'arbitrary or unjustifiable discrimination' under Article XX solely because one international negotiation resulted in an agreement while another did not.[62]

59 *US – Import Prohibition of Certain Shrimp and Shrimp Products*, WTO Appellate Body (1998) WT/DS58/AB/R, paras. 168–72.

60 *Ibid.*, para. 177.

61 *Ibid.*, para. 182.

62 *United States – Import Prohibition of Certain Shrimp and Shrimp Products, Recourse to Article 21.5*, WT/DS58/AB/RW (2001), p. 37.

The threshold test of arbitrary and unjustifiable discrimination is unlikely to be passed by a mere breakdown in *bona fide* negotiations.

Even if the conditions for resort to unilateral trade sanctions are found to exist however, the real problem with using them to pressurise reluctant states into reducing GHG emissions is that this would represent a desperate last resort. They might work against an oil-exporting state like Saudi Arabia, but could Europe really use them against China or the US? The only likely outcome would be a trade war. Legally, it might be possible in certain circumstances. Politically, it seems only likely to worsen relations.

3.8 Conclusions

International law cannot solve the problems posed by climate change, neither can international litigation. At best, international regulation based on the UNFCCC and the Kyoto Protocol provides a good basis for co-ordinated action by governments and the private sector, but it can only be effective to the extent that politicians allow it to be. The fundamental challenge is to secure a strong commitment from all parties to take the necessary measures, and therein lies the core of the problem. A global solution requires near global consensus if it is to work, and that has come only slowly and reluctantly on the part of some key states. The challenge at this point is essentially political rather than legal. For all of the reasons set out earlier there seems only limited scope for using human rights law, WTO law or the Law of the Sea as weapons to pressurise governments over climate change. In this context there really is no useful alternative to negotiation, except at the margins or in extreme cases.

While Europe is doing reasonably well at meeting its Kyoto commitments and promoting energy efficiency, given the modesty of what Kyoto requires that is hardly a surprise. Europe's attempt to lead by example on Kyoto and post-Kyoto negotiations has not been a notable success. Poor European diplomacy and bad negotiating tactics at Copenhagen were rescued by Mexico at Cancun. There is some movement by developing industrialised states, but the developed states are still unable to agree on a common vision of the way forward. The restored consensus is based on a lowest common denominator approach because, as we have seen, there is no viable alternative to consensus negotiations, but it represents only what is politically feasible, not what is scientifically necessary or technologically possible. It remains to be seen whether it generates measures sufficient to restrain global temperature rises to 2°C. Future progress will depend on the US and China, not on Europe, which has largely done all it can.

Part II
The integration challenge

4 Giving a voice to the environment by challenging the practice of integrating environmental requirements into other EU policies

Ludwig Krämer

Article 11 of the Treaty on the Functioning of the European Union (TFEU) states: 'Environmental protection requirements must be integrated into the definition and implementation of the Union policies and activities, in particular with a view to promoting sustainable development.' This provision, which is probably the most important environmental provision in the whole Lisbon Treaty, raises considerable implementation problems, for lawyers, policy-makers and administrations.

In considering the implications of this Article, this chapter is structured as follows. In the first section, Article 11 TFEU will be interpreted, following its wording, history, objective and purpose, and its relationship with other EU provisions. The second section will discuss the practice of EU institutions in dealing with Article 11 and explore ways to improve its application.

4.1 Article 11 TFEU in EU law

4.1.1 The meaning of Article 11 TFEU

Article 11 requires the integration of environmental protection requirements into all Union policies and activities. As there are numerous sectors of EU policy which might be affected,[1] this chapter will not try to discuss the integration into the different specific policies. Indeed, a presentation of the implications of Article 11 TFEU for all the different parts of EU's policies would require the writing of a book.[2] Suffice it here to mention that 'policies and activities'

---

1 The EU website http://europa.eu/pol/index_en.htm lists, apart from the environment, 31 policy areas, where the EU is active. In 28 of these, environmental requirements play or should play a role. These are: Agriculture; Budget; Competition; Consumers; Culture; Development and cooperation; Education, training, youth; Employment and social affairs; Energy; Enlargement; Enterprise; External relations; External trade; Fight against fraud; Food safety; Foreign and security policy; Humanitarian aid; Human rights; Information society; Institutional affairs; Internal market; Justice; Maritime affairs and fisheries; Public health; Regional policy; Research and innovation; Taxation; and Transport.

2 I have found the best book on the market to be Nele Dhont, *Integration of Environmental Protection Into Other EC Policies* (Groningen: Europa Law Publishing, 2003). However, even this book limits itself to detailed discussions of agriculture, energy and transport.

also include nuclear energy, because the EU has, since the entry into force of the Lisbon Treaties, a (shared) competence in matters of energy policy (Article 194 TFEU). Nuclear energy is part of energy issues in general, and the objectives of Article 194 TFEU cannot be pursued without taking into consideration nuclear energy and its contribution to the achievement of its objectives.[3]

The wording of Article 11 TFEU establishes a requirement ('must be'). It does not invite the addressees to deploy best efforts ('shall aim to'[4]) to reach integration, or to consider ('shall be taken into account';[5] 'shall take care'[6]) the integration of environmental requirements. Rather, the instruction given by the Treaty is absolute and clear.

The term 'integrated' is not defined in Article 11 TFEU or in any other provision of the Lisbon Treaty. This is surprising, as the *raison d'être* of the European Union is integration. In view of this, recital 1 of the Treaty on European Union (TEU) speaks of the 'process of European integration'. Recital 6 mentions the desire 'to deepen' the solidarity between the European peoples, recital 7 of the wish to 'enhance further' the functioning of the EU institutions, recital 8 of 'strengthening' of economies, recital 9 of the determination 'to promote' economic and social progress. The term 'promote' appears three times in Article 3 TEU which deals with the EU's objectives.

All this language, which expresses movement and not a static situation, shows that integration is a process of moving closer to the general or specific aims of the TEU. As regards Article 11 TFEU, its declared aim is 'promoting sustainable development'. Obviously, the provision is based on the concept that sustainable development presupposes a process of bringing environmental requirements closer to EU policies and activities. The decisive point is that 'integration' is not a single, isolated action, but that it is a continuous *process*; in this, integrating environmental requirements is not different from integrating the EU Member States into a European Union, or integrating immigrants into the running and the daily life of their host society.

This preliminary conclusion shows the failure of the EU approach, which was linked to the so-called Cardiff process. Following a request from the European Council at their meeting in Cardiff in June 1998, for eight different sectors of EU policy documents were elaborated by the Commission which established a strategy of how to integrate environmental requirements into these

---

3 The Court of Justice has recognised that the EU had competence, under the Euratom Treaty, for environmental matters: see Case C-29/99 *Commission v Council* [2002] ECR I-11221, paras 102–4. This did not prevent, however, the Council from mentioning the protection of workers and the public, but not of the environment, in Directive 2009/71 establishing a framework for the nuclear safety of nuclear installations OJ 2009 L 172/18. The environment was only mentioned in recital 5 of that Directive.

4 This wording is used in Article 8 TFEU on gender equality and Article 10 TFEU on discrimination.

5 Wording used in Article 12 TFEU on consumer protection.

6 Wording used in Article 14 TFEU on services in the general interest.

policies.[7] These documents were discussed once in the Council – and then the whole procedure stopped.[8] The institutions did not see or did not want to see that the integration requirement implies a continuous process. Of course, such a process may be brought to a halt for policy reasons; however, this means that the requirement of Article 11 TFEU is no longer complied with.

'Environmental protection requirements' is again a term not defined in the Treaties. Obviously, it refers to the environmental chapter, Articles 191 to 193 TFEU. These requirements include thus the objectives of EU environmental policy, laid down in Article 191(1) TFEU, which include preserving protecting and improving[9] the quality of the environment and a high level of protection. Furthermore, 'requirements' include the specific principles of environmental policy, laid down in Article 191(2) TFEU (precaution and prevention, the rectification of environmental impairment at source and the polluter pays principle). Indeed, it is not imaginable that these principles should apply in the environmental sector, but not in agriculture, transport or energy. With regard to agriculture, the Court of Justice has already recognised the application of the precautionary principle.[10] Finally, the aspects of Article 191(3) TFEU are also environmental requirements.[11]

Article 11 TFEU does not indicate who must integrate environmental requirements.[12] However, as the TEU imposes obligations on EU institutions and on Member States, it can be safely stated that the EU institutions shall have to integrate environmental requirements. When EU Member States implement EU policies and activities, they might also have to respect Article 11. Other institutions are not visible.

It follows thus from the wording of Article 11 TFEU that the EU institutions are under an obligation to continuously strive towards preserving and protecting the environment at a high level, and improving its quality, when they elaborate or implement EU policies and activities.

---

7 See Commission, COM (98) 716 and COM (99) 640 (transport), COM (98) 571 (energy), COM (99) 22 and COM (2000) 20 (agriculture), COM (99) 263 (internal market), COM (99) 36 and COM (2000) 264 (development), COM (2001) 143 (fisheries), COM (2000) 576 (economic questions), and SEC (2002) 271 (external affairs).

8 The concluding document was COM (2004) 394.

9 'Improving' again refers to a change of the existing degree of protection, not just to the maintenance of the status quo.

10 Case C-180/96 *United Kingdom v Commission* [1998] ECR.I-2265 para. 99; see also Joined Cases T-74-76/00 *Artegodan v Commission* [2002] ECR II-327, para. 184.

11 Article 191(3) TFEU provides, 'In preparing its policy on the environment, the Union shall take account of: available scientific and technical data; environmental conditions in the various regions of the Union; the potential benefits and costs of action or lack of action; the economic and social development of the Union as a whole and the balanced development of its regions.'

12 See on this R. Macrory, 'The legal duty of environmental integration: commitment and obligation or enforceable right?' in R. Macrory, *Regulation, Enforcement and Governance in Environmental Law* (Oxford: Oxford University Press, 2010), p. 567.

4.1.2 *History of Article 11 TFEU*

The integration requirement was an essential element of EU environmental policy, long before a section on the environment was inserted into the Treaty. Indeed, the First EU Environmental Action Programme of 1973[13] stated:

> Effects on the environment should be taken into account at the earliest possible stage in all the planning and decision-making processes. The environment cannot be considered as external surroundings by which man is harassed and assailed; it must be considered as an essential factor in the organization and promotion of human progress. It is therefore necessary to evaluate the effects on the quality of life and on the natural environment of any measure that is adopted or contemplated at national or Community level and which is liable to affect these factors.

This statement, which goes back to a joint declaration of the EU environmental ministers of October 1972, constitutes the origin of the provisions on integrating environmental requirements into other policies. At the same time, it was one of Europe's contributions to the global discussion on the environment. Indeed, the UN Stockholm Declaration on the Human Environment of 1972 did not contain any integration requirement.[14] Only the UN Rio Declaration on Environment and Development of 1992 included an integration formula, though in a rather soft form and formulated as a principle.[15]

An integration provision was first inserted into the EC Treaty in 1987, in Article 130r (1), with a wording which is slightly different from the present text: 'Environmental protection requirements shall be a component of the Community's other policies.' During the discussions of the Maastricht Treaty on European Union, fear was expressed that such a wording might be directly applicable (i.e. have 'direct effect').[16] Therefore, Article 130r was amended to

---

13 OJ 1973 C 112/1.

14 J. Jans, in 'Stop the integration principle?' (2011) 33 *Fordham International Law Journal* 1533, is of the opinion that Principle 13 of the Stockholm Declaration already contains an integration requirement. I do not share this opinion. Principle 13 reads: 'In order to achieve a more rational management of resources and thus to improve the environment, States should adopt an integrated and coordinated approach to the development planning so as to ensure that development is compatible with the need to protect and improve environment for the benefit of their population.'

15 Rio Declaration on Environment and Development, Principle 4: 'In order to achieve sustainable development, environmental protection shall constitute an integral part of the development process and cannot be considered in isolation from it.' One should add the word 'economic' before the term 'development', in order to see its applicability to industrialised countries.

16 As to direct effect, see, for example, Case C-240/09 *Lesoochranárske zoskupenie,* judgment of 8 March 2011, not yet reported: 'a provision ... must be regarded as directly applicable, when the provision contains a clear and precise obligation which is not subject, in its implementation or effects, to the adoption of any subsequent measures'.

read: 'Environmental protection requirements must be integrated into the definition and implementation of other Community policies'.

In preparation of the discussions of the Amsterdam Treaty, the Commission had suggested inserting a clause equivalent to Article 130r into the Treaty chapters on agriculture, transport and competition. However, the Intergovernmental Conference (IGC) thought that this would duplicate the integration clause too often. Thus, the IGC removed the clause from Article 130r (the present Article 191 TFEU) and inserted it as Article 6 into the introductory chapter of the EC Treaty, which applied to all sectors of EU policy. At the same time it added, at the request of Sweden, the mention of sustainable development. The Lisbon Treaties did not bring any substantive amendments to the provision.

It follows from this evolution that the authors of the EU Treaty deliberately drafted the integration requirement in a way that it applied to all EU policies and activities. In order to clarify this further, they even placed it at its present position in the TFEU, in the chapter with the title 'Provisions having general application'.

4.1.3 *The dual objective of Article 11 TFEU*

Article 11 TFEU obviously has a double objective: on the one hand, it endeavours to ensure that environmental protection is given sufficient attention and consideration, whenever the Union pursues one of its policies or activities. Thus, it is a provision with the objective to reach the objectives of EU environmental policy which are laid down in Article 191 TFEU. On the other hand, it aims to promote sustainable development. Sustainable development is also mentioned in the fundamental provision of Article 3(3) TEU; there it is stated that sustainable development is 'based on', amongst others, 'a high level of protection and improvement of the quality of the environment'. Seen in this context, Article 11 TFEU appears to mean that in order for sustainable development to be achieved, environmental requirements must be integrated into other EU policies. Or, expressed differently, sustainable development can only be reached when environmental requirements are integrated into other policies. If this is not the case, the 'basis', the foundation on which sustainable development is to be grounded, is not solid. In short: no sustainable development without the integration of environmental requirements into the other EU policies.

4.1.4 *The nature of Article 11 TFEU and Article 37 of the EU Charter of Fundamental Rights*

Looking at Article 11 TFEU viewed in the context of other provisions, the close relationship with Article 3(3) TEU was already mentioned. As sustainable development is one of the Union's principal objectives, and this objective must be 'based' on environmental protection, the consequence can only be that environmental protection must be taken care of and promoted whenever the EU acts. This relationship in Article 3 TEU between environmental protection and sustainable development, which was taken up in Article 11 TFEU, is not present in the case of the requirements of Article 8 TFEU (integrating gender equality), Article 9 TFEU (social issues), Article 10 (discrimination) or Article 12 TFEU (consumer protection). Not only is the wording of the integration requirement in these provisions less decisive, they do not refer to sustainable development. Nor does Article 3 TEU state that sustainable development is based on gender equality, social protection, consumer protection or absence of discrimination.

A similar pattern of drafting was made in Article 37 of the EU's Charter of Fundamental Rights,[17] which states: 'A high level of environmental protection and the improvement of the quality of the environment must be integrated into the policies of the Union and ensured in accordance with the principle of sustainable development.'

Here again, the instruction is clear and unambiguous ('must'). And the provision repeats the close relationship between the integration requirement and sustainable development;[18] such a relationship is not established for gender equality, consumer protection, social issues or absence of discrimination – which are all mentioned in the Charter.[19] In Article 37, the reference to two fundamental principles of EU environmental policy – a high level of protection and the improvement of environmental policy – is even more direct and explicit than in Article 11 TFEU. The content of Article 37 is, in substance, that the other EU policies should also pursue the objectives of high environmental standards and the improvement of environmental quality.

The obligation of Article 37 falls on the EU institutions; it need not be discussed here whether the provision also imposes an obligation on the administrations of Member States.

It follows from this that the EU institutions, offices and bodies have the obligation to make sure that a high level of environmental protection and an improvement of the quality of the environment is ensured. As Article 6(1) TEU stipulates that the provisions of the Charter have the same legal value as the EU Treaties, this obligation is legally binding.

Thus, the wording of Articles 11 TFEU and 37 of the Charter, the history of Article 11, its purpose and its relation with other provisions indicate that the integration requirement needs to be made operational, if the EU aims to work towards sustainable development. Sustainable development cannot be attained unless the requirements of environmental protection policy are included in the elaboration and implementation of the different EU policies.

---

17 Charter of Fundamental Rights OJ 2000 C 364/1.

18 This contribution will not discuss the question whether 'sustainable development' is a *principle*, as stated in Article 37 of the Charter and in recital 9 TEU, or rather an *objective*, as follows from Article 3(3) and (5) and Article 21(2.d) and (2.f) TEU. I am of the opinion that it is an objective.

19 See Charter of Fundamental Rights (*op. cit.*), Articles 23 (gender equality), 31 (social issues), 38 (consumer protection) and 21 (absence of discrimination).

The term 'policies' could lead to the conclusion that only strategic documents, such as Green or White Papers, programmatic decisions or Council and Parliament resolutions would have to integrate the environmental requirements. However, such an understanding would be incorrect: Article 11 explicitly includes the words 'in the elaboration and implementation'. Thus, it also aims to include in the term 'policies' the different individual legislative acts, executive and implementing decisions and other measures which the EU institutions, agencies, bodies and offices might take. Indeed, the EU's agricultural policy cannot be reduced to the statements of Article 39 TFEU, but needs to be, and is in practice, elaborated, shaped, fine-tuned, reviewed, updated and made operational by numerous specific decisions and measures; competition policy is not reduced to the rules laid down in Articles 101 TFEU and onwards, but is made operational through individual and generally applicable decisions; and environmental policy does not exhaust itself in the provisions of Articles 191–193 TFEU, but needs to be put into practice by decisions which make these Articles a reality in daily life. A 'policy' for a specific sector is always and necessarily composed of the specific measures and decisions which give some shape and content to the framework that was set in the Treaty provisions.

Therefore, the obligation to integrate environmental requirements into 'policies' includes the obligation to have these requirements also included in the different decisions and measures taken under the specific policies which the EU pursues.

It is clear, though, that a high level of environmental protection and an improvement of the quality of the environment – these are the two elements which Article 37 of the Charter obliges the EU administration to pursue – need not be realised by each individual measure. It is sufficient that overall a high level is aimed at and that the environment is improved.[20] Another question is whether there should not be an explanation or justification of the question to what extent the high protection level and the environmental improvement requirement are reached or promoted. I will come back to this.

Is the integration requirement an objective or a principle? Article 11 and Article 37 of the Charter are formulated in the strongest possible terms ('must be integrated'). There is no discretion left for the EU institutions to apply or not to apply the integration requirement in a specific situation. In contrast to that, principles require a weighing up or balancing process in applying them in a specific case. They are not formulated in the form of an instruction. For instance, the subsidiarity principle of Article 5 TEU requires a weighing up of whether the EU can do better than Member States ('not sufficiently achieved – better achieved'). The proportionality principle of the same Article has the weighing up element already in the term 'proportionality', as well as in the terms 'necessary to achieve'. According to Article 191(2) TFEU, damage *should* be rectified at source, but it is not stated that damage 'must' be

---

20 Case C-341/95 *Bettati* [1998] ECR I-4355.

rectified at source; the polluter *should* pay, not '*the polluter* must *pay*'. Moreover, as regards the Charter of Fundamental Rights, Article 37 is placed, together with other rights, in Chapter IV, entitled 'Solidarity'. It is not placed in Chapter V 'General provisions', which contains a certain number of principles concerning the interpretation and understanding of the Charter. It would thus be surprising if it were establishing legal *principles*. This would contradict its title and, more importantly, its very purpose which is the establishing of *rights* and *obligations* and not of principles.

Contrary to widespread opinion,[21] Article 11 TFEU therefore constitutes an objective of EU policy and not a principle.

4.2 Making the integration requirement operational

Little is gained from the conclusion that the integration requirement is an objective and not a principle. This may be illustrated with an example: it is undisputed – at least in western societies – that there is a human right concerning gender equality. This right is laid down in the UN Declaration of Human Rights. Article 8 TFEU proclaims it, Article 6(1) TEU states that the rights of the Charter on Fundamental Rights have the same *legal* value as the EU Treaties, and Article 23 of the Charter proclaims the equality of men and women, while its Article 21 prohibits any discrimination on grounds of sex. Yet, within the European Union, women obtain, on average, 18 per cent less salary than men.[22] Any attempt to make the right of gender equality a reality must therefore struggle to get such inequalities eliminated; and there is little use in having further discussions on the theoretical concept of gender equality.

4.2.1 The integration requirement and other policies

As a policy objective, the integration provision of Article 11 TFEU/Article 37 of the Charter imposes an obligation on the EU institutions to take the environmental objective of a high level of protection and the improvement of the quality of the environment into account. Article 7 TFEU states in this regard: 'The Union shall ensure consistency between its policies and activities, taking all its objectives into account.' This provision could be understood as meaning that the environmental objectives mentioned shall be considered as other, additional objectives of the transport, agricultural, fisheries, etc. policies and be treated as such.

---

21 Including myself, see L. Krämer, *EC Environmental Law* (6th edn, London: Sweet & Maxwell, 2007), p. 20.

22 See Eurostat, *Sustainable Development in the European Union: 2009 Monitoring Report of the EU Sustainable Development Strategy* (Luxembourg: Office for Official Publications of the European Communities, 2009), p. 208: 'In 2006 and 2007, the gross hourly earnings of employed women were on average 18% lower than those of men. This relative difference, which represents the (unadjusted) gender pay gap, had decreased marginally from 17.7 to 17.5%. The gender pay gap represents one aspect of gender inequality.'

However, such an understanding of Article 7 TFEU does not take account of the fact that, on the one hand, Article 11 TFEU/Article 37 of the Charter both refer to one of the fundamental objectives of the European Union: the achievement of sustainable development. This connection is not made in the EU Treaties in the case of its transport, agricultural, fisheries or other policies: sustainability does not require, for example, a high quality of transport policy or a full achievement of the objectives of agricultural policy, laid down in Article 39 TFEU. For this reason, there is a particular obligation for the EU institutions in the context of Article 7 TFEU to ensure that the different policies and activities take into account and work towards the objective of a high level of protection and an improvement of the quality of the environment.

On the other hand, Article 37 is part of the Charter of Fundamental Rights. Thus, it is intended to place a particular obligation on the EU institutions and administrations to see that the Article's objectives are achieved. There is no obligation comparable to Article 37 placed on the EU institutions in the transport, agriculture, fisheries or competition areas. Rather, the environmental sector stands out with regard to all other sectors of EU policy: indeed, it is, together with the sectors of social and consumer policy, the only ones which are mentioned in the Charter. And with regard to these two other sectors, it is the only one where the Charter states that its objectives shall be pursued in order to reach sustainable development.

These considerations justify the conclusion that while, according to Article 7 TFEU, all EU objectives shall be taken into account in the pursuance of EU policies, particular attention is to be given to the pursuit of a high level of protection of, and an improvement of the quality of, the environment.

4.2.2 *The right of access to information*

There is another string which is relevant here: EU law gives citizens and their organisations a fundamental right of access to environmental information which is held by EU institutions, agencies, bodies and offices. This right is laid down in the Aarhus Convention[23] to which the EU has adhered.[24] The Aarhus Convention is part of EU law.[25] Its provisions prevail over secondary EU legislation.[26]

The right of access to environmental information is laid down in a clear and unmistakable form: Article 1 of the Convention states:

> In order to contribute to the protection of the right of every person of present and future generations to live in an environment adequate to his

---

23 Convention on access to information, public participation in decision-making and access to justice in environmental matters, done on 25 June 1998 in Aarhus (Denmark).

24 Decision 2005/370 OJ 2005, L 124/1.

25 See Article 216(2) TFEU and Case C-240/09 *Lesoochranárske zoskupenie,* judgment of 13 March 2011, *op. cit.*

26 Case C-344/04 *IATA and ELFAA* ECR [2006] I-403, with further references.

or her health and well-being, each Party shall guarantee the rights of access to information, public participation in decision-making and access to justice in environmental matters in accordance with this Convention.

The right is given to any natural or legal person (Article 4);[27] a refusal to grant access may be challenged in Court (Article 9); exceptions to this right are specifically enumerated; they shall be interpreted restrictively. Administrations have the obligation to collect and disseminate environmental information (Article 5), etc.

Article 5 of the Aarhus Convention lays down a number of obligations for public authorities to disseminate environmental information. Article 5(7) then states: 'Each Party shall (a) publish the facts and analyses of facts which it considers relevant and important in framing major environmental policy proposals; (b) publish or otherwise make accessible available explanatory material on its dealings with the public.' Here, the Convention draws the link between the right of the citizen to have access to environmental information and the obligation of the administration to make this information publicly available.

If one reads this fundamental right of the public of access to environmental information together with the obligation flowing from Article 37 of the Charter for the EU administration, the conclusion must be that citizens have a right to be informed if and how the EU institutions ensure, in their policies and in their individual measures, that a high level of protection and an improvement of the quality of the environment is achieved.

This means that the EU institutions are obliged to inform, when they make proposals for legislation, adopt legislative or other acts, or take decisions which are capable of affecting the environment, how they complied with the obligation to ensure a high level of protection or to improve the quality of the environment. Otherwise, the rights and guarantees which flow for citizens from Article 37 of the Charter are in fact empty.

4.2.3 Access to information and the EU's obligation to improve environmental quality

This sounds a small step. However, the following three examples might illustrate what is meant by this.

A first example is as follows. In 2008, the Commission put forward a proposal for a review of Regulation 1049/2001 on access to documents.[28] In its explanatory memorandum, it raised the question whether there should be

---

27 Compare Article 15(3) TFEU which gives a right of access to documents to citizens of the Union and to any natural or legal person residing or having its registered office in a Member State.
28 Regulation 1049/2001 regarding public access to European Parliament, Council and Commission documents OJ 2001 L 145/43.

more access to documents allowed than in existing EU legislation when commercial interests were affected. The Commission explained:[29]

> Protection of commercial interests. Public authorities and the corporate sector feel that the current rules strike the right balance. However, journalists, NGOs and a majority of individual citizens claim that more weight should be given to the interest in disclosure. Therefore, the Commission does not propose to amend this provision.

Clearly greater openness and transparency on environmental matters is also in the interest of any environmental policy. Under Article 37 of the Charter and Article 11 TFEU, the Commission would have to explain its decision to side with public authorities – from all Member States? – and the corporate sector – why not siding with civil society? – and why its omission to improve access to documents in this specific situation ensures a high level of protection and constitutes an *improvement* of the quality of the environment.

There is no doubt that officials will be able to find arguments to explain why a change of the legislation was not appropriate. However, in that case, the Commission takes the responsibility of declaring openly (or is accountable for declaring) why it does not improve access to documents and, thereby, improve the possibility to protect the environment.

By way of a second example, in 2011, the Commission published a White Paper on transport.[30] The White Paper declared quite bluntly that 'the transport system is not sustainable'.[31] It developed a scenario ('roadmap') until 2050, based on a reduction of greenhouse gas emissions by 60 per cent, compared to 1990; it did not discuss the EU's own estimation that these emissions should be reduced by 85–95 per cent. The White Paper was based on an impact assessment[32] which discussed four different policy options. The impact assessment concluded that from an environmental point of view, option 2 would deliver the best results. The White Paper itself did not explicitly specify which option the Commission suggested. It proposed a number of goals and measures which were all oriented towards a more competitive and resource efficient transport system in the EU.

It is submitted that under Articles 37 of the Charter and 11 TFEU, the Commission was obliged to explain how it envisages a high level of environmental protection and an improvement of the quality of the environment to be achieved in the transport sector by 2050, and why it did or did not follow option 2 of the impact assessment which it itself qualified as the environmentally best option. In view of the Commission's own statement that the EU transport

---

29 COM (2008) 229, section 2.2.4. Emphasis added.
30 Commission White Paper, 'Roadmap to a Single European transport area – towards a competitive and resource efficient transport system' COM (2011) 144.
31 *Ibid.,* para. 13.
32 Commission, 'Impact assessment – accompanying document to the White Paper' SEC (2011) 358.

system is not sustainable, there would also be a need for an explanation if and how this sustainability will be achieved by 2050.

Such an explicit explanation would allow a discussion in the public domain, the European Parliament and the Council about whether and to what extent the issue of integrating environmental concerns into the future EU transport policy has been considered. This is not the case with the present White Paper.

The weaknesses of the *environmental* section in the Commission's impact assessment cannot be discussed here. Suffice it to say that the assessment is limited to some parameters;[33] that, for example, it is merely indicated that the noise levels would decrease due to a decrease in the number of cars and the increase in the number of electrical cars.[34] The loss of biodiversity and land use is only dealt with by commonplaces.[35]

Finally, a third example is as follows. In 2005, the Commission set up a Scientific, Technical and Economic Committee for Fisheries (STECF).[36] This Committee had the task, among others, to give, on its own initiative or on request by the Commission, an opinion on the fisheries management; STECF's opinions were to be published 'without delay' on the Commission's website.[37] The Commission was obliged to take the opinions into account when presenting proposals on fisheries management.[38] Furthermore, STECF was obliged to publish an annual report on the situation of fisheries.

The last STECF opinion published dates from 2008. No annual report has been published after the STECF report of November 2005.[39] This omission to disseminate information on the findings of the EU's own scientific committee has allowed the EU institutions to decide on fishing measures, in particular on total allowable catches, according to political but not environmental parameters.

It is submitted that in all three examples the Commission did not comply with its obligation under Articles 37 of the Charter and 11 TFEU, because it did not respect the fundamental right of access to information. Under these provisions, the Commission is obliged to inform the public – civil society, individuals – if and to what extent its proposal aims at a high level of protection of, and improves the quality of, the environment.

The general obligation to give reasons follows from Article 296(2) TFEU.[40] This provision only refers to legal acts. However, as there is a right of information

---

33 *Ibid.*, section 5.4. The parameters are climate change, local air pollution, noise levels, biodiversity loss and natural resources depletion.

34 *Ibid.*, parameters 224 and *infra*.

35 *Ibid.*, paragraph 235 and *infra*.

36 Commission Decision 2005/629 OJ 2005 L 225/18; amended by Commission Decision 2010/75 OJ 2010 L 37/52.

37 *Ibid.,* Article 12.

38 Regulation 2371/2002 on the conservation and sustainable exploitation of fisheries resources under the Common Fisheries Policy OJ 2002 L 358/59, Article 33.

39 See http://ec.europa.eu/fisheries/partners/stecf/reports/index_en.htm (accessed 28 April 2011).

40 Article 296(2) TFEU: 'legal acts shall state the reasons on which they are based'.

on the environment and a corresponding obligation of the EU institutions to make relevant information on policy proposals available, Article 296(2) TFEU expresses a more general obligation to account for the extent to which the measures or proposed measures ensure a high level of environmental protection and an improvement of the quality of the environment. This corresponds to the above-mentioned principle of good EU governance applicable to EU institutions and bodies: 'Each of the EU institutions must explain and take responsibility for what it does in Europe.'[41]

When an EU institution or body adopts or proposes a measures which is likely to affect the environment to a significant extent, it is under an obligation to explain – in the explanatory memorandum, in recitals or in another appropriate way – how this measure contributes – or omits to contribute – to a high level of environmental protection and to the improvement of the quality of the environment.

4.2.4 *Enforcing the obligation to improve environmental quality*

The enforcement of environmental objectives is a specific problem, because the environment has no social pressure group behind it which would press for a full application of the principles. Article 191 TFEU contains a number of environmental objectives which read well on paper but which are forgotten in daily practice. A good example is the objective to aim at a high level of environmental protection. The Court of Justice has declared that such a high level does not mean the highest level which is technically possible.[42] Furthermore, the high level need not be aimed at or achieved in all parts of the EU; it would be sufficient that the overall level of protection in the Union be increased, even if in some parts of it the EU measure would lead to a reduction of the protection level.[43] Finally, the Court declared that in complex matters such as the environment, the EU legislator has wide discretion to decide which measures should be taken and at which speed; the control by the Court would therefore have to be limited to examine whether this large amount of discretion had been exceeded.[44]

In practice, the EU institutions regularly take decisions in environmental matters and then declare that the adopted act constitutes a high level of environmental protection. They do not first assess what a high level is, and then measure the envisaged decision with regard to this parameter, but they do it the other way round.

With regard to the objective of integrating environmental requirements (achieving a high level of protection and the improvement of the quality of the environment), the conclusion above was that the fundamental right of

---

41 Commission, 'European Governance: A White Paper' COM (2001) 428, p.10.
42 Case C-233/94 *Germany v European Parliament and Council* [1997] ECR I-2405.
43 *Ibid.*
44 Case C-341/95 *Bettati* [1998] ECR I-4355.

information requires an explanation of how the objective of achieving a high level of protection and an improvement of the quality of the environment is to be achieved by the specific measure in question.

It is this right of information which is enforceable. An applicant could ask the EU institution or body to disclose information in this regard. And the answer by the institution could not only be controlled by the EU Courts as to whether the wide discretion was exceeded. As the answer constitutes 'information' and there is a fundamental right of access to information, the Courts would rather have to examine whether the answer is sufficiently precise and complete such as to comply with the obligation to inform the applicant.

The right of information exists with regard to every institution or body, as it is a fundamental right and as all EU institutions and bodies are obligated under Articles 37 of the Charter and 11 TFEU. Therefore, this right also applies when the Commission makes a proposal for a legal act.

Examples would be:

- regional funds legislation would have to explain why the diverting of structural funds money that was ear-marked for the environment to the financing of energy and transport projects[45] which very obviously and flagrantly contradicts Article 177(2) TFEU[46] constitutes a high level of protection of, and an improvement of the quality of, the environment;
- fisheries legislation which refers to 'scientific advice' in order to justify certain legislative measures would have to specify which scientific advice was used and give the reference;[47]
- a proposal for legislation on nuclear waste[48] would have to indicate why it constitutes a high level of environmental protection that the export of *nuclear* waste to third countries is not prohibited, whereas the export of *hazardous* waste to third countries is, as a rule, prohibited.

45 Regulation 1084/2006 establishing a Cohesion Fund OJ 2006 L 210/79, Article 2(1)(b): '(The Fund shall finance) the environment within the priorities assigned to the Community environment protection policy under the policy and action programmes on the environment. In this context, the Fund may also intervene in areas related to sustainable development which clearly present environmental benefits, namely energy efficiency and renewable energy and, in the transport sector outside the trans-European networks, rail, river and sea transport, intermodal transport systems and their interoperability, management of road, sea and air traffic, clean urban transport and public transport.'

46 Article 177(2) TFEU only allows the financing of 'environment and trans-European networks in the area of transport infrastructure'.

47 This was not done, for example, in the case of Regulation 41/2006 fixing for 2007 the fishing opportunities and associated conditions OJ 2007 L 15/1. The Council was obliged to take into account the report by the EU Scientific Committee STECF (recital 1). However, recitals 20 and 21 only refer to 'scientific advice', recital 23 to 'scientific investigations'. No reader can glean from this what advice the Council actually referred to, and why the measures that were decided constitute a high level of protection of, and an improvement of the quality of, the environment.

48 Commission Proposal for a directive on the management of spent fuel and radioactive waste COM (2010) 618.

It might well be that the EU institution in question declares that this or that measure or policy does not aim at an improvement of the protection of the quality of the environment. However, this then would at least clarify the policy of the Union or of the institution and, if there were a continuous or systematic disregard of the requirement to aim to achieve a high level of protection and an improvement of the quality of the environment, the Courts would have to examine whether the obligations of Articles 37 of the Charter and 11 TFEU have been breached.

4.2.5 *The necessity to develop a strategy for making Article 11 operational*

This approach of asking, via the right of citizens to know, the EU institutions to account for why they take this or that measure, why they adopt this or that decision or spend money on this or that issue, is the attempt to reduce the gap between the high, splendid words of the Lisbon Treaties on the protection of the environment and sustainable development, on the one hand, and, on the other hand, the daily practice of the EU institutions – which all too often does not even try to make the Treaty provisions on the environment operational.

The environment is an interest without a group: while agricultural policy (farmers), fisheries policy (fishermen), transport policy (persons who transport or are transported), competition policy (competitors), etc. all have strong, vested interest groups behind the policy, which groups discuss, influence, defend or attack, shape and lobby in favour of their interests, the environment as a diffuse interest has no such group behind it. One cannot consider environmental organisations to be such a group, because they normally act in the general, and not in their own, interest. Overall, they are as diffuse as the interest in the environment itself.

In order to make the above-mentioned right of information on environmental matters operational, it would therefore be necessary for environmental groups, journalists, academics, charities and human rights organisations to pool their forces and require that the EU institutions and bodies answer the question, via hundreds of specific, individual answers, how the environmental requirements are being integrated in daily practice into the EU's other policy sectors. In the same way as a democracy will not function without democrats, environmental protection – here, the integration of environmental requirements into other policies – will not function without persons who become active in making this integration a political, economic, social and environmental reality.

It is clear that persons, groups and organisations which are working in the environmental sector or are interested in the protection of the environment are hardly able to develop and implement such a strategy: their interests are too diverse, their priorities are too divergent and their sense of strategic cooperation is too undeveloped. This is the other side of the statement that the environment is an interest without a group. It is highly unlikely that such a concerted action will be able to be pursued at EU level, where one of the marked features is the absence of a *European* public opinion – as opposed to an Irish, British, French or Italian public opinion.

4.2.6 Governance and Articles 11 TFEU and 37 of the Charter

All this should not make us forget that the obligation to make Articles 11 TFEU and 37 of the Charter of Fundamental Rights a reality lies first of all with the EU institutions and bodies. The first obligation here would be to set up administrative structures to deal with the integration problem. In this regard, the EU Commission had already announced, in 1993, what could and should be done to improve environmental integration.[49] As mentioned above, later it changed policy with the aborted 'Cardiff Process' which went nowhere.

It may be interesting though, to review, one by one, the Commission's suggestions of the past[50] and to indicate where the EU stands today, almost twenty years later:

i)   All Commission proposals should be assessed with regard to their environmental effects; where such effects are likely to occur, an environmental impact assessment is to be made;

This approach was abandoned. There is an impact assessment of the economic, social and environmental effects of the Commission proposals. However: (a) the EU Treaties do not contain a requirement that economic requirements must be integrated into the policies of the Union, comparable to Article 11 TFEU and 37 of the Charter. Therefore, the general embedding of environmental issues into broader issues of general policy is itself a political decision which does not do justice to Articles 11 TFEU and 37 of the Charter; (b) the environmental part of the Commission impact assessments is normally very poor and insufficient; (c) the impact assessment is not open to a range of results, but is oriented to justify the political decision which was taken beforehand. The instrument of a general impact assessment which is, in practical terms, handled by the President of the Commission and the Secretariat, thus allows environmental initiatives to be stopped at a very early stage with the argument that, economically, the initiative would not be acceptable.

ii)   Proposals for new legal measures should, in the explanatory memorandum, describe and explain their environmental effects and the environmental costs and benefits;

This approach was abandoned. The vast majority of Commission proposals do not even touch upon environmental issues. The internal guidelines of the

---

49 Commission, SEC (93) 785; Press Release IP 97/636 of 11 July 1997.
50 That is, suggestions made in the documents referred to in the above note.

Commission for drafting an explanatory memorandum do not contain any requirement as to the description and assessment of environmental effects.

iii) The Commission annual work programme shall identify, with a green asterisk, those proposals that will have significant environmental effects;

This approach was abandoned.

iv) In all relevant Commission departments, contact persons for the integration of environmental requirements shall be designated;

Approach abandoned.

v) An inter-service group of director-generals shall be created, chaired by the director-general for the environment. This group shall have the task of discussing and coordinating environmental questions with other policy measures in order to achieve better integration;

Approach abandoned. Such a group does not exist.

vi) Within the Directorate-General for the environment, a specific administrative unit shall deal with the implementation of the EU environmental action programme and the integration of environmental requirements into other policies;

Directorate-General for the environment does not have such a unit.

vii) The Commission's annual report shall contain, for key policy areas, an indication of which environmental considerations were taken into account;

The EU's General Report on its activities does not contain such indications.[51]

viii) The Commission shall take a number of measures for 'green accounting' (waste management, procurement policies, etc.);

In 2002, the Commission decided to adhere to the European eco-management and audit scheme.[52] In 2008, it reported that 15 of its buildings in Bruxelles (30 per cent of the office space) adhered to the scheme.[53] The EMAS register

---

51 See the last General Report on the activities of the European Union (2010), available at http://europa.eu/generalreport/pdf/rg2010_en.pdf.
52 See Regulation 1221/2009 on the voluntary participation by organisations in a Community eco-management and audit scheme OJ 2009 L 342/1; this Regulation replaced earlier Regulations.
53 Commission, MEMO/08/688 of 11 November 2008.

of 2011 indicated that 12 Commission sites come under the EMAS scheme[54] – which means less than 25 per cent of the Commission office space.

    ix)   Progress in better integrating environmental requirements into other policies shall be regularly assessed;

The review of the fifth environmental action programme contained such an assessment.[55] Since then, the approach has been abandoned. In 2007, the Commission declared:[56]

> progress has been mixed. In the agricultural sector there have been fundamental reforms over the last 15 years that have moved towards seeing farmers as stewards of nature. However, the integration of environmental concerns into other areas has been less successful. The Cardiff process – which was set up in 1998 in order to institutionalise this type of integration – has not lived up to expectations.

This assessment is followed by one of the Commission's typical promises:[57]

> The Commission will produce a strategic framework in order to address the issue of policy integration. It will pay particular attention to the sectors where there is the greatest potential for policy synergies in order to improve the quality of the environment (agriculture, fisheries, transport, energy, regional and industrial policy and EU external relations).

To date – five years later – there has been no follow-up to this announcement. And the constitutional requirement to integrate environmental concerns into other policies has existed since 1987, thus for twenty-five years.

4.3 Concluding remarks

    i)   Article 11 TFEU and the equivalent provision of Article 37 of the Charter of Fundamental Rights contain an obligation for the EU institutions to integrate environmental requirements into the elaboration and implementation of the other EU policies and activities. These provisions do not only constitute principles.

    ii)   It follows from Articles 11 TFEU and 37 of the Charter that sustainable development, one of the major objectives of EU policy, requires the integration of environmental concerns into other policies. This

---

54 See www.emas-register.eu/search.php?base=base (accessed 2 May 2011).

55 Decision 2179/98 on the review of the Fifth Environment Action Programme OJ 1998 L 275/1.

56 Commission, Mid-term review of the Sixth Environment Action Programme COM (2007) 225, section 5.3.

57 *Ibid.*

means in clear terms that sustainable development cannot be reached without such integration.

iii) There is an obligation for the EU institutions and bodies to inform and explain how their policies and individual measures taken in the context of the different policies ensure a high level of protection and an improvement of the quality of the environment.

iv) To this obligation corresponds a right of the citizens to know if and how this obligation has been complied with. This right to know flows from the fact that the integration requirement is part of the Charter of Fundamental Rights.

v) A strategic, concerted action by civil society could make this right operational, by insisting on asking for explanations and justifications as to whether and how the high level of protection and the improvement of quality of the environment were made operational in the context of concrete measures. Eventually, this right to know would have to be enforced via the EU Courts.

vi) Such action could begin to give a voice to the environment which is cherished in words but all too rarely by action.

vii) Integrating environmental requirements into the elaboration and implementation of other EU policies remains a topic for Sunday speeches of politicians. In the daily practice of the EU institution and bodies, it does not play a role.

viii) The Commission, which is obliged to take or propose measures to integrate environmental requirements into other policies, obviously has no political will to do so. Further, it has not set up any governance mechanisms or working mechanisms to make the requirement of Article 11 TFEU and Article 37 of the Charter on Fundamental Rights operational.

The Nobel Prize winner Heinrich Böll once described a situation where the boss every morning proclaims: 'Today, something must happen.' And the choir of his colleagues answered every day, 'Today, something will happen'. This went on for decades, without anything happening. We are, with the integration requirement, not far away from this story: everybody agrees that there should be integration. And that's it.

5   The CAP in 2020

Vision or hindsight?

Joseph A. McMahon

5.1 Introduction

The *OECD–FAO Agricultural Outlook (2010–19)* indicated that the three major challenges facing agriculture in the run-up to 2020 would be climate change, global food chains, innovation and food security.[1] In discussing these topics, the OECD Agriculture Ministerial Meeting in February 2010 recognised:[2]

(a)   that an integrated approach to food security is needed involving a mix of domestic production, international trade, stocks, safety nets for the poor, and other measures reflecting levels of development and resource endowment, while poverty alleviation and economic development are essential to achieve a sustainable solution to global food security and hunger in the longer term;

(b)   that 'green growth' offers opportunities to contribute to sustainable economic, social and environmental development, that agriculture has an important role to play in the process, as do open markets that facilitate the sharing of technologies and innovations supportive of green growth, and that, in this context, care needs to be taken to avoid all forms of protectionism;

(c)   that climate change presents challenges and opportunities in reducing greenhouse gas emissions, in carbon sequestration, and in the need for adaptation.

The Communiqué continued by outlining a series of guidelines for governments as they adapt their agricultural policies. These include that farmers should be able to respond effectively to changing consumer and societal demands, that appropriate risk-management policies should be in place and that agricultural policy should be coherent with other policies, including environmental, consumer and development policies. Particular emphasis was placed on improving the environmental performance of agriculture.

---

1   Paris: OECD, 2010, pp. 43–46.
2   Available at www.oecd.org/document/2/0,3343,en_21571361_43893445_44664898_1_1_1_1,00.html (last accessed 24 January 2011). All websites noted in subsequent notes were last accessed on this date.

In April 2010, the European Commission initiated a widespread public consultation on the future of the Common Agricultural Policy (CAP), centred around four questions:

- Why do we need a CAP?
- What do citizens expect from agriculture?
- Why reform the CAP?
- What tools do we need for the CAP of tomorrow?

The resulting contributions were brought together and presented at a conference in July 2010.[3] In response to the four questions, there was support for a CAP at European level as opposed to a series of national policies. The policy would promote equality of competition, maintain the diversity of farming systems and ensure the delivery of important public goods. Such goods included environmental protection and biodiversity support and these goods would be realised whilst offering consumers high-quality food at affordable/reasonable prices. As for how this would be achieved, the responses suggested continuing the current method of support or refocusing the policy to link agricultural support more closely with the delivery of specific public goods. Among the many conclusions offered from the consultations was the suggestion that the European Union (EU) should 'take a strategic approach to CAP reform [and] go for total, not partial, solutions taking account of CAP challenges on the one hand and the interplay between the CAP and other internal and external EU policies on the other hand'.[4]

Using the consultation exercise, the Commission issued a paper on the options for reform in November 2010.[5] Reflecting the view that there should be a common policy built around two pillars, the Commission suggested that the three strategic aims of the policy in the period up to 2020 should be to guarantee long-term food security, to provide European citizens with high-quality food that is produced in a sustainable manner and to maintain the viability of rural communities. It suggested that:[6]

> Reform of the CAP must also continue, to promote the greater competitiveness, efficient use of taxpayer resources and effective public policy returns European citizens expect, with regard to food security, the environment, climate change and social and territorial balance. The objective should be to build more sustainable, smarter and more inclusive growth for rural Europe.

---

3 See http://ec.europa.eu/agriculture/cap-post-2013/conference/index_en.htm.

4 See http://ec.europa.eu/agriculture/cap-post-2013/debate/report/summary-report_en.pdf for a summary of the submissions. An executive summary is available at http://ec.europa.eu/agriculture/cap-post-2013/debate/report/executive-summary_en.pdf.

5 *The CAP towards 2020: Meeting the food, natural resources and territorial challenges of the future* COM (2010) 672.

6 *Ibid.*, p. 3.

For the Commission this would involve greener and more equitable measures in the area of market support (first pillar) whilst rural development measures (second pillar) would concentrate on competitiveness, innovation, climate change and the environment. The reform path according to the Commission would involve a choice between three broad policy options, the first of which would involve a gradual adjustment of the existing policy while tackling equity issues relating to the distribution of the Single Farm Payment (SFP) between Member States. The second option would involve a major overhaul of the policy to ensure that 'it becomes more sustainable, and the balance between different policy objectives, farmers and Member States is better met'.[7] The final option would involve a more far-reaching reform that would focus on environmental and climate change objectives that would be realised through the rural development pillar and would entail gradually moving away from market support measures.

This contribution examines the options identified by the Commission in more detail and how the environment has been impacted by the existing CAP and some of the changes introduced by the most recent reform of the CAP, which is usually referred to as the 2008 Health Check. The conclusions consider the reactions of the Council and the new co-legislator in agricultural matters, the European Parliament, to the proposals before offering some thoughts on whether the reform will promote a more environmentally friendly CAP. As for the scope of the environmental challenge facing the EU, some interesting facts are given in the Commission's consultation document for the impact assessment of the proposed reform.[8] This indicates that:[9]

- agriculture and forests cover 77 per cent of the EU territory (47 per cent agriculture). There are 13.7 million holdings with an average farm size of 12.6 ha and over 50 per cent of farms are managed by persons over 55. Between 0.2 and 2 per cent of utilised agricultural land is abandoned annually;
- 36.4 per cent of family farmers engage in another gainful activity;
- one-third of EU agricultural land is managed by farming systems delivering High Nature Value;
- Natura 2000 sites cover 10 per cent of agricultural areas;
- 65 per cent of assessments under the Habitats Directive[10] are unfavourable;
- 24 per cent of water abstraction is used for agriculture (only one-third of this is returned);
- 25 per cent of EU soil suffers from unsustainable erosion and 45 per cent has low organic matter content;

7 *Ibid.*, p. 12.
8 Available at http://ec.europa.eu/agriculture/cap-post-2013/consultation/consultation-document_en.pdf. The consultation period ended on 25 January 2011.
9 *Ibid.*, pp. 4–9.
10 Council Directive 92/43/EEC of 21 May 1992 on the conservation of natural habitats and of wild fauna and flora OJ 1992 L 206/7, as amended.

- there has been a substantial decline in fertiliser consumption and a decline in the use of plant protection products;
- non-CO_2 emission from agriculture fell by 20 per cent from 1990 to 2005. Emissions in agriculture are predicted to remain at current levels unless further action is taken. Agriculture currently represents 9 per cent of total European emissions;
- agriculture is a source of renewable energy and provides raw materials for bio-based products; and
- agriculture uses 2.4 per cent of final energy consumption in the EU.

5.2 Option 1: limited adjustment

Under this option in the first pillar, the current direct payment system would remain basically unchanged, although measures would be introduced to ensure a more equitable distribution of such payments, and existing market instruments would be simplified with stronger risk-management tools being introduced. In the second pillar, the orientation of the policy evident from the 2008 Health Check would be maintained with increased funding for the challenges posed by climate change, water, biodiversity and renewable energy. This option is essentially the 'business as usual' or limited adjustment option. The adjustment of the CAP to encompass the environmental dimension is a relatively recent phenomenon.

> As environmental difficulties have emerged, the EU has attempted to tackle them in a relatively imaginative way, although never addressing (until 1992) the central problem of price support; but the response has remained reactive, rather than to turn the environment into a central feature of agricultural policy.[11]

Enhancing the environmental dimension of the CAP began in earnest with the 1992 reforms which introduced environmental concerns into the operation of various common organisations of the market and a range of accompanying measures in addition to the existing agricultural structural measures.[12] Article 11 TFEU (formerly Article 6 EC) requires that 'environmental protection requirements must be integrated into the definition and implementation' of all Union policies and activities to promote sustainable development. In 1998 the Cardiff European Council invited all relevant Council formations to establish a strategy for environmental integration and sustainable development within

11 J. Ockenden and M. Franklin, *European Agriculture: Making the CAP Fit the Future* (London: Pinter, 1995), p. 44. They also noted the symbolic importance of the absence of an environmental aim from what is now Article 39 TFEU.
12 Regulations 2078–80/92 OJ 1992 L 215/85.

their respective policy areas and this necessitated a further rethink of the environmental dimension of the CAP.[13]

In relation to agriculture, the resulting Decision of the Parliament and the Council set the priority objectives of the Community to be:[14]

> ... better to integrate market, rural development and environmental policies with a view to securing sustainable agriculture, notably in the framework of the reform process launched by the Commission's Agenda 2000 proposals by:
>
> — integrating environmental considerations into agricultural policy making and taking appropriate steps to ensure that specific environmental objectives are achieved pursuant to the process of the reform of the common agricultural policy;
> — considering the scope for the incorporation of additional environmental considerations into agricultural policies.

In addition to these objectives, the Decision goes on to specify other objectives. These include the promotion of sustainable farming, a comprehensive approach to rural development and a more integrated strategy for reducing the risks to human health and the environment arising from the use of pesticides and plant-protection products. The need for a more sustainable CAP would be a hallmark of the Agenda 2000 proposals, which described the effects of 1992 reforms on the environment as 'mixed'.[15]

A start had thus been made on the integration of environmental protection requirements into the definition and implementation of the CAP. The Agenda 2000 document envisaged further integration on two fronts: internally, the process of incorporating environmental concerns into the operation of the CAP would continue and, externally, the Commission advocated the need to begin international trade negotiations on new issues, such as environmental standards in agriculture.[16] On the former it was noted that:[17]

> In the coming years, a prominent role will be given to agri-environmental instruments to support a sustainable development of rural areas and respond to society's increasing demand for environmental services. The measures aimed at maintaining and enhancing the quality of the environment shall be reinforced and extended.

13 EU Bulletin 6–1998, I.11.34. See also the reaffirmation of this invitation by the December 1998 Vienna European Council, EU-Bulletin 12–1998, I.8.78–71.
14 Decision 2179/98 OJ 1998 L 275/1.
15 COM (97) 2000, Part 1, Chapter III.1.
16 *Ibid.*, Part 1, Chapter III.2.
17 *Ibid*, Part 1, Chapter III. 4.

Increased budgetary resources being allocated to these measures would assure this prominent role but they would remain complementary, or 'accompanying measures', to price support and production control measures. The primacy accorded to these latter measures confirmed the preservation of farmers' income rather than the pursuit of environmental goals and rural development remained the essential core of the CAP. A similar conclusion emerged with respect to rural development policy, which the Agenda 2000 recognised as being 'a juxtaposition of agricultural market policy, structural policy and environmental policy with rather complex instruments and lacking overall coherence'.[18] As the 1999 Commission Communication on Sustainable Agriculture pointed out:[19]

> The philosophy underpinning the environmental aspects of CAP reform is that farmers should be expected to observe basic environmental standards without compensation. However, wherever society desires that farmers deliver an environmental service beyond this base-line level, this service should be specifically purchased through agri-environmental measures.

Despite this comment, Article 24 of Regulation 1257/1999, which established the framework for Community support for rural development as from 1 January 2000, offered support on the basis of the income foregone (additional costs resulting from the commitment given) and the need to provide an incentive.[20]

In recognition of increasing public concern about the nature of agriculture, the agri-environmental measures also allowed assistance to be offered for the promotion of animal welfare and production methods that improved the quality of agricultural products intended for human consumption. Existing schemes to support farming in less favoured areas would continue under this category of measures, although the purpose of such support was now to ensure continued agricultural land use, thereby contributing to maintenance of a viable rural community and to maintain the countryside. Also included within this area, as a result of the Regulation, was support for areas with environmental constraints – in the words of Article 13, 'to ensure environmental requirements and safeguard farming'. In addition, Article 14(2) required farmers to 'apply good farming practices compatible with the need to safeguard the environment and maintain the countryside, in particular by sustainable farming'. Under Article 29 of Regulation 445/2002, good farming practice was defined as 'the standard of farming which a reasonable farmer would follow in the region concerned' and the Member States were required to establish in their rural development plans verifiable standards that ensure compliance with general mandatory environmental requirements.[21]

18 *Ibid.*, Part 1, Chapter III. 1.
19 'Directions Towards Sustainable Agriculture' COM (1999) 22, pp. 20, 22.
20 OJ L 1999 160/80.
21 OJ 2002 L 74/1.

The integration of environmental concerns into the CAP would continue after agreement was reached on the Agenda 2000 reforms at the Berlin European Council. In December 1999 the Helsinki European Council adopted a strategy for integrating the environmental dimension into the CAP, which set specific objectives on such matters as soil degradation, the reduction of risks arising from the use of agrochemicals, the quality and balanced use of water, and landscape and biodiversity preservation.[22] A 2002 report for the Directorate-General for Agriculture by the Institute for European Environmental Policy identified the principal environmental concerns arising from agriculture and used the understanding so generated to explore the scope for further integration of environmental goals into the CAP. The conclusions of the report addressed the need for more effective implementation of existing environmental policy, but as for the primary focus of the study, the conclusion was:[23]

> There is a need to develop agri-environment programmes as a primary integration measure within the second pillar. This would result in sub-stantially greater application of schemes in most Member States, with a commensurately increased budget. Agri-environment measures provide a means of targeting specific environmental concerns in a direct way, with the flexibility to develop and amend specific rules to match local requirements.

However, it was recognised that there were limits to such schemes – in particular, it was unclear whether they would provide a sufficient income for farmers – so further decoupling was recommended in the first pillar of the CAP. As for environmental policy, one of the goals of the Sixth Environmental Action Programme agreed in 2002 was 'Encouraging more environmentally respon-sible farming including, where appropriate, extensive production methods, integrated farming practices, organic farming and agro-biodiversity, in future reviews of the CAP, taking account of the need for a balanced approach to the multifunctional role of rural communities'.[24]

In the midst of these developments, the Commission Communication on the mid-term review of the Agenda 2000 reforms was published.[25] The 2003 mid-term review introduced the SFP to improve the overall market orientation of agriculture and to promote greater environmental protection by the removal of production-specific incentives. Subsequently, the 2008 CAP Health Check acknowledged the central role played by agriculture in protecting and enhancing biodiversity, in managing and protecting water resources and in

---

22 EU Bulletin 12–1999, I.14.46–50. See also, 'The Biodiversity Action Plan for Agriculture' COM (2001) 162, and Regulation 870/2004 OJ 2004 L 162/18 launching a Community programme on the conservation, characterisation, collection and utilisation of genetic resources in agriculture.

23 D. Baldock, J. Dwyer and J. Sumpsi Vinas, *Environmental Integration and the CAP* (Madrid: Institute for European Environmental Policy, 2002), p. 106.

24 Decision 1600/2002 OJ 2002 L 242/1.

25 COM (2002) 394.

tackling climate change.[26] Key to these objectives are the cross-compliance criteria, which are classified into the following areas: animal welfare;[27] animal health;[28] public health;[29] and the environment. There are five cross-compliance criteria which relate to environmental protection. Two of these relate to the contribution of agriculture to nature conservation, namely Directive 79/409 on the conservation of Wild Birds, and Directive 92/43 on the conservation of Natural Habitats and of Wild Fauna and Flora.[30] Although the two Directives establish a comprehensive legal framework to protect biodiversity within the EU, it has been noted that, 'in reality, Member States' implementation record in relation to each Directive has been less than impressive'.[31] The Commission has emphasised that the CAP must do more to protect biodiversity through the support of environmentally friendly farming practices.[32] The Member States also have an important role to play in this area, as sitting alongside the cross-compliance criteria is a requirement for the Member States to develop codes of practice on maintaining land in good agricultural and environmental condition as a further eligibility requirement for the SFP.

A further two Directives in the cross-compliance criteria deal with water pollution caused by the use of nitrates (Directive 91/676) and certain dangerous substances (Directive 80/68).[33] Pollution is defined in the Nitrates Directive as the direct or indirect discharge of nitrates from agricultural sources 'into the aquatic environment, the results of which are such as to cause hazards to human health, harm to living resources and to aquatic ecosystems, damage to amenities or interference with other legitimate uses of water'.[34] Waters with a nitrate content above a certain threshold are regarded as being polluted and an obligation is imposed on the Member States to designate all lands draining into those waters as being 'Nitrate Vulnerable Zones'.[35] Within such zones an action programme must be implemented to reduce the level of nitrate pollution, irrespective of the source of such pollution. These two Directives are part of a wider EU programme with respect to water which includes the Urban

---

26 See Regulations 72–74/2009 OJ 2009 L 30/1.
27 See Directives 98/58 OJ 1998 L 221/23, 91/629 OJ 1991 L 340/28 and 91/630 OJ 1991 L 340/33.
28 See Directive 2008/71 OJ 2008 L 213/31 on the identification and registration of pigs, Regulation 1760/2000 OJ 2000 L 204/1 on the identification and registration of bovine animals and Regulation 21/2004 OJ 2004 L 5/8 on the identification and registration of ovine and caprine animals.
29 See Directive 96/22 OJ 1996 L 125/3, Directive 91/414 OJ 1991 L 230/1 and Articles 14, 15, 17(1) and 18–20 of Regulations 178/2002 OJ 2002 L 31/1.
30 Respectively, OJ 1979 L 103/1 and OJ 1992 L 206/7.
31 B. Jack, *Agriculture and EU Environmental Law* (Farnham: Ashgate Publishing, 2009), p. 157.
32 See *Preparing for the 'Health Check' of the CAP Reform*, COM (2007) 722, p. 9. See also *Biodiversity Plan for Agriculture: Implementation Report* COM (2001) 162.
33 Articles 4 and 5 of Directive 91/676 OJ 1992 L 375/1 and Directive 80/68 OJ1980 L 20/43/1.
34 Article 2(j) of Directive 91/676 OJ 1992 L 375/1.
35 *Ibid.*, Article 3(2). The threshold is 50mg/l is based on standards recommended by the World Health Organisation. Under Article 3(5) Member States may alternatively declare their whole national territory to be a Nitrate Vulnerable Zone.

Waste Water Treatment Directive and the Water Framework Directive; Article 22 of the latter provides for the repeal of Directive 80/68 by 22 December 2013.[36]

In early 2010 the Commission reported on the implementation of the Directive 91/676 for the period 2004–7. This was the first report covering all 27 Member States.[37] The report indicated that some 21 million tons of nitrogen fertiliser and nearly 17 million tonnes of nitrogen from animal husbandry were used annually in this period within the EU as a whole. It also indicated that 15 per cent of monitoring stations had average nitrate concentrations greater than 50mg/l, which is the level set by the Directive for water to be regarded as polluted; the non-binding target of 25 mg/l, which had been initially set in Directive 75/440, had been exceeded in a further 21 per cent of monitoring stations.[38] Eight Member States were identified as having increasing trends of pollution in more than 30 per cent of their monitoring stations compared with the previous period; Ireland was included in this list.

Looking specifically at water and Ireland, the Irish Environmental Protection Agency (EPA) in a report of 2008 identified the main threat to surface water quality as being eutrophication, which comes mainly from agricultural manures and fertilisers, sewage and detergents.[39] For the period 2004–2006, the 2008 report indicated that the percentage of water bodies at risk of failing to meet the targets set by the Water Framework Directive for good water by 2015 in Ireland were: 64 per cent of rivers; 64 per cent of lakes; 53 per cent of estuarine waters; 27 per cent of coastal waters; and 62 per cent of ground-water. On the latter, the EPA reported that approximately 30 per cent of all samples taken between 2003 and 2005 showed bacteriological contamination, with such contamination occurring at least once in the period 2003–5 at 52 per cent of all monitoring locations. However, the EPA's latest report, published in March 2011, indicates that there have been improvements in water quality. For example, significant investment in facilities for the storage of livestock slurry and manure at a farm level and decreasing sales of fertiliser have improved the quality of groundwater with just over 15 per cent of groundwater now being classified as poor under the Water Framework Directive. Similar improvements were made in the other categories (lakes, rivers, estuarine and coastal waters). However, the 2011 report also recognises that continuing efforts will be needed to maintain these improvements and to

36 Respectively Directive 91/271 OJ 1991 L 135/40 (as amended by Directive 98/15 OJ 1998 L 67/29) and Directive 2000/60 OJ 2000 L 327/1. Pending the repeal and replacement of Directive 80/68, its provisions are supplemented by Directive 2006/118 OJ 2006 L 372/19.

37 COM (2010) 47.

38 *Ibid.*, p. 3. Directive 75/440 (OJ 1975 L 194/26) dealt with the quality of surface waters intended for drinking water abstraction.

39 EPA, *Water Quality Report: Water Quality in Ireland (2004–2006)* (Wexford: EPA, 2008) Available at www.epa.ie/downloads/pubs/water/waterqua/waterrep/#d.en.25320.

reverse the negative effects of agriculture in this area.[40] A similar picture emerges for the other environmental areas listed in cross-compliance criteria.

Viewed in the light of the above developments, in terms of the options for CAP reform proposed by the Commission in November 2010, Option 1, the limited adjustment option, should lead to a harmonisation of the SFP across all the Member States, and as a result give encouragement to agriculture in the new Member States where the sector remains important for social and economic reasons. The focus of the policy would remain income support for 'active' farmers, with this concept still to be refined. There would also be some changes to the market management measures, especially in the area of risk management, and this would allow the EU to cope more efficiently with exceptional situations such as those that arose in the dairy sector in 2009. Public intervention and private storage would continue to be features of the first pillar. As for the second pillar, there would be strengthening of measures in accordance with the 2008 Health Check (climate change, water, bio-diversity and renewable energy) but the increase in funds for these measures would be limited. Overall, the extent to which this reform scenario would refocus the policy in the way that was noted in the public consultations that preceded the Commission's Communication may be doubted.

A more integrated approach is supported by the results of the Scenar-2020 study when it was updated in 2009.[41] This took account of recent developments in identifying trends for European agriculture and the rural economy up to 2020 in light of projections in rural demography, agricultural technology and markets and the natural and social constraints on land use.[42] The results indicated a decline in the agricultural economy (confirming the 2006 Scenar-2020 study) in terms of both income and employment, which is unevenly distributed across the EU. Growth in agricultural incomes continues to lag behind growth in other sectors.[43]

---

40 EPA, *Water Quality in Ireland Report (2007–2009)* (Wexford: EPA, 2011) Available at www.epa.ie. downloads/pubs/water/waterqua/WaterQuality0709.pdf.

41 P. Nowicki *et al.*, *Scenar 2020-II – Update of Analysis of Prospects in the Scenar 2020 Study* (Brussels: European Commission, Directorate-General Agriculture and Rural Development, 2009). For details of the previous study see http://ec.europa.eu/agriculture/publi/reports/scenar2020/index_en.htm.

42 The study used three possible options (pp. 24–28) which are broadly similar to those identified by the Commission. The first scenario (a reference scenario equivalent to the integration approach) involved a nominal reduction in CAP budget, a full decoupling of the SFP, and a significant increase in resources available under the second pillar. Under this scenario, there would also be a WTO agreement on reform of agriculture that would include the elimination of export subsidies. A conservative scenario (equivalent to the limited adjustment scenario) assumes that the 2008 Health Check results are largely maintained, with direct payments being slightly reduced and a significant increase in second pillar resources. The final scenario is liberalisation (equivalent to the Commission's third option) under which all trade-related measures (including SFP and market instruments) would be discontinued and there would be a 100 per cent increase in the second pillar.

43 *Ibid.*, Table 3.7 (p. 97). Under the liberalisation scenario, income losses exceed 35 per cent in four Member States – the Czech Republic, Denmark, Ireland and the UK. Agricultural employment falls in four Member States (Austria, Finland, Ireland and Sweden) as a result of a reduction in second pillar payments (Figure 3.29, p. 108).

Although there is an increase in arable production, yield improvements would lead to a reduction in agricultural land use (and agricultural land prices).[44] Crops used for biofuel production fare better than others but there will be negative effects here if second generation biofuels emerge. There are significant changes in livestock production with more open international markets, especially in beef. There would be positive environmental effects arising from decreased use of nitrates and lower methane emissions but this would have to be weighed against the negative effects of land abandonment. The more integrated approach would obviously have to address this issue.

5.3 Option 2: greater integration

There would be a (substantial) re-design of direct payments under the second option with the basic rate serving as income support and a compulsory additional aid for those extra costs associated with realising the public goods demanded from agriculture.[45] Further additional payments would be available to compensate for specific natural restraints and a new scheme would be introduced for small farms. In the second pillar, the Commission would propose measures to ensure that existing instruments would be better aligned with priorities in the areas of the environment, climate change and/or restructuring and innovation at national/local levels. Whereas the first option envisaged risk-management measures under the first pillar, this option would see the introduction of such measures as part of second pillar measures to ensure income stabilisation and to compensate for substantial income losses.[46] It is implicit in the Commission document that it is this option which will lead to 'green growth in the agricultural sector and the rural economy as a way to enhance well being by pursuing economic growth while preventing environmental degradation'.[47]

Increased competitive pressures arising from a more open international trading system (and the need to feed an expanding population) will lead to greater specialisation and intensified production and so the greater integration option can be seen as a response to the need to create incentives within the CAP promoting more sustainable agricultural practices. Within the existing policy such incentives are located in the poorer second pillar but under this option they would become a more prominent feature of the first pillar addressing issues such as climate change and the environment. On climate change, land use, land-use change and forestry is not part of the EU's greenhouse gas reduction commitment, although the Commission is due to report in 2011 on

---

44 *Ibid.*, p. 107. The effect is variable across the EU with a strong decrease in the number of arable crops farms in Ireland, Austria, Finland and Sweden.

45 *The CAP towards 2020*, p. 12 and Annex.

46 As a result of being moved from Pillar 1 under the limited adjustment option to Pillar 2 under the greater integration option (Option 2), implementation of risk management options would be a matter of discretion for the Member States.

47 *The CAP towards 2020*, p. 6.

the possible inclusion of this sector in the future. As for the impact of climate change at a European level, the Scenar 2020-II study indicated:[48]

> Climate change and the energy challenge will affect all regions. Regions in the Mediterranean part of Europe seem to be more exposed to these challenges, whereas northern and western European regions appear to be less at risk. However, the impact depends on climate change scenarios which may vary considerably over time.

There is little doubt that changes in climate will affect agricultural production but the nature of those changes is uncertain at a global level and may be minimised if there is an open international trading system.[49]

As for the local impact of climate change, the EPA recognises that Ireland faces significant challenges if it is to meet its emissions targets for greenhouse gases under the EU climate change package. Emission levels peaked at about 68.3 million tonnes of CO_2 equivalent in 2005 and are projected to fall to just above 65.3 million tonnes of CO_2 equivalent by 2020 but a further reduction of 5.2 million tonnes could be made with additional measures.[50] The 2020 EU Effort Sharing target requires a 20 per cent reduction from 2005 levels for those sectors not covered by the Emissions Trading Scheme, which includes agriculture. The latest emission projections for agriculture show the three main sources of emissions as enteric fermentation (47 per cent), manure management (28 per cent) and nitrogen application to soils (20 per cent) with total emissions decreasing by 5 per cent by 2020 to 17.8 million tonnes of CO_2 equivalent.[51] The agriculture sector is the largest source of emissions in Ireland at 29 per cent of total emissions in 2009, so meeting the mandate of the climate change package will be a major challenge, especially if the food processing sector is included.[52]

As part of the debate on how to respond to this challenge, a 2009 report from the Irish Institute for International and European Affairs (IIEA) offered suggestions for enhancing the environmental sustainability of Irish farming, which balances this goal against those of a stable income for farmers and enhancing the competitiveness of Irish agricultural products.[53] This corresponds

48 *Ibid.*, p. 55.
49 See G. Nelson, 'Agriculture and Climate Change' in P. Boulanger and P. Messerlin (eds), *2020 European Agriculture: Challenges and Policies* (Washington, DC: German Marshall Fund of the US, 2010) for further discussion.
50 See EPA, *Ireland's Greenhouse Gas Emissions and Projections 2010–2020* (Wexford: EPA, 2010), Appendix 1. Available at www.epa.ie/downloads/pubs/air/airemissions/EPA_GHG_Emission_Projections_2010.pdf.
51 *Ibid.*, p. 14.
52 See www.epa.ie/environmentinfocus/indicatordashboard/greenhousegasemissionsbysector/. The percentage for 1990 was 36 per cent.
53 M. Dowling *et al.*, *From Farm to Fork: A Sustainability Enhancement Programme for the Irish Agri-Food Industry* (Dublin: IIEA, 2009).

well with the goals set more generally for European agriculture in the Commission proposals. For primary production, what was proposed was a 'whole farm-scale strategy' that included extending the grazing season, reducing finishing times, improved sward quality, increased use of clover in swards, earlier slurry application times, dietary manipulation and, where economically feasible, a transition to organic farming.[54] With the exception of the latter, these proposals could form part of the requirement to keep land in good agricultural and environmental condition which is necessary to receive the SFP. Beyond animal farming, the report also proposed greater agricultural carbon sequestration through greater afforestation (current levels in Ireland are less that half of that needed to have a sustainable forestry sector), greater cultivation of biomass products (current levels in Ireland are at 5 per cent of what is estimated as possible levels of production) and a possible expansion of the production of biofuels.[55]

Directive 2009/28, the Renewable Energy Directive, mandates that a 20 per cent share of final energy consumption in the EU must come from renewable sources by 2020 with each Member State's contribution differentiated in accordance with their respective starting points.[56] The Directive also mandates that a 10 per cent share for renewables in the transport sector is achieved with considerable emphasis placed in meeting this target on the role of biofuels, which are defined in Article 2 as 'liquid or gaseous fuel for transport produced from biomass'. The imposition of a binding target for the use of biofuels in the transport sector is justified on a number of different bases, including the ease with which transport fuels may be traded between Member States. Thus if domestic production is unable to keep pace with demand, fuels could be imported from other Member States and/or from other countries. The EU is now the world's largest producer of biodiesel and the fourth largest producer of bioethanol. An additional justification for the imposition of binding targets is offered by reference to the need to provide investors with certainty and an enabling environment for continued technological development for renewable energy more generally.

The Directive requires biofuels used to meet these targets to adhere to certain sustainability standards and compliance with these standards is also required so as to be eligible for financial support.[57] The core sustainability criterion requires biofuels to achieve a minimum level of 35 per cent

---

54 *Ibid.*, pp. 13–17.
55 *Ibid.*, pp. 19–20. See also pp. 21–22 for discussion of renewable energy development.
56 OJ 2009 L 140/6. Annex I of the Directive contains national overall targets for each Member State's share of energy from renewable sources which, taken together, will secure a share of 20 per cent of final energy consumption from renewables by 2020.
57 *Ibid.*, Article 17. Identical sustainability criteria have been included in the recent amendment to the Fuel Quality Directive (Directive 2009/30 OJ 2009 L 140/88) and the Commission has recommended that Member States adopt the same sustainability criteria for biomass (*Report on sustainability requirements for the use of solid and gaseous biomass sources in electricity, heating and cooling* COM(2010) 8).

greenhouse gas savings; by 2017 this figure is set to increase to 50 per cent.[58] Article 17 goes on to provide further sustainability criteria. For example, raw materials used to produce biofuels should not be obtained from land with high biodiversity value, which includes primary forests and other wooded land where there is no indication of human activity, as well as areas designated for nature protection purposes. Raw materials taken from areas for the protection of rare, threatened or endangered eco-systems are not permitted to be taken into account for the purposes of meeting the targets or receiving financial support. However, an exception is provided if it can be shown that the production of biofuel feedstocks did not interfere with conservation efforts. Raw materials taken from highly diverse grassland are also ineligible for use to meet the targets set out in the Directive, which also discourages the use of high-carbon-stock lands such as wetlands to produce biofuel feedstocks. Peatlands are additionally singled out as deserving of special attention due to their high carbon value and as such, raw materials derived from such areas will not be deemed to conform to the Directive's sustainability criteria unless it can be proved that production of the material did not result in the drainage of previously undrained areas. The sustainability criteria apply regardless of whether the raw material is imported or domestically produced.[59] In the case of domestically produced feedstocks, however, Article 17(6) also requires producers to adhere to the standards relating to good agricultural and environmental condition.

Ensuring compliance with the designated sustainability criteria is under Article 18 a matter for Member States, who are required to ensure that economic operators show that the sustainability standards have been adhered to and that they submit reliable data setting out their adherence to the designated criteria. In demonstrating compliance with the sustainability criteria, economic operators must adopt a 'mass balance' system under which feedstocks are partly traceable to their source.[60] Member States are required to produce a National Action Plan detailing the strategy they will adopt to fulfil the sustainability criteria for biofuels as well as to verify compliance with the scheme.[61] As the sustainability criteria in this area are fully harmonised, Member States are not permitted to require economic operators to adhere to additional criteria.

The introduction of sustainability requirements is noteworthy not so much for which factors are considered as deserving of protection under such a scheme but rather for the concerns which are left out. Social issues such as labour and land-use rights are not included within the auspices of the sustainability

---

58 For biofuel production beginning after 1 January 2017, the figure will be 60 per cent.

59 The Commission is tasked with monitoring the supply of biofuels to the EU market in an effort to achieve an appropriate equilibrium between imported and domestic supply.

60 The Commission is to monitor and report on the effectiveness of a mass balance system in maintaining the integrity of the verification system.

61 Guidance upon this is provided in Commission Decision (EC) 2009/548 establishing a template for National Renewable Energy Action Plans under Directive 2009/28 OJ 2009 L 182/33.

scheme and, more crucially, the impact of biofuel production upon food prices is merely to be monitored. However, under Article 17(7), the Commission may propose corrective action if evidence shows that biofuel production has a significant impact on food prices, but no guidance is provided as to the meaning of 'significant' or the types of corrective action envisaged. In addition, while concern for social issues, water and air protection as well as indirect land use changes, restoration of degraded land and the avoidance of excessive water consumption are mentioned within the Directive, they are not operationalised through the introduction of specific criteria but instead form part of future reporting requirements imposed upon the Commission under Article 23.

The debate about whether biofuel production mitigates greenhouse gas emissions is continuing and for their part the IIEA considered that further research would be necessary to ensure that production of oilseed rape meets the sustainability criteria set out in Directive 2009/28.[62] However, this was only one aspect of their proposed 'whole farm-scale strategy' and other aspects included biodiversity enhancement, animal-welfare promotion and improved water quality and management.[63] As noted, it is clear that a number of the IIEA's proposed changes can be implemented by changes to the good agricultural and environmental conditions and the existing cross-compliance criteria and the continuation of cooperation between farmers financed under the second pillar (for example, in biomass, biofuels and anaerobic digesters). This is consistent with the Commission's Option 2 – the greater integration option. However, unlike the IIEA report, it is not a whole-industry approach, as that report also addresses the sustainability of the food processing industry and the retail sector. The Commission's failure to address such issues raises the question of what 'integration' means in this context.

For the Commission, Option 2 would link the SFP with the provision of public goods (benefits for the environment, climate change, etc.) and proposes a division of the SFP into three parts, which would further reduce the link between support and the historical type and level of production, thus promoting greater equity between farmers and Member States. (Coupled support would, however, still be possible at the discretion of a Member State.) The three elements are: a basic rate for all active farmers; additional aid to compensate for the extra costs associated with realising an improved environmental outcome (e.g. permanent pasture, green cover, crop rotation and ecological set-aside); and payments to compensate for specific natural restraints. This three/four-fold division of income support raises the question of whether it is in accordance with the simplification agenda for the CAP. Under the proposal, active farmers would be eligible for environment payments and payments for specific natural constraints under both pillars, which would increase the relative share of the Rural Development pillar in overall spending. This is hardly consistent

---

62 Dowling *et al.*, *From Farm to Fork*, p. 20.
63 *Ibid.*, pp. 23–25.

with the objective of a simpler CAP. It also raises the questions of whether the additional environmental payment under Pillar 1 would be more effective and efficient than equivalent payments under Pillar 2 and the balance between the specific natural constraints under Pillar 1 and the less-favoured-areas payment under Pillar 2. In both cases there may be a transfer of resources from Pillar 2 to Pillar 1.

The basic rate will still be conditional on fulfilling the cross-compliance criteria and maintaining land in good agricultural and environmental condition. How prominent this feature will be is a decision that has yet to be made, as is the decision on the period during which these changes will be implemented. In deciding on this balance, the fact that farm income has stagnated – the decline following 2008 has brought levels back to what they were fifteen years ago – will have to be taken into account, and the Commission Communication promises that any reform would limit the 'gains and losses of Member States by guaranteeing that farmers in all Member States receive on average a minimum share of the EU-wide average level of direct payments'.[64] So, for example, if the relationship between these three elements were to be 50:40:10 (basic rate:environmental payment:specific payment) this would yield greater benefits to the environment than one in which the relationship was 90:5:5. It is the balance between these three elements, ultimately to be decided by the Council and the European Parliament, which will determine the extent to which this particular option meets its goal of ensuring that the CAP becomes 'more sustainable and that the balance between different policy objectives, farmers and Member States is better met'.[65]

5.4 Option 3: liberalisation or re-focusing

The integration approach – Option 2 – meets the 2010 Policy Principles identified by the OECD Agriculture Ministers as promoting 'green growth', addressing the issue of climate change and improving environmental performance. However, the focus on these types of measures could also be a feature of the third option presented by the Commission. This option, the most radical presented, would involve the phasing-out of existing direct payments and the abolition of all market measures, although there would be limited payments for the provision of environmental public goods and specific natural constraints and a disturbance clause that could be activated in the event of severe crises. Most measures under this option would be in the second pillar and would focus on the environment and climate change.

The (earlier) leaked version of the Commission paper identified Option 3 as follows:[66]

---

64 *The CAP towards 2020*, p. 8.

65 *Ibid*, p. 12.

66 Available at http://capreform.eu/wp-content/uploads/2010/10/communication-leak.pdf (original emphasis).

Those requesting a more *radical* reform of the CAP advocate moving away from income support and most market measures, and focusing entirely on environmental and climate change objectives. This alternative could have the advantage that it would allow for a clear focus of the policy. However, this would lead to a significant reduction in production levels, farm income, and number of farmers for the most vulnerable sectors and areas, as well as cause land abandonment in some areas and intensification of production in other areas, with serious potential environmental and social consequences. This option would thus imply a loss of synergies between the economic, environmental and social dimensions of the CAP.

When it was officially released, this option was drafted as follows:[67]

Another option would be a more far reaching reform of the CAP with a strong focus on environmental and climate change objectives, while moving away gradually from income support and most market measures. Providing a clear financial focus on environmental and climate change issues through the Rural Development policy framework would encourage the creation of regional strategies in order to assure the implementation of EU objectives.

It is difficult to imagine that the Commission wishes this option to be taken seriously! Others have taken this option as the way forward.

A 2010 Declaration by a group of leading agricultural economists, entitled *For an Ambitious Reform of the Common Agricultural Policy*, concluded: 'Policymakers must show more reform ambition for the post-2013 CAP if they are serious about the Europe 2020 strategy and the EU's high-level environmental commitments.'[68] The need for ambitious CAP reform, in their opinion, was motivated by the fact that the policy does not at present adequately fulfil important objectives in relation to the environment, competition and development. They advocated five guiding principles for a new CAP. Under the first principle, public goods would be targeted which would involve the phasing out of subsidies that are not differentiated on the basis of these objectives and this would include the SFP. Rural poverty alleviation would be designated a matter of social policy rather than falling under the CAP. The environment would be a focus of the policy under the second principle with measures concentrating on biodiversity protection, climate change mitigation and water management. The remaining principles call for greater market orientations, a focus on food security at a global level and subsidiarity.

---

67 *The CAP towards 2020*, p. 12.
68 Available at www.reformthecap.eu/declaration/. See also 'A Common Agricultural Policy for European Public Goods', 2009 Declaration by a Group of Leading Agricultural Economists, available at www.reformthecap.eu/posts/declaration-on-cap-reform.

Support for some of these arguments actually emerges from the Commission's consultation document for the impact assessment of the proposed CAP reform. The document acknowledges that the state of European farming is such that it would be difficult to reorient the policy towards greater environmental sustainability.[69] The Commission does not recognise that farm household income may be more than income from farming, as other members of the household, including some farmers, have non-farm incomes.[70] This makes justification of a CAP directed at income support harder to justify. Of greater significance is that the document suggests that concerns about food security in Europe are misplaced and that agriculture's positive contribution to the environment is questionable.[71]

A 2010 proposal from five non-governmental organisations (NGOs) for a new CAP notes:[72]

> Farming and wider land management are key activities for addressing some of the greatest challenges facing mankind this century. Stemming the collapse of biodiversity, mitigating and adapting to climate change, and maintaining plentiful and clean water resources, are some of the environmental challenges that require profound changes to the ways in which Europe's land resource is used and managed.

Eschewing a 'greenwash' of the existing policy instruments, the proposal sets out a system of public payments rewarding farmers for the provision of public goods while maintaining that the 'polluter pays principle' should apply to all farming activity.[73] Farmers would not be paid for respecting existing legislation even if it required the provision of a public good.[74] As a prerequisite for receiving payments, the proposal would require environmental legislation to be respected and the current cross-compliance criteria would be maintained as a baseline for all payments. However, the following would be added to the criteria: the Water Framework Directive; the future Soil Framework Directive;

---

69 http://ec.europa.eu/agriculture/cap-post-2013/consultation/consultation-document_en.pdf, p. 2: 'In effect, short-term survival dominates the perception of many farmers over the long-term, broader perspective.'

70 *Ibid.*, p. 9. See also, J-C. Bureau, 'Why are we so lousy at measuring farm incomes' (30 July 2010). Available at http://capreform.eu/why-are-we-so-lousy-at-measuring-farm-incomes/.

71 *Ibid.*, p. 2, 'The concern regarding food security is less about the overall availability of supply in Europe, but rather about the role of the EU within a world-wide context.'

72 See www.birdlife.org/eu/pdfs/Proposal_for_a_new_common_agricultural_policy_FINAL_100302.pdf, p. 2. The five non-governmental organisations are Birdlife International, European Environmental Bureau, European Forum on Nature Conservation and Pastoralism, International Federation of Organic Agriculture Movements and World Wide Fund for Nature.

73 *Ibid.*, pp. 5 and 13. The proposal also suggests additional environmental legislation, for example, on protection against conversion of permanent grassland and removal and deliberate damage of landscape elements (pp. 14–15).

74 *Ibid.*, p. 15. Exceptions would be made for Nature 2000 management and river basin management plans.

the Sustainable Pesticide Use Directive; the emission reduction elements of the future Industrial Emissions Directive; and the Regulation on Maximum Residue Levels in Food. Existing training and advisory services would inform and advise farmers on how to comply with their legal obligations.

At a general level the following points should be made. Application of the polluter pays principle would represent a sea-change in agriculture, which up to now has used the pay-the-polluter principle. It also poses the challenge of measuring pollution not at a single point (i.e. a factory) but for some forms of production across a geographical area. Furthermore, imposing climate change costs on agriculture could result in these being passed on to the consumer through higher food prices or, if domestic production is not competitive, increased imports which may increase domestic food insecurity and lead to domestic land abandonment. Any emissions scheme would also have to calculate the positive contribution made by agriculture to climate change. Whilst solutions may be found to the measurement problems and to the design of an emissions scheme (especially if imposed internationally to reduce the negative impacts), these points indicate that what is being proposed by the NGOs is a fundamental re-design of the architecture of the existing CAP.

As for the architecture of the new CAP there would be five support schemes, agreed at the EU level and for which the Member States would establish national or regional programmes, in addition to wider support measures addressing sustainable land management and rural development.[75] The five area-based schemes would be:

- Basic Farm Sustainability Scheme – 'to support farmers and land managers that commit to a set of concrete and meaningful best practice rules that can deliver better land stewardship and more sustainable farming'.[76] Among the proposed commitments would be a requirement for crop rotation, a maximum livestock density and good practices for water management and soil erosion.
- High Nature Value (HNV) System Support Scheme – to 'support the maintenance (or recovery) of farming systems that deliver high levels of public goods but are threatened by marginalisation, abandonment or conversion'.[77] Each Member State would identify its HNV farming system on basis of farm-level criteria. Payments under this scheme would be in addition to the Basic Scheme and could be combined with the Organic System Support payments.
- Organic System Support Scheme – to support the continuing development of organic farming in the EU in accordance with Regulation 834/2007.[78]

---

75 *Ibid.*, pp. 22–27. These support measures would include capital investment grants, support for management planning and cooperation and support for rural communities threatened by abandonment.
76 *Ibid.*, p. 16.
77 *Ibid.*, p. 18.
78 OJ 2007 L 189/1.

- Targeted Agri-Environmental Schemes – to address specific environmental problems not supported under other schemes. Agreements would last between five and ten years and could be concluded on a collective basis with farmers in a particular region. Payments would be calculated on an income foregone/cost incurred formula and could be combined with payments under other schemes.
- Natura 2000 and Water Framework Directive Scheme – 'to provide compensation for income loss and cost incurred by mandatory and territorially explicit prescriptions'.[79]

Each of these schemes would be implemented in accordance with a series of operational principles.[80] These specify, for example, that payments would be made on a contractual basis and would be targeted at the achievement of specific and well-defined policy objectives with results being quantifiable against baselines. The general principles of the scheme would be agreed at the EU level with details being agreed at the national/regional level (and approved by the Commission) in accordance with a strategy for the use of the various schemes (also to be approved by the Commission to ensure spending coherence). The end result would be the realisation of the objective of creating an environmentally sustainable CAP for which the framework is set at EU level but implementation is through national/regional programmes. It would fall short of a re-nationalisation of the policy but would fully embrace the concept of subsidiarity.

The positions advocated by the group of leading agricultural economists and by the NGO submission would result in a fundamentally different CAP and would address all of the policy prescriptions identified by the OECD Agriculture Ministers. However, it should be noted that similar proposals in the past, such as the Buckwell Report, although highly commendable, have fallen at the hurdle of political acceptability.[81] Given the reaction of the Member States to date to the proposed reform of the CAP it is unlikely that any major liberalisation or refocusing will occur in the immediate future.

5.5 Conclusion

The period beginning in 2013 is shaping up as a challenge for European agricultural markets. New trading conditions, new financial perspectives, the disappearance at Community level of export refunds – which will require all Community products to position themselves on the world market under competitive conditions – and greater market volatility,

---

79 www.birdlife.org/eu/pdfs/Proposal_for_a_new_common_agricultural_policy_FINAL_100302.pdf, p. 21
80 *Ibid.*, pp. 10–13.
81 Report of an Expert Group, *Towards a Common Agricultural and Rural Policy for Europe* (1997). Available at http://ec.europa.eu/agriculture/publi/buck_en/index.htm.

amongst other factors, make for a more uncertain backdrop against which the CAP will have to continue to meet its objectives. The EU must have an agricultural model with the tools necessary to stabilise markets and deal with price volatility, a model in which the economic activity of agriculture provides farmers with fair incomes that reflect their contribution to society and in which farming is the mainstay of life in rural areas.[82]

This was how a Presidency paper from Spain to the February 2010 Agriculture Council characterised the challenges facing the CAP. The emphasis on the income-support objective suggests that radical change may not be how the EU will meet these challenges. The paper endorsed the objectives of the CAP in Article 39 TFEU and other Member States expressed broad support for the paper.[83] A subsequent Franco-German position paper maintained that the original objectives of the policy 'are still valid today'.[84] It considered that two new challenges would lead to a wider vision of the CAP: the adaptation of the policy to the new global environment and the needs and demands of European citizens. To meet these challenges, the paper argued for the continuation of the reform path set out in successive reforms, confirmed by the 2008 Health Check.

Although greater market orientation in the CAP is endorsed, the Franco-German position paper suggested that countervailing measures are needed 'to buffer the devastating effects of growing price volatility and market crises' but risk-assessment measures to stabilise farm incomes over time, such as insurance and mutual funds, would be investigated by Member States on a voluntary basis. The two pillar structure would be maintained, and once the budget for each pillar had been decided there would be no modulation between pillars. The paper rejects national co-financing of expenditure under the first pillar and an EU-wide flat rate for direct payments, arguing that the rate should be set with regard to the net budget positions of Member States. Greater flexibility is supported on the distribution of direct payments and in rural development policies and measures to address new challenges (e.g. further streamlining of the cross-compliance criteria) would 'take very carefully into account the financial implications for each Member State'. Decisions on the future CAP budget would be made 'when decisions are made on all policies and the entire EU financial framework'.

Debate within the Council was crystallised by an informal meeting of the Agriculture Council held under the Belgian Presidency in September 2010.[85]

---

82 *Future of the CAP: Market Management Measures in the Years after 2013* (15 February 2010). Available at http://register.consilium.europa.eu/pdf/en/10/st06/st06063.en10.pdf.

83 See www.consilium.europa.eu/uedocs/cms_data/docs/pressdata/en/agricult/113353.pdf, meeting of the Agriculture Council of 22 February 2010.

84 See http://capreform.eu/franco-german-position-on-future-of-the-cap/ for further details of the paper titled 'Franco-German position for a strong CAP beyond 2013 – new challenges and expectations for food biomass and the environment.'

85 See http://register.consilium.europa.eu/pdf/en/10/st15/st15339.en10.pdf.

The results of the meeting indicated that there was no questioning of the two-pillar structure but it was noted that they should be complementary with tasks divided between pillars. As for the first pillar a balance would have to be struck between income support and the rewarding of farming's contributions to the provision of public goods. A safety net would also be necessary for cases of extreme price volatility and crises. Ministers recognised that the future CAP would have to address issues of competitiveness, climate change and biodiversity while also contributing to food security in a sustainable way. They concluded that the budget for agriculture should allow agriculture to fulfil its objectives. Debates within the Council since the publication of the Commission Communication suggest that major changes to the policy are not contemplated.[86] However, the decision is no longer solely for the Council because as a result of the Lisbon Treaty the European Parliament is now a co-legislator in agricultural matters.

As for the European Parliament's Committee on Agriculture and Rural Development, its June 2010 report suggested that the main challenge for the CAP after 2013 would be ensuring food security at a European and global level, but the aim of increased food production will have to be balanced against the challenge of climate change.[87] A more competitive European agriculture would tackle climate change and promote innovation through green growth whilst ensuring balanced territorial development. A fairer and more sustainable CAP would be delivered through five building blocks. Direct support would be offered in the first building block, Food Security and Fair Trade, using area-based payments with basic cross-compliance criteria; coupled payments would be limited and capped. Sustainability, the second building block, would be achieved through contractual climate change top-ups based on clear targets. Both of these building blocks would be funded through the EU budget with remaining blocks being co-financed.[88] Agriculture across Europe, the third building block, would involve continuing reform of the Less Favoured Areas payment to ensure farming activity across the EU, supporting local food production and meeting the challenge of land abandonment. Outcome agreements and territorial contracts would be a feature of the fourth building block, Biodiversity and Environmental Protection, which would cover agri-environmental measures for the majority of agricultural land, water and soil improvement and organic and high nature value farming. The final building block, Green Growth, would adopt an integrated approach to rural development with additional measures on climate change and green energy. The differences

---

86 See, for example, www.consilium.europa.eu/uedocs/cms_data/docs/pressdata/en/agricult/118455.pdf, meeting of the Agriculture Council of 13 and 14 December 2010. See also, the meeting of 24 January 2011, see www.consilium.europa.eu/uedocs/cms_data/docs/pressdata/en/agricult/118939.pdf.

87 See PE 439.972v0200 *Report on the future of the Common Agricultural Policy after 2013* (Rapporteur George Lyon), available at www.europarl.europa.eu/sides/getDoc.do?pubRef=-//EP//NONSGML+REPORT+A7-2010-0204+0+DOC+PDF+V0//EN& language=EN.

88 The EU would also finance safety nets to cope with price volatility and food crises.

between this proposal and the views expressed by the Council would suggest a possible conflict between the two institutions. However, the extent of the conflict may not be significant as both institutions are in agreement on the fundamentals (greater integration of environmental concerns and the promotion of rural development) but are likely to disagree on the budgetary settlement.

Legislative proposals are due from the Commission in June 2011 and it is probable that the second option, greater integration, will be chosen. However, a number of questions remain to be answered. These include: the definition of an active farmer; the balance between elements of the Pillar 1 payment; the relationship between the cross-compliance criteria (and the good agricultural and environmental condition requirement) and the additional environmental payment; the relationship between the payment for specific natural constraints under Pillar 1 and the Less Favoured Area payment under Pillar 2; the balance between the two pillars; the impact of the changes on the Rural Development pillar; and the budgetary settlement for agriculture. Answers to these questions will determine what sort of CAP emerges from the current reform process.

6   The integration challenge

Integrating environmental concerns into other EU policies

Owen McIntyre

6.1 Introduction

Despite the fact that the principle of environmental integration was first introduced into the Community legal order almost 30 years ago, by means of the Third Environmental Action Programme adopted in 1983, its precise normative character and substantive content remain unclear. In common with the other guiding principles which are meant to provide a basis for European Union action on the environment, the impact and justiciability of the stipulation that environmental requirements must be integrated into the definition and implementation of other EU policies and activities remains fraught with uncertainty. Following the failure of the so-called 'Cardiff process', by means of which the Union institutions attempted to formalise procedures and institutional mechanisms for the practical implementation of the principle in the context of EU decision-making, and the introduction into the TFEU of a host of new integration principles requiring consideration of a range of additional policy objectives and requirements in general EU policy-making, this uncertainty has been exacerbated.

This volume includes two contributions which aim to shed light on the true legal meaning and policy implications of the principle of environmental integration in the post-Lisbon era. The first, by Ludwig Krämer,[1] seeks to identify the essence of the obligation imposed upon policy-makers by the principle and concludes that it, amongst other things, involves a duty to make available to the public information on whether and how environmental protection requirements have been addressed in measures adopted in other, related policy fields. The second, by Joseph McMahon,[2] outlines the ongoing developments in relation to the proposed reform of the EU Common Agricultural Policy (CAP) and, in so doing, provides a fascinating insight into the practical means employed to integrate environmental factors into one such policy area in the post-Lisbon era.

1 L. Krämer, 'Giving a Voice to the Environment by Challenging the Practice of Integrating Environmental Requirements into Other EU Policies', Chapter 4 of this volume.
2 J. A. McMahon, 'The CAP in 2020: Vision or Hindsight?', Chapter 5 of this volume.

6.2 Origins of the principle of environmental integration

Though it may be possible to trace the origins of the principle of environmental integration to the very first attempts to formulate a Community environmental policy,[3] it is more commonly associated with the Third Environmental Action Programme (EAP).[4]

As the Third EAP, covering the period 1982–86, was largely concerned with the introduction of the internal market (due to be completed by 1992) and with the role of environmental policies in that process, it is hardly surprising that it should have first set out the Community principle of integration of 'concern for the environment into the policy and development of certain economic activities ... and thus promot[ing] the creation of an overall strategy making environmental policy a part of economic and social development'.[5] This formulation of the principle of integration now appears prescient in light of the subsequent emergence of the concept of sustainable development, and reminds us how central to the latter concept the integration of potentially conflicting policy objectives remains.[6] Indeed, it is no coincidence that the

---

3 In fact, Krämer, in section 4.1.2, notes that the First EAP of 1973, OJ 1973 C 112/1, stated:

> Effects on the environment should be taken into account at the earliest possible stage in all the planning and decision-making processes. The environment cannot be considered as external surroundings by which man is harassed and assailed; it must be considered as an essential factor in the organisation and promotion of human progress. It is therefore necessary to evaluate the effects on the quality of life and on the natural environment of any measure that is adopted or contemplated at national or Community level and which is liable to affect these factors.

4 OJ 1983 C 46/1.

5 *Ibid.*, at pp. I, 8. See further, A. Syngellakis, 'The Concept of Sustainable Development in European Community Law and Policy' (1993) 24 *Cambrian Law Review* 59, at p. 64. Professor Jan Jans traces 'elements' of the principle back to Principle 13 of the 1972 Declaration of the United Nations Conference on the Human Environment, (the 'Stockholm Declaration'), UN Doc. A/CONF.48/14/Rev.1 (16 June 1972):

> 'In order to achieve a more rational management of resources and thus to improve the environment, States should adopted an integrated and coordinated approach to their development planning so as to ensure that development is compatible with the need to protect and improve the environment for the benefit of their population.'
>
> (See, J. H. Jans, 'Stop the Integration Principle?' (2010) 33 *Fordham International Law Journal* 1533, at p. 1535)

6 For example, in 2002 the International Law Association (ILA) identified seven fundamental principles of sustainable development law, including 'the principle of integration and interrelationship, in particular relating to human rights and social, economic and environmental objectives', which it generally regarded as having a firm status in various fields of international law. See International Law Association, *New Delhi Declaration of Principles of International Law Relating to Sustainable Development* (London: ILA, 2002), at p. 9. See also, the dicta of International Court of Justice Judge Christopher Weeramantry in the *Gabčíkovo-Nagymaros (Hungary v. Slovakia) Case*, ICJ Reports (1997) 7 at p. 88, recognising that the integration of environmental and developmental issues is now a fundamental issue in international law.

original EC Environmental Impact Assessment (EIA) Directive[7] was adopted during the life of the Third EAP, as the requirements inherent to this Directive can be regarded as an example of the practical application of the principle of integration. However, progress on the realisation of the approach required under the integration principle was otherwise very modest and, despite the express inclusion of the principle in the Third EAP and the adoption of the EIA Directive during the term of the Programme, 'the fact remains that the bulk of Community environmental legislation continued to address environmental problems in the traditional vertical pattern of adopting measures with regard to a specific medium e.g. air, water, sea, noise, etc.'[8]

It was under the changes to the EC Treaty introduced by the 1986 Single European Act (SEA) that the principle of integration was elevated to the status of a legally binding requirement under EC law. The SEA added a Title VII to the EC Treaty, consisting of Article 130r, s and t, which for the first time conferred an express competence upon the Community institutions to act for the protection of the environment. In addition to listing the original objectives of Community environmental policy,[9] Article 130r also set down the basic principles which were henceforth to guide Community environmental policy-making, including the unequivocal requirement that 'environmental protection requirements shall be a component of the Community's other policies'. Though this new Treaty stipulation, in combination with Article 162 of the Treaty of Rome which required the Commission to adopt its rules and procedures so as to ensure that it operated in accordance with the provisions of the Treaty, clearly required the Commission to adopt a procedure for consideration of the environmental implications of each proposal for Community legislation that it drafted, for some years the Commission's rules of procedure did not provide specific means to this effect.[10] Indeed, it was not until June 1993 that the Commission announced a number of internal procedural mechanisms, under the auspices of the Fifth Environmental Action Programme (1992–2000), for taking account of environmental considerations at an early stage of preparation of Commission measures.[11] From 1993, each Commission Directorate General (DG) was required to assess the environmental

---

7 Council Directive 85/337/EEC of 27 June 1985 on the assessment of the effects of certain public and private projects on the environment, OJ 1985 L 175/40.

8 Syngellakis, 'The Concept of Sustainable Development in European Community Law and Policy', at p. 64.

9 Including 'to preserve, protect and improve the quality of the environment'; 'to contribute towards protecting human health'; and 'to ensure a prudent and rational utilisation of natural resources'.

10 *Règlement Intérieur de la Commission* OJ 1963 No. 17–63/41/CEE; Art. 21 required proposals to be circulated to all other interested services merely 'in order to avoid any overlap and to obtain their agreement and their observation'. See D. Baldock *et al.*, *The Integration of Environmental Protection Requirements into the Definition and Implementation of Other EC Policies* (London: Institute for European Environmental Policy, 1992) at p. 26, cited by Syngellakis, 'The Concept of Sustainable Development in European Community Law and Policy', at p. 65.

11 *Integrating the Environment into Other Policy Areas Within the Commission* IP (93) 427, 2 June 1993.

impact of measures or programmes and, where the impact was expected to be significant, to have an environmental impact study prepared.[12]

The Fourth EAP,[13] which coincided with the adoption of the Single European Act and ran from 1987–92, emphasised the need for integration even more clearly than the Third EAP. It discussed the concept at length and highlighted the principal policy areas for which the integration of environmental policy objectives would be necessary, including agriculture, competition, social policy, energy, tourism, transport, regional policy development and cooperation.[14] However, it might be regarded as 'a vivid illustration of the deficit in implementing the pronouncements on environmental policy integration' that the Community institutions omitted to address the environmental implications of the internal market as an integral part of the 1985 White Paper on Completing the Internal Market[15] and the subsequent 1992 legislative programme.[16] This omission led to the setting up by the Commission in 1988 of a Task Force on the Environment and the Internal Market whose 1989 report provided an 'unequivocal endorsement of the integration of environmental protection into the restructuring and modernization of the Community, anticipated through the Internal Market programme'.[17]

The amendments to the Treaty of Rome introduced by the Maastricht Treaty (TEU)[18] in 1992 further enhanced the imperative character of the principle of environmental integration, by introducing into the revised Environment Title XVI a new formulation of Article 130r that required that environmental protection requirements must be 'integrated into the definition and implementation of other Community policies'. In addition, the TEU introduced the principle of sustainable development into both the European Union and European Community legal orders and thereby placed considerable emphasis upon a concept that inevitably relies upon the integration of environmental considerations into other policy areas as a means of giving it practical effect.[19] This renewed emphasis reflects the policy position taken under the Fifth Environmental Action Programme, *Towards Sustainability*,[20] which ran from

---

12 Commission Internal Communication SEC (93) 785 final, 3 June 1993, and Manual of Procedures of the European Commission, para. 9.5.4. See O. Stokke and J. Forster, *Policy Coherence in Development Cooperation* (London: Frank Cass Publishers, 1999), at p. 340.

13 OJ 1987 C 328/13.

14 *Ibid.,* para. 2.3.28.

15 COM (85) 310 final, 14 June 1985.

16 Syngellakis, 'The Concept of Sustainable Development in European Community Law and Policy', at p. 66.

17 *Ibid.*

18 Treaty on European Union, OJ 1992 C 191. For a detailed discussion of the implication for EC environmental policy of the TEU, see D. Wilkinson, 'Maastricht and the Environment: The Implications for the EC's Environment Policy of the Treaty on European Union' (1992) 4/2 *Journal of Environmental Law* 221.

19 For example, Article 2 of the TEU sets as one of the objectives of the Union the achievement of 'balanced and sustainable development', while the TEU also amended Article 2 of the EC Treaty so as to compel the Community to promote 'sustainable and non-inflationary growth respecting the environment'.

20 COM (92) 23 final, 27 March 1992. See further, D. Fleming, *The Fifth Environmental Action Programme* (European Environment Special Supplement, European Research Press, 1992).

1992 to 2000 and identified the 'integration of environmental protection into the activities of critical actors and economic sectors as ... the key mechanism in the realization of the programme'.[21] In this regard it identified industry, energy, transport, agriculture and tourism as the targeted priority policy sectors. By the early 1990s some of the institutional machinery of environmental integration had been established, with environmental units having been set up in Commission DGs concerned with such policy areas as agriculture, transport, energy and fisheries, while a number of integrative consultation documents had been issued in relation to such policy areas.[22]

However, it was arguably not until the amendments to the EC Treaty introduced in 1997 by the Treaty of Amsterdam that the principle of environmental integration was placed on an appropriate legal footing. The key change in respect of environmental policy brought about by this Treaty[23] was the elevation of the integration principle, which had been contained in the former Article 130r, to Article 6 in Part I of the revised Treaty of Rome. It was entirely correct that it should have been moved from the environmental provisions of the Treaty, to which it had no useful application, to where it could apply to the various areas of Community policy covered by the Treaty and into the definition and implementation of which environmental protection requirements had now to be integrated. Thus, the Amsterdam amendments 'exported' the integration principle from the environmental provisions of the Treaty and promoted it to the status of a 'general principle' applicable to the entire EC Treaty.[24] The revised Article 6 expressly linked environmental integration to the principle of sustainable development, the constitutional significance of which was now made abundantly clear by means of its inclusion as one of the primary aims of the Community under Article 2.[25] Revised Article 6 was considerably more explicit about the remit of the principle's application, expressly applying it to all the activities and policies listed in Article 3 of the revised EC Treaty.[26] Article 3 contained a long list of such activities

---

21 Syngellakis, 'The Concept of Sustainable Development in European Community Law and Policy', at p. 69.
22 Including: *Sustainable Mobility* COM (92) 46 final, 20 February 1992; *Industrial Competitiveness and Environmental Protection* SEC (92) 1986 final, 4 November 1992; and *Agriculture and the Environment* COM (88) 338 final, 8 June 1988. See Syngellakis, 'The Concept of Sustainable Development in European Community Law and Policy', at p. 71.
23 OJ 1997 C 340/1. For a detailed discussion on the implications of the Amsterdam Treaty for Community environmental policy, see R. Macrory, 'The Amsterdam Treaty: An Environmental Perspective', in D. O'Keeffe and P. Twomey (eds), *Legal Issues of the Amsterdam Treaty* (Oxford: Hart Publishing, 1999), p. 171.
24 Jans, 'Stop the Integration Principle?', at pp. 1537–38. On this controversial point, see further S. Kingston, *Greening EU Competition Law and Policy* (Cambridge: Cambridge University Press, 2012), p. 107.
25 The revised Article 2 of the EC Treaty now provided, *inter alia*, that, 'The Community shall have as its task ... to promote throughout the Community a harmonious, balanced and sustainable development of economic activities'.
26 Article 6 provided that, 'Environmental protection requirements must be integrated into the definition and implementation of the Community policies and activities referred to in Article 3, in particular with a view to promoting sustainable development'.

and policies, including measures relating to the common commercial policy, the internal market, the free movement of persons, agriculture and fisheries, transport, employment, economic and social policy, environment, industry, research and technology, health protection, culture, development cooperation, international trade, consumer protection, energy, civil protection, tourism and equality. Thus, the Amsterdam Treaty amendments put it beyond doubt that sustainable development was now one of the overarching objectives of the EC Treaty and that a broadly applicable principle of environmental integration was one of the essential means for achieving this objective.

The period following the adoption of the Amsterdam Treaty witnessed frenetic developments relating to practical implementation of the integration principle. The Commission reviewed its 1993 internal communication and suggested a range of new measures in a 1997 communication which, however, also highlighted the inherent difficulties in implementing the principle, noting that 'the measures to integrate the environment into sectoral policies are still not fully internalised by the services of the Commission in operational terms'.[27] Specifically, this communication concludes that the various administrative arrangements intended to ensure integration of environmental requirements, including 'Environmental Evaluations' of all Commission activities, 'Environmental Impact' assessments of new legislative proposals, the use of so-called 'Green Stars' by DGs to identify proposals which may have significant environmental consequences, and the appointment of 'Integration Correspondents' within each DG, tended to operate in an informal, unsystematic and uncritical manner.[28] Therefore, the European Council held in Luxembourg in December 1997 tasked the Commission with development of a strategy on environmental integration,[29] which was adopted by the Cardiff European Council of June 1998, thus giving rise to the so-called 'Cardiff process'. This ongoing process had resulted in the development of practical requirements for the Commission and for the Council. In particular, relevant formations of the Council were invited to establish strategies for achieving environmental integration within their own policy areas, starting with the Transport, Energy and Agriculture Councils, before moving on to the Development, Internal Market, Industry, General Affairs, Ecofin and Fisheries Councils. However, even though the Commission elaborated policy documents for each of these Council formations setting out a strategy on how to integrate environmental requirements into their respective areas of policy,[30] Krämer points out in this volume that

---

27 Communication C (97) 1844, at p. 1.
28 *Ibid.*, at pp. 8–10. Krämer, in section 4.2.6, outlines each of these proposed measures and highlights the fact that all have effectively been abandoned.
29 *Partnership for Integration – A Strategy for Integrating Environment into EU Policies* COM (98) 333, June 1998.
30 COM (98) 716 and COM (99) 640 (transport); COM (98) 571 (energy); COM (99) 22 and COM (2000) 20 (agriculture); COM (99) 263 (internal market); COM (99) 36 and COM (2000) 264 (development); COM (2001) 143 (fisheries); COM (2000) 576 (economic questions); and SEC (2002) 271 (external affairs). In relation to agriculture, McMahon, 'The CAP in 2020: Vision or Hindsight?', at section (2),

'[t]hese documents were discussed once in the Council – and then the whole procedure stopped'.[31] Indeed, Krämer's conclusions about 'the failure of the EU approach, which was linked to the so-called Cardiff process'[32] are echoed by the Commission's own 2004 stocktaking exercise on the implementation of the principle of environmental integration, which concludes: 'However, environmental integration commitments are still largely to be translated into further concrete results for the environment. To date, the Cardiff process has failed to deliver fully on expectations. It suffers from several shortcomings.'[33]

Article 11 of the newly adopted Treaty on the Functioning of the European Union (TFEU),[34] the principal treaty currently providing for the operation of the Union institutions, reproduces almost identical wording to that of Article 6 of the revised EC Treaty.[35] However, whereas '[o]n each occasion that the EEC Treaty was amended, the integration principle was strengthened' as '[e]ach round of revisions enhanced the profile and its impact', Jans argues that '[t]he Lisbon Treaty brought an end to that pattern'.[36] Indeed, the context in which it is placed in the TFEU has resulted in even greater uncertainty in respect of its true legal status and implications. For example, the proliferation of integration principles under the Lisbon Treaty requiring that a wide range of policy objectives, additional to those relating to the environment, are to be taken into account in defining and implementing European Union policies generally, has raised new uncertainties about the priority accorded to, and justiciability of, the principle of environmental integration.[37]

A slightly different articulation of the environmental integration principle was included in Article 37 of the 2000 Charter of Fundamental Rights of the European Union, which provides that 'A high level of environmental protection and the improvement of the quality of the environment must be integrated into the policies of the Union and ensured in accordance with the principle of sustainable development'.[38] While the Charter was non-binding upon the Community institutions at the time of its adoption, the new Article 6 of the post-Lisbon TEU now provides that the Charter 'shall have the same legal value as the Treaties', thus conferring upon Article 37 of the Charter the same legal status as that enjoyed by Article 11 of the TFEU. Both now clearly bind

highlights that Decision 2179/98 OJ 1998 L275/1 sets out the Community's objectives in integrating environmental requirements into the CAP, though these appear rather vague and non-specific.

31 See Krämer, in section 4.1.1.
32 *Ibid.*
33 Commission, *Integrating Environmental Considerations Into Other Policy Areas – a Stocktaking of the Cardiff Process* COM (2004) 394 final, 1, June 2004, at p. 31.
34 OJ 2010 C 83/47.
35 See note 26. Article 11 TFEU provides that, 'Environmental protection requirements must be integrated into the definition and implementation of the Union's policies and activities, in particular with a view to promoting sustainable development'.
36 See Jans, 'Stop the Integration Principle?', at pp. 1538 and 1547.
37 Articles 7–10 and 12–13 TFEU. See further *infra*.
38 OJ 2000 C 364/1.

the Union institutions, though the principle is set out differently in each and, arguably, somewhat more narrowly under the Charter.[39]

6.3 Legal nature and implications of the principle of environmental integration

One key question which arises is that of which 'environmental protection requirements' must be integrated into the definition and implementation of the Union's policies and activities. It seems reasonable to conclude that the objectives of environmental policy set out under Article 191(1) TFEU must be taken into account in related sectoral policy measures, although these objectives appear quite general and normatively indeterminate and non-imperative in nature.[40] More significantly, it seems clear that the principles set out under Article 191 (2), on which Union environmental policy is to be based, are to apply to other policy areas.[41] While we have a somewhat clearer understanding of the practical means available for implementing these principles, at least in the context of environmental measures,[42] examples of their inclusion in non-environmental measures remain relatively few.[43] By referring to '[a] high level of environmental protection and the improvement of the quality of the environment', both objectives expressly listed under Articles 191(1) and (2) TFEU, the wording of Article 37 of the Charter of Fundamental Rights might be taken to suggest

---

39 See Jans, 'Stop the Integration Principle?', at p. 1544.
40 Article 191(1) provides that,
   'Union policy on the environment shall contribute to pursuit of the following objectives:

   − preserving, protecting and improving the quality of the environment,
   − protecting human health,
   − prudent and rational utilisation of natural resources,
   − promoting measures at international level to deal with regional or worldwide environmental problems, and in particular combating climate change.'

41 The first paragraph of Article 191(2) provides that,

   Union policy on the environment shall aim at a high level of protection taking into account the diversity of situations in the various regions of the Union. It shall be based on the precautionary principle and on the principles that preventive action should be taken, that environmental damage should as a priority be rectified at source and that the polluter should pay.

42 For example, in the Waste Framework Directive, Directive 2008/98/EC OJ 2008 L 312/3, the principle of rectification at source is given practical effect by means of the principles of self-sufficiency and proximity, set out under Article 16 of the Directive. In addition, the polluter pays principle is elaborated upon in Article 14, while guidance on the precautionary and preventive principles is included in Recital 30 to the Directive.
43 By way of example, Krämer, in section 4.1.1, points to the European Courts' recognition of the application of the precautionary principle to the agriculture policy area in Case C-180/96 *United Kingdom v. Commission* [1998] ECR I-2265, para. 99 and in Joined Cases T-74-6/00 *Artegodan v. Commission* [2002] ECR II-327, para. 184.

that each of the aims and principles set out under these provisions are to apply to all EU policies. Further, the principle of 'coherence' or 'consistency' of EU law would appear to confirm that the general aims of Articles 191(1) and (2) come within the scope of the 'environmental protection requirements' alluded to in Article 11 TFEU.[44] In addition, it would appear that 'the policy aspects referred to in [A]rticle 191(3) TFEU should not *a priori* be excluded' from other sectoral policy measures,[45] though they only provide broad policy guidance and might even be regarded as justifying derogations from the foregoing requirements set out under Articles 191(1) and (2).[46] Also, Article 191(3) itself merely requires that these factors should be taken into account.

As regards the question of *who* must integrate environmental protection requirements, Krämer points out that the TFEU is silent on the issue, but notes that:

> as the TEU imposes obligations on EU institutions and on Member States, it can be safely stated that the EU institutions have to integrate environmental requirements. When EU Member States implement EU policies and activities, they might also have to respect Article 11.[47]

Hession and Macrory, writing at the time of the Amsterdam Treaty amendments to the EC Treaty, also conclude that the principle of environmental integration applies to 'all relevant Community institutions and Member States in so far as they are charged with implementing Community policies'.[48] As regards Community institutions, they further suggest that 'these would encompass at the very least all those Community bodies involved in defining or implementing

---

44 On the principle of coherence, see A. Von Bogdandy, 'Founding Principles of EU Law: A Theoretical and Doctrinal Sketch' (2010) 16 *European Law Journal* 95, p. 109. See further, K. Lenaerts and T. Corthaut, 'Towards an Internally Consistent Doctrine on Invoking Norms of EU Law', in S. Prechal and B. van Roermund (eds), *The Coherence of EU Law* (Oxford: Oxford University Press, 2008), 495. On the principle of consistency, see C. N. K. Franklin, 'The Burgeoning Principle of Consistency in EU Law' (2011) 30 *Yearbook of European Law* 42–85.

45 Jans, 'Stop the Integration Principle?', at p. 1533.

46 Article 191(3) provides that,
'In preparing its policy on the environment, the Union shall take account of:

– available scientific and technical data,
– environmental conditions in the various regions of the Union,
– the potential benefits and costs of action or lack of action,
– the economic and social development of the Union as a whole and the balanced development of its regions.'

47 Krämer, in section 4.1.1.

48 M. Hession and R. Macrory, 'The Legal Duty of Environmental Integration: Commitment and Obligation or Enforceable Right', in T. O'Riordan and H. Voisey (eds), *The European Union and Sustainable Development* (London: Frank Cass, 1998), 100–112, reproduced in R. Macrory, *Regulation, Enforcement and Governance in Environmental Law* (Oxford: Hart Publishing, 2010), 567–83, at p. 575.

Community policy, including the Council of Ministers, the European Investment Bank and the European Parliament'.[49] As regards Member States, Hession and Macrory conclude that they are bound by the principle when acting within the Council of Ministers and involved in the 'design' of policy, as well as when taking responsibility for the 'implementation' of such policy, though in this latter role '[m]uch would depend on the level of discretion granted at national level, and the extent to which a failure at national level to integrate an environmental dimension could frustrate the effect' of the principle.[50] They provide the example of a national body given responsibility for the distribution of Union funds.[51] Though this conclusion is undoubtedly sound in principle, the applicability of the principle of environmental integration to Member State measures for the implementation of EU policy is effectively undermined by the severely limited utility of the principle as grounds for judicial review of such actions.[52]

While there can be little doubt that the integration principle is firmly established as a solemn legal requirement set out under the founding Treaties of the European Union, doubts linger as to its precise normative character and significance. In fact, the principle of environmental integration can be understood as having an impact on EU law and policy-making in several distinct ways.

First of all is its so-called 'enabling function', whereby it extends the limits of the Union's legal competences as governed by the Treaties. Under the so-called 'principle of conferral' or 'specific powers doctrine', 'the Union shall act only within the limits of the competences conferred upon it by the Member States in the Treaties to attain the objectives set out therein'.[53] However, in light of the principle of environmental integration, the Union institutions enjoy competence to take additional legal measures to ensure protection of the environment whenever they are acting in furtherance of a wide range of EU policies, including agriculture, transport, energy, development aid, trade and external relations, internal market and competition policy, commercial policy and regional policy. The ECJ has supported this function of the principle in cases such as *Concordia Bus Finland*, where it confirmed that environmental objectives may be pursued in the context of public procurement.[54] Essentially, in

---

49 *Ibid.*

50 *Ibid.*

51 This was the central question at issue in the *Mullaghmore* case, Case T-461/93 *An Taisce and WWF (UK) v. Commission* [1994] ECR II-733, though it was never considered as the case was ruled inadmissible on procedural grounds, a decision confirmed on appeal in Case C-325/94 [1996] ECR I-3727. See Hession and Macrory, 'The Legal Duty of Environmental Integration', at p. 577.

52 See text below. If such utility is restricted at the EU level due to the complexity of implementing EU environmental protection requirements and to the wide discretion enjoyed by EU institutions in this regard, these difficulties are likely to be exacerbated at the Member State level.

53 Article 5(1) of the post-Lisbon Treaty on European Union OJ 2010 C 83/13.

54 Case C-513/99 *Concordia Bus Finland Oy Ab v. Helsingin Kaupunki* [2002] ECR I-7213.

this role, '[t]he environmental integration principle broadens the objectives of the other powers laid down in the TFEU and thus limits the role of the specific powers doctrine in environmental policy'.[55]

In addition, the principle may perform a 'guidance function', whereby 'European law may — and indeed must — be interpreted in the light of the environmental objectives of the TFEU, even with respect to areas outside the environmental field'.[56] Several of the other guiding principles of EU environmental policy, first incorporated into the EC Treaty by means of the Single European Act and Maastricht Treaty amendments, have been applied by the ECJ as aids to the interpretation of secondary legislation on the environment. For example, in the *Waddenzee* case the requirement to conduct an appropriate assessment of the likely ecological impacts of plans or projects under the Habitats Directive[57] was interpreted in light of the precautionary principle,[58] while the definition of waste under the Waste Framework Directive was extended having regard to the polluter pays principle[59] and preventive and precautionary principles[60] in the *Van de Walle* case, although in this case the implications proved quite unwelcome.[61] The principle of environmental integration itself played an important role in justifying the application of the precautionary principle, a guiding principle of EU environmental policy, to the protection of public health in the *Artegodan* case.[62] Jans also argues that the principle has played a key role 'in justifying recourse to the Cassis de Dijon mandatory requirements, which now include environmental protection, to justify a directly discriminatory barrier to trade'.[63] Though the principle of environmental integration has now been elevated to the status of a general principle of EU law, its function as an aid to the interpretation of the rules of EU law remains closely connected to the guiding principles of EU environmental law set out under Article 191(2) TFEU. For the purposes of legislative interpretation, the principle possesses no inherent substantive values, but extends the relevance of the Article 191(2) principles beyond the narrow confines of EU environmental policy.

Finally, as one might reasonably expect, the principle of environmental integration can serve as a ground for reviewing the validity of an EU measure adopted

55 Jans, 'Stop the Integration Principle?', at p. 1541.

56 *Ibid.*

57 Council Directive 92/43/EEC OJ 1992 L 206/7, Article 6(3).

58 Case C-127/02 *Landelijke Vereniging tot Behoud van de Waddenzee and Anr v. Staatsecretaris van Landbouw, Natuurbeheer en Visserij* [2004] ECR I-7405, para. 44.

59 Case C-1/03 *Van de Walle* [2004] ECR I-7613, paras. 48 and 58.

60 *Ibid.*, para. 45. See also, Opinion of AG Kokott, 29 January 2004, paras. 24–25, referring to Joined Cases C-418/97 and C-419/97 *ARCO Chemie Nederland and Others* [2000] ECR I-4475, para. 38 *et seq.* and Case C-9/00 *Palin Granit and Vehmassalon kansanterveystyön kuntayhtymän hallitus* [2002] ECR I-3533, para. 23.

61 See further, O. McIntyre, 'The All-Consuming Definition of "Waste" and the End of the "Contaminated Land" Debate? Case C-1/03: *Van de Walle*' (2005) 17 *Journal of Environmental Law* 109.

62 Joined Cases T-74, 76, 83, 85, 132, 137, 141/00 [2002] ECR II-4945, para. 183. See Jans, 'Stop the Integration Principle?', at p. 1541.

63 *Ibid.*, citing Case C-379/98 *PreussenElektra AG v. Schhleswag AG* [2001] ECR I-2099.

in respect of a policy sector with the potential to impact upon the environment, where that measure may have failed to comply with, or at least take full account of, the essential environmental requirements of EU environmental policy. However, it would appear that the usefulness of such a general principle for the judicial review of measures taken by the Union institutions in the exercise of their significant legislative discretion is very severely limited. In the *Bettati* case, which involved a challenge to the validity of Ozone Regulation 3093/94, the Court, while accepting that the environmental objectives, principles and criteria of the former Article 130r must be respected by the Community legislature in implementing environmental policy, nevertheless found that:

> in view of the need to strike a balance between certain of the objectives and principles mentioned in Article 130r and of the complexity of the implementation of those criteria, review by the Court must necessarily be limited to the question whether the Council, by adopting the Regulation, committed a manifest error of appraisal regarding the conditions for the application of Article 130r of the Treaty.[64]

If the scope for judicial review of environmental measures on the basis of the environmental requirements set out under the Treaty is limited, it stands to reason that the scope for judicial review on these grounds of measures which are not primarily environmental is even more limited. Though the *Bettati* case did not concern review for compliance with the integration principle, which has since been elevated to the status of a general principle and articulated in an unequivocally imperative manner, the principle inevitably involves the extended application of the requirements of Articles 191(1) and (2). If each Union institution enjoys 'a wide discretion regarding the measures it chooses to adopt in order to implement the environmental policy',[65] it necessarily enjoys an even broader discretion in respect of measures adopted in other policy sectors where environmental requirements are only one of a number of issues to be considered.[66]

6.4 The principle of environmental integration post-Lisbon

Uncertainty regarding the normative implications of the principle has only been exacerbated by the new Treaty regime ushered in post-Lisbon.[67] For instance,

---

64 Case C-341/95 *Bettati v. Safety Hi-Tech Srl* [1998] ECR I-4355, at paras 34–35 (emphasis added).
65 *Ibid.*, at para. 32.
66 On the 'proliferation' of integration principles under the post-Lisbon TFEU, requiring integration of a wide range of EU policy objectives additional to environmental requirements, see text below.
67 Though some commentators trace the first attempt to downgrade the principle of environmental integration to the text of the Draft Treaty Establishing a Constitution for Europe issued by the Convention on the Future of Europe under the chairmanship of Valéry Giscard d'Estaing on 20 June 2003, which sought to exclude the principle from the opening part of the proposed constitutional treaty. See further, J. H. Jans and J.Scott, 'The Convention on the Future of Europe: An Environmental Perspective' (2003) 15 *Journal of Environmental Law* 323.

it is of great significance that the principle of environmental integration is now but one integration principle among many included under the TFEU. Article 8 TFEU requires that the Union '[i]n all its activities ... shall aim to eliminate inequalities, and to promote equality, between men and women', effectively a principle of gender equality integration. Rather more generally, Article 9 TFEU provides that:

> In defining and implementing its policies and activities, the Union shall take into account requirements linked to the promotion of a high level of employment, the guarantee of adequate social protection, the fight against social exclusion, and a high level of education, training and protection of human health.

Thus, Article 9 might be understood as requiring the integration of considerations arising under a number of economic and social rights, each in itself quite nebulous and uncertain.

Article 10 TFEU in turn provides that, 'in defining and implementing its policies and activities, the Union shall aim to combat discrimination based on sex, racial or ethnic origin, religion or belief, disability, age or sexual orientation' – a principle of non-discrimination integration. Under Article 12 TFEU, 'consumer protection requirements shall be taken into account in defining and implementing other Union policies and activities' – a principle of consumer protection integration. Further, Article 13 TFEU introduces a principle of animal welfare integration, requiring that, 'In formulating and implementing the Union's agriculture, fisheries, transport, internal market, research and technological development and space policies, the Union and the Member States shall, pay full regard to the welfare requirements of animals'. In addition to the specific sectoral integration principles listed above, Article 7 TFEU introduces a broad requirement that '[t]he Union shall ensure consistency between its policies and activities, taking all of its objectives into account in accordance with the principle of conferral of powers'. This principle of 'consistency' would appear to amount to a principle of 'general' or 'universal' integration of policy objectives, bringing all policy requirements listed under the TFEU into play and requiring that each must be considered in the adoption of every measure to which it might be relevant. Understood strictly, it would make redundant all of the specific sectoral integration principles listed above.

In terms of legal clarity, it does not help that each of the new, post-Lisbon sectoral integration principles is articulated somewhat differently, ranging from stipulations that the Union institutions 'shall aim' to meet, 'shall take into account' or 'shall ensure consistency between' certain sectoral policy objectives, to one requiring that the Union and Member States 'shall pay full regard' to certain sectoral requirements. While the principle of environmental integration is stated in the most imperative manner of all the post-Lisbon sectoral integration principles, with Article 11 TFEU requiring that '[e]nvironmental protection requirements must be integrated', there can be no doubting the conclusion that the 'true proliferation of integration principles' under the Lisbon Treaty[68] has resulted in a significant downgrading of environmental integration. Obviously, a dramatic increase in the range and number of interests to be accommodated in the policy-making process makes that process of accommodation very much more complex and markedly reduces the relative weight to be accorded to any one type of interest. Of course, it might yet prove significant that the version of environmental integration set out under Article 37 of the Charter of Fundamental Rights of the European Union, itself now enjoying the status of a treaty provision, would appear to be rather narrower in scope than Article 11 TFEU, only requiring integration of a 'high level of environmental protection and the improvement of the quality of the environment ... into the policies of the Union'. As it does not mention the 'activities' of the Union, nor require integration as regards the 'definition and implementation' of Union policies, Article 37 might be understood to be less relevant to specific measures and decisions and to the practical application of EU law and, thus, to be less justiciable. Jans expresses concern that 'an interpretation of [A]rticle 11 TFEU in line with the Charter may result in a further downgrading'.[69]

On the other hand, Krämer stresses the close relationship between the principle of environmental integration, as articulated under both Article 11 TFEU and Article 37 of Charter of Fundamental Rights, and the fundamental Union objective of promoting sustainable development. Article 3(3) of the TEU includes sustainable development as one of the fundamental, overarching objectives of the European Union[70] and Krämer suggests that the connection between Articles 11 TFEU and 3(3) TEU 'appears to mean that in order for sustainable development to be achieved, environmental requirements must be integrated into other EU policies'.[71] Regarding the proliferation of integration principles to include the objectives of other areas of sectoral policy, he further points out that:

> [n]ot only is the wording of the integration requirement in [Articles 8,9, 10 and 12 TFEU] less decisive, they do not refer to sustainable development. Nor does Article 3 TEU state that sustainable development is based on gender equality, social protection, consumer protection or absence of discrimination.[72]

On this basis, Krämer re-interprets the significance of the principle of 'consistency' set down under Article 7 TFEU so that it cannot be understood 'as meaning that the environmental objectives mentioned shall be considered

---

68 Jans, 'Stop the Integration Principle?', at pp. 1544–45.
69 *Ibid.*, at p. 1544.
70 Article 3(3) TEU provides, in part, that, 'The Union ... shall work for the sustainable development of Europe based on ... a high level of protection and improvement of the quality of the environment.'
71 Krämer, o in section 4.1.3.
72 *Ibid.*, in section 4.1.4.

as other, additional objectives of the transport, agricultural, fisheries, etc. policies and be treated as such'.[73] Instead, remembering that Article 11 TFEU and Article 37 of the Charter both refer to one of the fundamental objectives of the Union, he concludes that 'there is a *particular obligation* for the EU institutions in the context of Article 7 TFEU to ensure that the different policies and activities take into account and work towards the objective of a high level of protection and an improvement of the quality of the environment' (emphasis added).[74] In addition, he points out that '[t]here is no obligation comparable to Article 37 [of the Charter] placed on the EU institutions in the transport, agriculture, fisheries or competition areas ... [so that] ... the environmental sector stands out with regard to all other sectors of EU policy'.[75] Though social and consumer policy are mentioned in the Charter, it is only in respect of the principle of environmental integration that the Charter requires its objectives to be pursued in accordance with the fundamental objective of sustainable development.

However, it is obvious that the political 'voice' previously afforded to the environment by the principle of environmental integration is now in danger of being drowned out by the din of all the other policy objectives which are required to be integrated into general EU policy-making. Jans refers to this phenomenon as the 'minestrone effect', whereby, '[l]ike the mixture of ingredients in minestrone, decision-making on the basis of multiple integration principles could result in measures where the component elements are still visible, but not as sharply and clearly as before'.[76] He expresses concern over the possibility that certain environmental standards might be diluted or offset through a process he calls 'reversed integration', that is 'a process by which certain environmental standards, such as environmental quality standards or emission standards, are lowered as a consequence of the requirement that other than environmental interests are to be taken into account'.[77] McMahon provides an interesting glimpse at the practice of integration post-Lisbon and outlines in some detail the environmental factors highlighted in the Commission's recent Consultation Document for the Impact Assessment for the proposed reform of the CAP.[78]

In addition, the proliferation of sectoral integration principles is likely to limit the justiciability of the principle of environmental integration in quite specific ways. The requirement of Union institutions to take account of and balance a broad range of policy objectives and requirements inevitably strengthens and extends the discretionary powers of these institutions and makes it rather less likely that the ECJ would find that such discretion has

73 *Ibid.*, in section 4.2.1.
74 *Ibid.*
75 *Ibid.*
76 Jans, 'Stop the Integration Principle?', at pp. 1546–47.
77 *Ibid.*, at p. 1547.
78 Krämer, in section 4.1.

been exceeded. Citing the case law of the ECJ in the context of the CAP, Jans predicts that 'the ECJ will show even more deference to the EU's political institutions than before in this balancing act and will become even more reluctant to reach the conclusion that the European legislator committed "a manifest error of appraisal"'.[79]

Also, under the specific powers doctrine, or the so-called 'principle of conferral',[80] the key brake on creeping Union competence under the Treaties, the multiplicity of integration principles clearly extends the competence of the Union institutions to take legally binding measures to ensure that myriad sectoral policy objectives are pursued, or at least taken into account, when decisions are being taken in almost any area of EU policy-making. In addition to making EU measures more difficult to review, this effect 'makes it more difficult to draw a clear line between Union and Member State competences'.[81] Indeed, recognising the implications of the principle of consistency in terms of the extension of Union competence, Article 7 TFEU makes express, if somewhat weak and uncertain, reference to the principle of conferral of powers.[82]

6.5 Normative content of the integration obligation

It only remains to examine what exactly the obligation to integrate environmental requirements, to the extent that it is enforceable or justiciable, requires of policy-makers in practical terms. Hession and Macrory summarise the obligatory policy requirements envisaged under the principle of environmental integration as follows:

- a contribution towards the objectives of preserving, protecting and improving the quality of the environment, protecting human health, and the prudent and rational utilization of natural resources;
- a high level of protection;
- adherence to the four principles of precaution, prevention, rectification at source, and polluter pays; and
- the need to take into account certain additional factors including the diversity of situations within various regions of the community, available

---

79 Jans, 'Stop the Integration Principle?', at p. 1546, referring to the test identified by the Court for the judicial review of a measure adopted by a Union institution for failure to respect one of the guiding principles of EU environmental policy in Case C-341/95 *Bettati v. Safety Hi-Tech Srl* [1998] ECR I-4355, at pp. 17–18.

80 According to Article 5(1) of the post-Lisbon Treaty on European Union, 'the Union shall act only within the limits of the competences conferred upon it by the Member States in the Treaties to attain the objectives set out therein'.

81 Jans, 'Stop the Integration Principle?', at pp. 1546 and 1540.

82 Article 7 TFEU provides, 'The Union shall ensure consistency between its policies and activities, taking all of its objectives into account and in accordance with the principle of conferral of powers.'

scientific and technical data, and the potential costs and benefits of action or inaction.[83]

However, this general account leaves certain questions unanswered. Notably, it remains unclear whether the principle requires compliance by policy-makers engaged in related sectoral policy areas with any and all standards set down under EU environmental directives and regulations. In many cases such standards may be contained in environmental directives which are addressed to Member States rather than the relevant Union institutions.

In this regard, Krämer focuses on the right of access to information, which he regards as absolutely central to the practical implementation of the principle of environmental integration. Specifically, considering the fundamental right of the public of access to environmental information, set out in the Aarhus Convention[84] and in EU secondary legislation,[85] together with Article 37 of the Charter and Article 296(2) TFEU, requiring that 'legal acts shall state the reasons on which they are based', he concludes:

> This means that the EU institutions are obliged to inform, when they make proposals for legislation, adopt legislative or other acts, or take decisions which are capable of affecting the environment, how they complied with the obligation to ensure a high level of protection or to improve the quality of the environment. Otherwise, the rights and guarantees which flow for citizens from Article 37 of the Charter are in fact empty.[86]

However, he proceeds to list three recent, illustrative examples of EU initiatives, relating to access to EU institution documents and to the transport and fisheries policy areas, where the Commission has failed to comply with this principle of 'good EU governance'.[87] This understanding of the normative content of the obligation of environmental integration corresponds with that of Hession and Macrory, who suggest that '[t]he duty to integrate environmental requirements is suggestive of procedural rather than substantive protection'.[88] They note that '[a] familiar requirement often imposed on administrative bodies is to "take into consideration" certain factors, implying that once taken on board

---

83 Hession and Macrory, 'The Legal Duty of Environmental Integration: Commitment and Obligation or Enforceable Right', at pp. 578–79.

84 UNECE Convention on access to information, public participation in decision-making and access to justice in environmental matters, 38 *ILM* (1999) 517 (Aarhus, 25 June 1998).

85 Decision 2005/370 OJ 2005 L 124/1.

86 Krämer, in section 4.2.2.

87 *Ibid.*, in section 4.2.3, where he cites the 2001 Commission White Paper on Governance, which states that, 'Each of the EU institutions must explain and take responsibility for what it does in Europe' (see Commission, *European Governance*, COM (2001) 428, at p. 10).

88 Hession and Macrory, 'The Legal Duty of Environmental Integration: Commitment and Obligation or Enforceable Right', at p. 579.

they may be rejected if they conflict with other goals', though they caution that it does have some substantive normative significance by reminding us that 'the terminology of the integration duty implies more than this; conflict with other areas does not entitle environmental requirements to be dismissed'.[89] Thus, in the field of environmental protection, procedural duties are very largely concerned with the collection, management, analysis, sharing and consideration of information relevant to environmental impacts, benefits or performance. Indeed, Krämer lists the measures previously suggested by the Commission in the context of the Cardiff process, all now abandoned, to give practical effect to the principle. These included a system for assessing the environmental effects of Commission proposals, measures for describing and explaining environmental effects and environmental costs and benefits of proposals, the clear identification of those proposals that will have significant environmental effects in the Commission's annual work programme as well as an indication of which environmental considerations were taken into account in relation to proposals adopted, a number of measures for 'green accounting', and regular assessments of progress on integrating environmental requirements into other policies.[90] Clearly, each of these initiatives, which must be regarded as essential for the effective implementation of the principle of environmental integration, is in some way concerned with identifying and communicating environmental information related to the proposal in question.

6.6 Conclusion

The chapters included in this volume on the principle of environmental integration make a timely and significant contribution towards assisting understanding of this difficult yet vitally important principle of EU law.[91] Krämer's analysis of the principle, as essentially requiring the provision of information to the public on the steps taken to ensure integration of environmental factors into decision-making in other related policy areas, re-ignites discussion on the measures needed to give the principle practical effect, a discussion that had largely ceased since the abandonment of the Cardiff process. In turn, McMahon's chapter in this volume outlines the ongoing process of CAP reform, highlighting the aim of delivering important public goods, in particular environmental protection and biodiversity support. Thus it provides an important insight, not only into the practical means of integrating environmental considerations into Union agricultural policy, but also into the interplay between the requirements of environmental protection and the objectives of

89   *Ibid.*, at pp. 579–80.
90   Krämer, in section 4.2.6.
91   For example, Krämer notes, on p. 83: 'This provision [Article 11 TFEU] which is probably the most important environmental provision in the whole Lisbon Treaty, raises considerable implementation problems, for lawyers, policy-makers and administrations.'

other policy areas also required to be integrated into the CAP, such as consumer protection, human health, food security, rural development, competitiveness and innovation. Together, these authors have made a seminal contribution to exploring the practical legal implications and limitations of the EU principle of environmental integration in the post-Lisbon era.

Part III

The enforcement challenge

7 Mind the gap

Difficulties in enforcement and the continuing unfulfilled promise of EU environmental law

*Suzanne Kingston**

7.1 Introduction

It is axiomatic that without adequate enforcement even the best-intentioned law will remain a dead letter. While the scope of substantive EU environmental law continues to expand, we are not witnessing the parallel improvement in the state of the European environment that one might expect. An authoritative recent confirmation of this is the European Environment Agency's (EEA) report of November 2010, *The European Environment – State and Outlook*.[1] The report makes uncomfortable reading. Of the sixteen discrete environmental 'issues' identified by the EEA, the EU was, as at 2010 and viewed as a whole, meeting its targets in respect of only three (namely, the climate change target of reducing greenhouse gas emissions by 20 per cent by 2020,[2] the waste management targets set for recycling,[3] and the water pollution targets for pollution from point sources and bathing water quality).[4] Within all other areas – including in relation to the EU's energy efficiency and renewables goals, all of its other waste policy goals, its water and air quality and air pollution goals, and all of its biodiversity goals[5] – the EU is not meeting its environmental targets.[6]

Such unsatisfactory outcomes cannot, of course, be attributed *in toto* to inadequate enforcement of EU environmental measures. In many vital areas, agreement has not yet been reached at EU level on appropriate legislation (as, for instance, in the case of the long-awaited Soil Framework Directive, proposed

---

* I thank Andrew Jackson and the participants in the Irish European Law Forum, Dublin 2011, for their comments on a draft of this contribution.
1 European Environment Agency, *The European Environment: State and Outlook* (Copenhagen: EEA, 2010).
2 On the EU's climate and energy package, see http://ec.europa.eu/clima/policies/brief/eu/package_en.htm.
3 European Parliament and Council Directive 94/62/EC of 20 December 1994 on packaging and packaging waste OJ 1994 L 365/10, as amended.
4 See generally, http://ec.europa.eu/environment/water/index_en.htm.
5 The EEA divides these targets into four categories: (1) stabilising pressure on ecosystems from eutrophication; (2) achieving favourable conservation status for important habitats and species; (3) halting the loss of biodiversity; and (4) preventing further soil degradation. See EEA, *The European Environment*, at p. 18.
6 *Ibid.*, summary chart at pp. 18–19.

by the Commission in 2006 but still under discussion in the Council,[7] and in the case of the Access to Justice Directive, discussed further below). More broadly, many fundamental problems result not from the content and (lack of) enforcement of EU environmental legislation as such, but from the lack of consideration given to environmental concerns in non-environmental legislation, in the sense of legislation with a legal basis other than Article 192 TFEU. Nonetheless, a significant improvement in the enforcement of EU environmental law would bring undeniable benefits, not only from an environmental quality perspective, but also in terms of ensuring a basic respect for the rule of law within the EU.

With this in mind, this contribution seeks to revisit[8] the issue of EU environmental enforcement and to highlight some of the key challenges in this area at present. The analysis is structured around what may be termed the three pillars of environmental enforcement within the EU: the European Commission; national authorities; and private parties, with particular focus on the first and third pillars.

7.2 The European Commission as enforcer: the changing nature of the infringement action

The first pillar of environmental enforcement is the Commission. One of the first things that EU law students learn about this institution is of course its role as guardian of the Treaties. This is expressed formally in the Treaty in Article 17 TEU (formerly Article 211 EC), which provides that the Commission 'shall ensure the application of the Treaties, and of measures adopted by the institutions pursuant to them. It shall oversee the application of Union law under the control of the Court of Justice of the European Union ... '. Yet the way in which the Commission in practice exercises this function has changed considerably in recent years, and in a manner which raises some rather fundamental questions about the nature of the infringement action in environmental cases, and its future role within the panoply of remedies for breach of EU environmental law. As such, despite the fact that these differences represent, in most cases, changes in practice, rather than changes in the law as such, they merit serious scrutiny.

---

7 See Proposal for a Directive of the European Parliament and of the Council establishing a framework for the protection of soil and amending Directive 2004/35/EC COM(2006) 232 final. Although the European Parliament delivered an opinion on the draft Directive in 2007, at the time of writing no political agreement had yet been reached in the Council. See the Progress Report prepared by the General Secretariat for the Council, 7100/10 of 10 March 2010.

8 For previous discussions of the issue, see M. Hedemann-Robinson, *Enforcement of European Union Environmental Law: Legal Issues and Challenges* (Abingdon: Routledge, 2007); A. Jordan, 'The Implementation of EU Environmental Policy: a Policy Problem Without a Political Solution?' (1999) 17 *Environment and Planning* 69; and S. Dillon, 'The Mirage of EC Environmental Federalism in a Reluctant Member State Jurisdiction' (1999) 8 *N.Y.U. Environmental Law Journal* 1.

A first point to note is the Commission's shift towards prioritisation of certain types of infringement case. In its 2007 Communication, 'A Europe of Results – Applying Community Law', the Commission indicated its intention to prioritise three categories of cases, namely:

a)   non-communication of national measures transposing directives or failure to respect other notification obligations. Post-Lisbon, the Commission's hand has been strengthened in cases of failure to notify transposition measures for directives, as the Court is empowered pursuant to Article 260(3) TFEU to impose fines and/or penalty payments in such cases without any need for a follow-on action.[9] In a 2011 Communication, the Commission made clear its intention to rely on this provision 'as a matter of principle' in *all* non-communication cases falling within its scope.[10] In 2010, environmental cases accounted for 115 of 470 non-communication cases pending (i.e. almost one quarter), with the Commission reporting that deadlines are 'regularly missed by a large number of Member States'.[11] It seems inevitable, therefore, that Article 260(3) TFEU will frequently be employed in environmental cases;[12]
b)   breaches of EU law raising 'issues of principle or having particularly far-reaching negative impact for citizens'; and
c)   failure to respect Court judgments declaring the existence of infringements (i.e. Art. 260(2) TFEU cases). In this case, compliance is expected within an average of 12–24 months, subject to the 'specific circumstances of exceptional cases'.[13]

The scope of category (b) in the specific context of the environmental sector was further expanded upon by a 2008 Communication, in which the Commission stated that it considered the following breaches to fall within this category:

•   non-conformity of 'key legislation' viewed as presenting a significant risk for correct implementation of environmental rules, which means breaches of (provisions of) directives that 'set the main framework' for environmental protection;[14]

---

9   Article 260(3) TFEU provides for such a possibility in the case of failure to notify measures transposing a 'directive adopted under a legislative procedure'.
10   Commission Communication on implementation of Article 260(3) TFEU OJ 2011 C 12/1, para. 17.
11   Commission, 28th Annual Report on Monitoring the Application of EU Law (2010) COM (2010) 588 final (29 September 2011), pp. 5–6.
12   See, for instance, Commission Press Release, 'Environment: Commission takes Poland to Court over air quality and marine policy legislation and urges compliance with the Nitrates Directive' IP/11/1434 of 24 November 2011.
13   Commission Communication on implementing European Community Environmental Law COM (2008) 773, at p. 8.
14   *Ibid.*

- systematic breaches of environmental quality or other requirements presenting 'serious adverse consequences or risks' for human health or aspects of nature with 'high ecological value' (i.e. contravention 'repeatedly or on a significant scale' of particularly important environmental obligations or key procedural or activity-related obligations, such as those requiring landfills to operate under a waste permit). Here, the Commission states that it intends to 'focus on systemic breaches of central provisions of environmental directives', as this is generally a 'more efficient and equitable' approach;[15]
- breaches of 'core, strategic obligations on which fulfilment of other obligations depends' (e.g. failure to designate sites under the Habitats Directive, or to come up with appropriate waste management plans);
- breaches concerning large infrastructure projects or projects involving EU funding, particularly in cases where irreversible ecological damage may arise.[16] In such situations, the Commission indicated its intention to seek interim measures in suitable cases where the (rather strict) conditions for grant of this remedy are made out. The Commission has since done so successfully in a number of cases in situations where natural resources could have been irreversibly damaged by the time the Court delivered a judgment in the main action.[17] Evidently, however, in cases where interim measures are obtained, their effectiveness is dependent on the Member State's respect for the Court's judgment.[18]

The effect of prioritisation is, it would seem, that unless an issue falls within one of the prioritised categories set out, the issue will in practice be unlikely to be pursued by the Commission – at least in the short term, and subject perhaps to the possibility of greater resources being made available to the Commission.[19]

---

15 *Ibid.*, at p. 9.

16 *Ibid.*

17 See, for instance, the Orders of the President in Case C-193/07 R *Commission v Poland*, not published in the ECR and also Case C-503/06 R *Commission v Italy*, Order of the President of February 27, 2007 [2007] ECR I-19, Case C-76/08 R *Commission v Malta*, Order of the President of April 24, 2008 [2008] ECR I-64, Case C-573/08 *Commission v Italy*, Order of the President of December 10, 2009 [2009] ECR I-0000. See generally, M. Hedemann-Robinson, 'Enforcement of EU Environmental Law and the Role of Interim Measures' (2010) 19(5) *European Energy and Environmental Law Review* 204.

18 A case in point is Malta's breach of the Birds Directive in relation to bird hunting. While the Commission successfully obtained interim measures against Malta pending the outcome of Article 258 TFEU infringement proceedings (see Case C-76/08 R *Commission v Malta*, Order of the President of April 24, 2008 [2008] ECR I-64), followed by judgment against Malta in those proceedings (Case C-76/08 *Commission v Malta* [2009] ECR I-8213), it has subsequently brought Article 260(2) TFEU proceedings against Malta for failure to comply with that judgment. See Commission Press Release of 28 October 2010, 'Commission Requests Malta to Comply with Court Ruling on Bird Hunting' IP/10/1409.

19 Note, however, the Commission's statement that '*all complaints and infringements will be dealt with*': Commission Communication on implementing European Community Environmental Law COM (2008) 773, at p. 8. However, this is a rather minimal guarantee that can, it would seem, be satisfied simply by issuing a response to a complaint without pursuing it further.

The legality and consequences of bringing actions for systemic, rather than individual, breaches were famously considered by the Court of Justice in *Commission v Ireland* (Case C-494/01), in which the Commission argued that the situations raised in twelve separate complaints with regard to illegal waste activities constituted evidence not only of the twelve separate infringements, but also of a general and persistent, or systemic, breach of Ireland's obligations under the Waste Directive.[20] The Court came down strongly on the Commission's side, following Advocate General Geelhoed, who had argued forcefully that this was necessary in order to increase the effectiveness of EU environmental law, in view in particular of the relative scarcity of resources on the part of the Commission to investigate complaints and the interests of efficiency in grouping complaints together.[21] Importantly, the Court ruled that the consequences of a plea of systemic breach were that, in respect of that plea, the normal rule that all arguments and evidence to be relied upon against the Member State must be contained in the Reasoned Opinion did not apply. Rather, 'the production of additional evidence intended, at the stage of proceedings before the Court, to support the proposition that the failure thus alleged is general and persistent cannot be ruled out in principle'.[22] In such cases, therefore, the Commission's hand is strengthened considerably, not least in that, once the Court has found a systemic breach to exist, the Commission can continue to gather evidence from environmental NGOs and other sources in any follow-on Article 260 TFEU proceedings. Further, in relation to the burden of proof, the Court noted that it was enough for the Commission to adduce 'sufficient' evidence to show that a Member State's authorities had developed a repeated and persistent practice contrary to the Directive; once this threshold had been reached, the burden shifted to the Member State to challenge the information produced and consequences flowing therefrom.[23] The Court has since confirmed the validity of the systemic breach approach in a number of other judgments.[24]

Commission v Ireland (Case C-494/01) – currently the subject of Article 260(2) TFEU proceedings[25] – indicated a good deal of empathy on the Court's part for the difficulties faced by the Commission in attempting to monitor the vast area of the EU's environment without its own environmental enforcement inspection service. At the time, in supporting the Commission's position, the Advocate

---

20 The relevant directive in force at the time was Council Directive 75/442/EEC of 15 July 1975 on waste OJ 1975 L 194/39, as amended. See further, P. Wennerås, 'A New Dawn for Commission Enforcement under Articles 226 and 228 EC' (2006) 43 *Common Market Law Review* 31.

21 Opinion in Case C-494/01 *Commission v Ireland* [2005] ECR I-3331

22 *Commission v Ireland*, para. 37.

23 *Ibid.*, at para. 47.

24 See, for instance, Case C-135/05 *Commission v Italy* [2007] ECR I-3475; Case C-189/07 *Commission v Spain* [2008] ECR I-195.

25 At the time of writing, the administrative stage of Article 260(2) TFEU proceedings had been commenced (although the matter had not been lodged with the ECJ).

General was very much motivated by a desire to increase the effectiveness of EU environmental law in practice.[26] The establishment of a 'general and persistent' breach category was intended to add to the Commission's armoury, rather than to replace entirely other types of infringement cases. Yet, in effect, the unintended consequence of this and similar judgments seems to have been that, in practice, infringements will only rarely be pursued by the Commission if they fall outside one of the categories deemed important pursuant to the 2008 Communication. While the Commission's discretion in selecting infringement cases has long been recognised to be extremely broad, the explicit prioritisation movement goes one step further: it effectively confirms that a large chunk of potential environmental infringements will *not* normally be pursued by the Commission. This is in line with indications given by Commissioner Potočnik that, while improving implementation of EU environmental law constitutes one of the priorities of his tenure, his aim is to develop 'a risk-based, systemic approach to enforcement, as opposed to an *ad hoc* complaint-based approach'.[27] For citizens unfortunate enough to be faced with a problem that lies outside the Commission's priority areas, therefore, this will not feel like increased effectiveness of EU law at all.

Alongside the prioritisation movement, a further important shift in the Commission's enforcement role is reflected in its institution of the EU Pilot scheme in April 2008.[28] The scheme seeks to establish a dialogue between the Commission and Member States in the former's efforts to answer enquiries or respond to complaints, including as to potential infringements of EU law. As such, Member States may be contacted directly by the Commission via a confidential online database, with correspondence and complaints referred for comment and resolution, and a network of contacts created in Member States to operate the system. Should complainants or correspondents choose to allow their identity to be revealed, the Member State replies directly to that individual or organisation with information and, where possible, suggestions as to how the problem(s) can be resolved.[29] However, the Commission retains the power to take the matter further and launch Article 258 TFEU proceedings if it so wishes. The Commission now considers that the scheme has gone beyond the experimental stages to become a 'well-established working method' on its

---

26 A personal observation as the present author was a *référendaire* in Advocate General Geelhoed's cabinet at the time.

27 J. Potočnik, 'Achieving our Objectives by Effective Implementation' SPEECH/11/440 of 15 June 2011 (Environment Commissioner, 2010–present).

28 This scheme was announced in the 2007 Commission Communication, 'A Europe of Results – Applying Community Law' COM (2007) 502 final, at p. 7.

29 See P. Koller and L. Cashman, 'Implementing EC Environmental Law: Compliance Promotion and Enforcement by the European Commission' (2009) 6(1) *Journal for European Environmental and Planning Law* 1, at p. 8. EU Pilot does not apply to non-communication cases, and at the time of writing applied only in 25 of the 27 Member States (with Malta and Luxembourg not yet in the system). See the Commission's Second Evaluation Report on EU Pilot, SEC (2011) 1629, 21 December 2011.

part,[30] complementing the CHAP central registry for complaints and enquiries created in September 2009. All complaints and enquiries are first registered in CHAP, and then transferred to the EU Pilot if the Commission needs to obtain further factual or legal information or to provide the Member State in question with an opportunity to propose a solution compliant with EU law.[31]

The aim of the Pilot initiative is in principle a laudable one: an increase in cooperation and partnership between the Commission and Member States, involving Member States at an early stage while at the same time aiding the Commission's task in obtaining information. This can be viewed as a move towards a more network-based style of governance in enforcement,[32] which had been announced in the 2001 White Paper on European Governance, as well as in the 2007 Communication mentioned above, which set out the overarching principles that the Commission would apply to enforcing of EU environmental law.[33] A cooperative approach also fits with the Article 4(3) TEU principle of sincere cooperation, whereby the 'Union and the Member States shall, in full mutual respect, assist each other in carrying out tasks which flow from the Treaties'. From a resource perspective, this carries the advantage of shifting some of the burden of responding to complaints and comments from the Commission to Member States.

Yet this approach also raises potential issues about the objectivity and reliability of the information received pursuant to this process: at its most basic, Member States are being asked to help inform the Commission about matters which may potentially lead to an infringement action against them. Further, from a complainant's perspective, being put in touch with the very national authorities which are, in the complainant's view, disregarding EU law may seem far from satisfactory.

The Commission's confirmation that a correspondent will always receive an evaluation by the Commission of the response of the Member State authority goes some way to alleviating such concerns.[34] It is striking, however, that in fully 87 per cent of environmental cases dealt with through the Pilot scheme up to September 2011, the Commission services considered that responses provided by Member States were acceptable and allowed the file to be closed.[35]

---

30 Commission's Second Evaluation Report on EU Pilot, *ibid.,* at p. 7.

31 In 2010, only 17 per cent of the 4035 cases created in CHAP went on to be transferred to EU Pilot, with 9 per cent transferred to infringement proceedings and the rest closed by the Commission without necessitating transfer: *28th Annual Report on Monitoring the Application of EU Law (2010)* COM (2011) 588 final, 29 September 2011. See also on CHAP, the *27th Annual Report on Monitoring the Application of EU Law (2009)* COM (2010) 538 final, at p. 7.

32 See, for instance, I. von Homeyer, 'Emerging Experimentalism in EU Environmental Governance' in C. Sabel and J. Zeitlin, *Experimentalist Governance in the European Union* (Oxford: Oxford University Press, 2010).

33 COM (2007) 502 final, at p. 7. See also, the emphasis on networks in environmental information gathering in the Commission Communication 'Improving the Delivery of Benefits from EU Environment Measures: Building Confidence through better Knowledge and Responsiveness', COM (2012) 95 final, pp. 7 and 10.

34 See the Commission's First Evaluation Report on EU Pilot COM (2010) 70 final; and Second Evaluation Report on EU Pilot, SEC (2011) 1629, 21 December 2011, at p. 3.

35 Annex to Second Evaluation Report on EU Pilot, *ibid.,* at p. 17.

This once again underlines the relatively small likelihood of environmental complaints leading to the opening of an infringement action nowadays. The statistics available to date on the operation of the EU Pilot scheme and CHAPs confirm this analysis. While environmental complaints comprised 666 (or almost 20 per cent) of total complaints made to the Commission in 2010 – making this the most complained-about sector[36] – and 76 (or almost 22 per cent) of total complaints registered to the Pilot scheme in 2010,[37] only 20 (or 8.2 per cent) of the infringement cases opened following a complaint in that year were in the environmental sector.[38] In contrast, by far the highest proportion (40, or 21 per cent) of the cases opened on the Commission's own initiative in 2010 concerned the environmental sector,[39] and 169 (or almost 20 per cent) of the non-communication cases opened by the Commission.[40]

The story told by these figures seems clear: while a large number of complaints continue to be made to the Commission alleging breach of environmental law on the part of Member States, only a fraction ever lead to a case being opened. Rather, in the environmental sector, the Commission is very much focused on own initiative cases, where it acts in accordance with the enforcement priorities that it has set, as well as non-communication cases. While this position fits with the 2008 Communication, it is to be contrasted with the balance in other sectors – such as Justice, where 33 cases were opened on foot of complaints in 2010, as compared to just three own initiative cases.[41]

There are also legitimate concerns that the effect of the Commission/Member State dialogue created by the Pilot scheme may in many cases be simply a prolongation of the length of the infringement action that ultimately ensues. According to the Commission's December 2011 report on the Pilot scheme, the average time taken by Member States to respond to the concerns raised was 67 days (i.e. just under the ten-week guideline set for Member States under the scheme), with the average time for follow-on responses from the Commission adding an additional 102 days.[42] All this must be added to the length of time inherent in issuing and receiving a response to a letter of formal notice and Reasoned Opinion, as well the almost 17-month average length of time for direct actions at the judicial stage, i.e. from the date when the application is lodged with the Court.[43]

Overall, the Commission's 2010 *Annual Report on Monitoring the Application of EU Law* concluded that the Commission's perception of the functioning of

---

36 *28th Annual Report on Monitoring the Application of EU Law* (2010) COM (2010) 588 final (29 September 2011), Annex I, Table 1.1.A.
37 *Ibid.*, Table 1.5.1.
38 *Ibid.*, Table 1.4.A.
39 *Ibid.*
40 *Ibid.*
41 *Ibid.*
42 Von Homeyer, 'Emerging Experimentalism in EU Environmental Governance', p. 5.
43 See the *2010 Annual Report of the Court of Justice of the EU* (Luxembourg: Publications Office of the European Union, 2011), Statistics on Judicial Activity, at p. 96.

the EU Pilot scheme in its first two years had been 'very positive'.[44] More generally, the Commission states that *all* of its own initiative cases, as well as all of the complaints it chooses to transfer from CHAP, will be entered first into the Pilot scheme, in replacement of the normal practice of sending an administrative letter before any formal step is taken (although this does not exclude the possibility of proceeding in exceptional cases directly to formal infringement proceedings).[45] In general, however, only non-communication cases will henceforth be opened as infringement cases directly, by-passing the Pilot scheme. The significance of the Pilot scheme looks set to increase, therefore, bringing with it a greater reliance on the cooperation of Member State authorities and, potentially, a very different experience for some complainants.[46]

Viewed in conjunction with the prioritisation movement discussed above, it is hard to avoid the conclusion that the nature of the Commission's role in enforcing EU environmental law is in the process of changing rather fundamentally. In particular, the role of complaints in triggering infringement proceedings appears now at best marginal, unless one happens to be complaining about a matter which the Commission in any event views as one of its priority areas (i.e. one's complaint falls within a broader systemic breach, or relates to a breach of a particularly important directive or obligation, or to a large infrastructure project, or non-communication of transposing measures, or failure to comply with an ECJ judgment). Moreover, should one's complaint fall outside these categories, no matter how well-founded, one may well find oneself left to deal with the very national authorities whom one likely approached in the first place, and who failed to act at that stage. It is easy to see the difficulties with which the Commission is faced – in particular, a lack of resources to investigate and bring infringement cases, coupled with an unwillingness on the part of Member States to grant a mandate for, for instance, an EU environmental enforcement agency (although such an agency is presently being considered in the waste sector),[47] means that it is simply not possible to pursue all well-founded complaints. Yet the consequent exclusion of many

---

44 Koller and Cashman, 'Implementing EC Environmental Law', p. 8.

45 See Second Evaluation Report on EU Pilot, von Homeyer, 'Emerging Experimentalism in EU Environmental Governance', p. 5.

46 See L. Krämer, 'The Environmental Complaint in EU Law' (2009) 6(1) *Journal for European Environmental & Planning Law* 13, who observes that, 'the Commission's activities over the last years with regard to environmental complaints give the impression that the Commission wants to get rid of such complaints. Citizens who disturb, by their complaints, the smooth relationship between the national and the Commission's administrations, are a nuisance' (at p. 31).

47 See Milieu et al., *Study on the Feasibility of the Establishment of a Waste Implementation Agency*, 7 December 2009, available at http://ec.europa.eu/environment/waste. See, however, against the proposal of a Waste Implementation Agency, European Parliament resolution of 2 February 2012 on the issues raised by petitioners in relation to the application of the Waste Management Directive, and related directives, in the Member States of the European Union (2011/2038/INI). See also, the Commission suggestion of increasing the role for the EEA in monitoring environmental enforcement, and instituting an EU level environmental inspection capacity, in Commission Communication 'Improving the Delivery of Benefits from EU Environment Measures', pp. 6 and 8.

complainants from the enforcement process is, to say the least, ironic in the context of a movement towards network-based, multi-level environmental governance within the European Union. Given the continuing restrictions on enforcement at national level (discussed below), it is difficult to see how these developments ensure adequate respect for the rule of law. A solution would be, in the short term, to increase the resources available to the directorate responsible for enforcement and compliance within DG Environment and, in the longer term, to allow complainants to gain a remedy elsewhere by improving access to environmental justice at national level, as discussed in section 7.4.

7.3 National authorities as enforcers: the pressure of harmonisation

National authorities constitute a second, and vital, pillar of enforcement of EU environmental law. As a matter of EU law, all national authorities – from central government, to state agencies, to the police – are of course subject to the Article 4(3) TEU principle of sincere cooperation, which obliges Member States to take 'any appropriate measure' to ensure fulfilment of their Treaty obligations, and to 'facilitate the achievement of the Union's tasks'. In principle, therefore, national authorities play the crucial role of ensuring on-the-ground enforcement in circumstances where the Commission has neither the resources nor the competence to do so.

While in theory it is for Member States to decide precisely how they wish to organise their own environmental enforcement systems, a battle has been ongoing over the limits of this discretion, and the extent to which harmonisation of enforcement techniques at EU level is legitimate and necessary. This is nothing new, being at the heart, for instance, of the dispute over whether the European Environment Agency should have the competence to monitor the application of environmental law – a position supported by the European Parliament,[48] but ultimately rejected at the behest of a number of Member States.[49] More recently, the battle was particularly evident in the hotly contested criminal sanctions saga where, following the ECJ's determination that Article 192 TFEU constituted the proper legal basis for criminal penalties that were essential for combating serious environmental offences, the Directive on the Protection of the Environment through Criminal Law was passed in 2008, for which the transposition period expired in December 2010.[50] Nonetheless, in *Ship Source Pollution*, the Court emphasised that determination of the 'type and level of the criminal penalties to be applied' did not fall within the Community's sphere of competence.[51]

---

48 See OJ 1990 C 96/114.
49 See Krämer, 'The Environmental Complaint in EU Law'.
50 Case C-176/03 *Commission v Council* [2005] ER I-7879 Directive 2008/99/EC of the European Parliament and of the Council of 19 November 2008 on the protection of the environment through criminal law OJ 2008 L 328/28.
51 Case C-440/05 *Commission v Council* [2007] ECR I-9097, para. 70.

Article 83(2)(1) TFEU, inserted by the Lisbon Treaty, not only codifies, but also expands, the Court's jurisprudence in this regard, in providing that directives may establish minimum rules with regard to the definition of criminal offences *and sanctions* where this is 'essential to ensure the effective implementation of a Union policy' in an area which has already been subject to harmonisation measures.

The next front in the battle, albeit not (yet) litigated before the ECJ, is the field of environmental inspections and, in particular, the extent to which Member States should be the ones who decide how and when to carry out such inspections. To date, while binding inspections provisions exist in rare sectoral directives,[52] the principal instrument on the matter at EU level has been the 2001 Recommendation on Minimum Criteria for Environmental Inspections (RMCEI), a non-binding document arrived at in a victory for the Council, which preferred a non-binding recommendation, over the European Parliament, which preferred a binding directive on inspections.[53] However, in an excellent illustration of the 'hardening' of soft law, the RMCEI principles have recently been transposed into binding law in the form of Article 23 of the Industrial Emissions Directive, which recasts the IPPC Directive[54] and has a transposition date of 7 January 2013.[55] This provision obliges Member States, within the field of IPPC installations, to set up a system of environmental inspections to examine the 'full range' of relevant environmental effects, to draw up an environmental inspection plan that addresses a range of specified matters, and to 'regularly' draw up programmes for routine environmental inspections, as well as carrying out non-routine inspections to investigate serious environmental complaints.

Nonetheless, the idea of moving towards binding inspections provisions more generally remains highly contentious, with conflicting views evident on this issue even within DG Environment itself. Thus, while it was originally indicated that a future Commission Communication on implementing EU environmental law and policy may include proposals for 'action on partial harmonization of the standards on the implementation and enforcement of EU environmental legislation through inspections' which may – potentially – lead to a Proposal for a horizontal directive replacing RMCEI,[56] it was then indicated that non-binding techniques of improving inspections will be preferred, including the possibility of instituting 'partnerships' with national

---

52 See, for instance, Council Directive 96/82/EC of 9 December 1996 on the control of major-accident hazards involving dangerous substances OJ 1997 L 10/13 ('Seveso II'), as amended, Article 18.

53 OJ 2001 L 118/41.

54 See Directive 2008/1/EC of the European Parliament and of the Council of 15 January 2008 concerning integrated pollution prevention and control OJ 2008 L 24/8.

55 Directive 2010/75/EU of the European Parliament and of the Council of 24 November 2010 on industrial emissions (integrated pollution prevention and control) OJ 2010 L 334/17.

56 See the Commission's roadmap, 'Communication on Implementing EU Environmental Law and Policy: a Common Challenge', available at http://ec.europa.eu/governance/impact/planned_ia/docs/2011_env_007_common_challenge_en.pdf.

inspectorates.[57] This approach would build, therefore, on the soft law techniques already being employed in this area by IMPEL (the EU Network for the Implementation and Enforcement of Environmental Law),[58] and would be disappointing for those hoping for a more robust approach to harmonising inspection standards.

A final recent development of interest in terms of enforcement by national authorities relates not so much to increasing the effectiveness of enforcement through harmonisation, but rather through consolidation. Of particular interest here are the major environmental permitting and enforcement reforms recently implemented within the UK. Under the Environmental Permitting (England and Wales) Regulations 2010, the UK has switched from a system whereby each of the many Directives requiring permitting (ranging from waste operations to landfill to the titanium dioxide industry) was transposed into national law individually, to a unified regime whereby a single permitting framework is employed, with schedules transposing the Directives incorporating the detailed requirements of the Directives by reference, and without re-drafting.[59] This is a significant step, based upon the idea that, by making the law more user-friendly, not only will compliance improve, but compliance costs will also decrease. This change has been implemented alongside a fundamental reform in sanctions whereby, rather than relying principally on criminal sanctions, new far-reaching powers to impose civil sanctions, including financial sanctions of up to £250,000, have been granted to the UK's Environment Agency and Natural England in Part 3 of the Regulatory Enforcement and Sanctions Act 2008 and its implementing Regulations.[60] Such sanctions are subject to satisfaction of the criminal standard of proof, i.e. beyond reasonable doubt.

These changes reflect a creative approach to environmental regulation that is to be welcomed: compliance is facilitated and incentivised not only by simplifying requirements, but also by increasing the danger that infringers will be subject to proportionate sanctions imposed directly by the relevant environmental agency (in a manner comparable to, for instance, the fining powers of the Office of Fair Trading for breach of competition law). However, it is not necessarily an approach that is transposable to all Member States.[61]

---

57 See the speech by Commissioner Potočnik, 'Achieving our Objectives by Effective Implementation' SPEECH/11/440 of 15 June 2011. Ultimately, in the 2012 Commission Communication 'Improving the Delivery of Benefits from EU Environment Measures', both the legislative (hard law) and partnership (soft law) options were kept on the table.

58 See http://impel.eu/. IMPEL has, *inter alia*, developed guidance documents on environmental inspections, helped national authorities to apply these, and carried out a peer review programme (the IMPEL review initiative) to further support authorities with the implementation of RMCEI.

59 The Environmental Permitting (England and Wales) Regulations 2010 (2010 No. 675).

60 Regulatory Enforcement and Sanctions Act 2008 (2008 c. 13). See generally, R. Macrory, 'Reforming Regulatory Sanctions – a Personal Perspective' (2009) 11(2) *Environmental Law Review* 69.

61 In Ireland, for instance, any attempt to institute administrative sanctions may run into constitutional difficulties, due to the requirement that criminal charges must be tried by jury (Constitution of Ireland, Article 38.5). This could mean that a constitutional amendment, which must be passed by referendum,

7.4 Private parties as enforcers: the access to justice challenge

A third major area of difficulty in the enforcement of EU environmental law, and one that has perhaps received most attention in recent years, is of course the role of private parties and the considerable ongoing limitations on access to environmental justice in many jurisdictions within the EU.

7.4.1 Access to environmental justice before the EU Courts

Not least amongst the jurisdictions exhibiting such limitations is the EU itself. As is well known, direct access to the EU Courts by private parties is subject to the tremendous restriction of having to satisfy the Article 263(4) TFEU test of direct and individual concern. In cases where a measure other than an EU decision addressed to the applicant is being challenged, the Court in *Plaumann* interpreted individual concern in a manner that effectively requires the applicant to demonstrate that it is affected by the EU measure in a different manner to any other person.[62] As will be recalled, the effect of the Court's decisions in cases such as *Greenpeace*, *EEB* and *WWF-UK* is that this test is effectively impossible to satisfy in cases of challenges to EU measures on environmental grounds.[63]

In *Greenpeace*, the applicant organisation had argued forcefully that the application of the standard *Plaumann* test to an environmental challenge would create a 'legal vacuum in ensuring compliance with Community environmental legislation, since in this area the interests are, by their very nature, common and shared'.[64] This situation, combined with the Court's affirmation in cases like *ADBHU* that environmental protection constituted one of the 'Community's essential objectives', meant in the applicants' view that a different interpretation of Article 263(4) TFEU must be adopted for environmental challenges. The Court rejected this argument, confirming application of *Plaumann* and holding that effective judicial protection could be ensured by national courts (in that case, by a challenge to the national decision authorising the construction of power plants allegedly in breach of the EIA Directive).[65]

More recently, in *EEB*, the General Court was asked to reconsider the matter in the context of a challenge to a Commission decision on plant protection products by two prominent environmental NGOs, the Brussels-based

---

would be necessary. The question of the necessity of a constitutional amendment would, however, ultimately be for the Supreme Court of Ireland to decide.

62 Case 25/62 *Plaumann* [1962] ECR 95.

63 The lines of jurisprudence in which the Court has adopted a more relaxed approach to standing – for instance, where an applicant has a specific right to be involved in the administrative procedure which gave rise to the decision under challenge (see, e.g., Case C-309/89 *Codorniu* [1994] ECR I-1853); or where the applicant can demonstrate that it belongs to a closed class of applicants whose interests the EU is bound to take into account (see, e.g., Case 11/82 *Piraiki-Patraiki* [1985] ECR 207) – do not generally apply to environmental challenges.

64 Case C-321/95 P *Greenpeace* [1998] ECR I-1651, at para. 18. See also, Case T-219/95 *Danielsson* [1995] ECR II-3051.

65 *Greenpeace, ibid*, paras. 27–35.

European Environmental Bureau and the Dutch Stichting Natuur en Milieu, which had special consultative status at EU and Dutch levels respectively.[66] While the applicants argued that the right to effective judicial protection in environmental matters would be breached by application of the strict *Plaumann* test, they did not explicitly rely on the Aarhus Convention, which was approved by the EU by Decision in 2005.[67] The Court rejected the applicants' arguments and held that the standard *Plaumann* test applied in this case: despite the applicants' special status as consultative bodies at EU and national levels, respectively, they did not benefit from any specific 'procedural guarantees' in the EU decision-making process in the way, for instance, complainants in competition proceedings do.[68]

In *WWF-UK*, the Court of Justice confirmed this approach in an action brought by an environmental NGO for the partial annulment of a Regulation fixing the total allowable catches in respect of cod fishing for the year 2007 in areas covered by a previous Regulation establishing measures for the recovery of cod stocks.[69] Despite the fact that WWF-UK was a member of the regional advisory council for the North Sea, which has consultative status in fisheries matters within that area and has the right to submit recommendations on such matters, this did not amount to a sufficient procedural guarantee for WWF-UK to be individually concerned.[70]

The undeniable lacuna in judicial protection to which this situation gives rise has been partially addressed by the amendment to Article 263(4) TFEU brought about by the Lisbon Treaty, which now provides that natural or legal persons may institute proceedings not only against an act addressed to them or that is of direct and individual concern to them, but also to 'a regulatory act which is of direct concern to them and does not entail implementing measures'. It is clear that this provision must be viewed in the context of the debate about the deficiencies of *Plaumann* in the (non-environmental) *UPA* case, in which Advocate General Jacobs had sharply criticised *Plaumann* for

---

66 Joined cases T-236/04 and T-241/04 *EEA and Stichting Natuur en Milieu v Commission* [2005] ECR II-4945.

67 Council Decision 2005/370 of 17 February 2005 on the conclusion, on behalf of the European Community, of the Convention on access to information, public participation in decision-making and access to justice in environmental matters OJ 2005 L 124/3.

68 *Ibid.*, para. 62.

69 Council Regulation (EC) No 41/2007 of 21 December 2006 fixing for 2007 the fishing opportunities and associated conditions for certain fish stocks and groups of fish stocks, applicable in Community waters and, for Community vessels, in waters where catch limitations are required OJ 2007 L 15/1; Council Regulation (EC) No 423/2004 of 26 February 2004 establishing measures for the recovery of cod stocks OJ 2004 L 70/8.

70 Order of the Court of 5 May 2009 in Case C-355/08 P *WWF-UK* [2009] ECR I-73. See also, Order of the Court of 26 November 2009 in Case C-444/08 P *Região autónoma dos Açores* [2009] ECR I-200 (Autonomous Region of the Açores did not have standing to challenge an EU fisheries regulation on the ground that the regulation, by opening up its territory to non-Portuguese vessels, would damage its marine environment).

failing to provide effective judicial protection, in potential breach, *inter alia,* of the requirements of the fundamental right to a fair trial under Article 6 of the European Convention of Human Rights.[71] This was particularly so in the case of a challenge to an EU Regulation, where there would be no national implementing measures to seek to challenge in national courts. While recognising this gap, the Court in *UPA* declined to follow its Advocate General, effectively attributing a constitutional status to *Plaumann* by holding that the test could only be altered by Treaty amendment.[72] Viewed in this light, it might have seemed logical to interpret the amended Article 263(4) TFEU as allowing challenges to EU Regulations that are of direct concern and that do not entail implementing measures. A narrower view, however, is that the provision distinguishes between regulatory and legislative acts, with the latter defined by Article 289(3) TFEU as 'legal acts adopted by legislative procedure' (i.e. the EU's ordinary or special legislative procedures set down in the Treaty).[73] By that reading, only acts of direct concern which do not entail implementing measures *and* have not been adopted by legislative procedure fall under this provision.

In *Inuit Tapiriit Kanatami,* which concerned a challenge to a Regulation on trade in seal products,[74] the General Court came down strongly in favour of this narrower meaning of 'regulatory act', holding that this term does not extend to all acts of general application, and in particular does not include legislative acts.[75] The General Court expressly rejected the applicants' argument that a broad interpretation of the term was necessitated by the Aarhus Convention, but using reasoning that leaves much to be desired. In particular, it gave no substantive analysis of this issue or of the requirements of the Aarhus Convention, confining itself to stating that 'the Treaty established a complete system of legal remedies and procedures designed to ensure judicial review of the legality of acts of the institutions' and that the 'provisions of international conventions may not depart from those rules of primary law of the European Union'.[76]

This reasoning is insufficient and, in itself, unconvincing, although part of the problem may have been that the matter was not argued properly before the Court.[77] In particular, it is difficult to see how the principal judgment cited by the General Court in support of its position – *Kadi and Al Barakaat International Foundation v Council and Commission* – necessitates the view that

---

71 Case C-50/00 P *UPA* [2002] ECR I-6677.

72 *Ibid.*

73 Articles 289(1) and (2) TFEU. See also, the distinction between legislative and regulatory acts contained in Article 207(6) TFEU.

74 Regulation (EC) No 1007/2009 of the European Parliament and of the Council of 16 September 2009 on trade in seal products OJ 2009 L 286/36.

75 Case T-18/10 *Inuit Tapiriit Kanatami and Others v European Parliament and Council of the European Union,* Order of the General Court of 7 September 2011. See, para. 49, where the General Court relies in support of its interpretation on the history of negotiating what became Article 263(4) TFEU in the drafting of the Constitutional Treaty.

76 *Ibid.*, para. 55.

77 See *ibid.*, paras. 53–54, criticising the applicants' arguments in relation to the Aarhus Convention.

the Aarhus Convention is irrelevant to the interpretation of Article 263(4) TFEU.[78] In that case, which concerned the interrelationship between the EU and UN legal orders, the ECJ affirmed that Community measures must always comply with the EU's human rights requirements, even where such measures ultimately flow from the UN legal order. *Kadi* can hardly be interpreted as meaning that the Aarhus Convention should not be taken into account in interpreting a provision of EU primary law, in circumstances where that provision is open to interpretation in a variety of ways, and the principles contained in the relevant international convention (access to information, public participation and access to justice in environmental matters) undoubtedly form part of the EU legal order.

In other words, this is not – as with *Kadi* – a case of a conflict between fundamental principles of two legal orders, but one of synergy. The ECJ's judgment on appeal will, therefore, be of great interest.[79] While it is unlikely that the ECJ will interpret the meaning of 'regulatory act' so as to encompass legislative acts, it is notable that the Aarhus Convention itself makes a fundamental distinction between decisions of public bodies acting in legislative and non-legislative capacities (with only the latter category falling within the scope of the duty to ensure access to review procedures for decisions, acts and omissions of a 'public authority' under that Convention).[80] In this sense, therefore, it may be open to the ECJ to confirm the relevance of the Aarhus Convention while emphasising that no conflict between the EU and Aarhus in fact exists.[81]

Aside from the meaning of 'regulatory act', a number of further questions relating to the interpretation of Article 263(4) TFEU have also arisen before the General Court to date. In *Arcelor*, the General Court held a challenge by a steel producer to the EU Emissions Trading Scheme Directive to be inadmissible.[82] The Court ruled that the new Article 263(4) TFEU would not have an effect on the matter, because Member States had a 'broad discretion' with regard to the implementation of the Directive. As a result, the Directive could not amount to a regulatory act which 'does not entail implementing measures' within the meaning of that provision. The result of the Court's judgment is that challenges to Directives will not as a rule fall under this provision.[83]

---

78 Joined Cases C-402/05 P and C-415/05 P *Kadi and Al Barakaat International Foundation* v *Council and Commission* [2008] ECR I-6351.

79 Case C-583/11, application not yet published in the OJ (pending).

80 See Article 2(2) of the Aarhus Convention and, for instance, the Compliance Committee's findings and recommendations in case ACCC/C/2008/32 (EC), 14 April 2011, para. 70.

81 See the Compliance Committee's findings and recommendations in case ACCC/C/2008/32 (EC), 14 April 2011, para. 92, which may be read as suggesting a similar approach.

82 Case T-16/04 *Arcelor v European Parliament and Council*, judgment of the General Court of 2 March 2010, para. 23.

83 While the General Court proceeded to give a view in that case, it declined to do so in its Orders in *Norisk Nickel* and *Etimine*, on the basis that Article 263(4) TFEU only applies to actions lodged with the Court after the entry into force of the Lisbon Treaty (1 December 2009) or where the three-month deadline for bringing such an action expired after this date. Case T-532/08 *Norilsk Nickel*, Order of the Grand Chamber of the General Court of 7 September 2010, para. 72; Case T-539/08 *Etimine*, Order of the Grand Chamber of the General Court of 7 September 2010, at para. 78.

The debate on access to environmental justice before the EU Courts, which had up until recently been played out primarily as a dialogue between the EU's own institutions (in particular the Court) and the Member States (as authors of the Treaty), has now shifted forum with the lodging of a complaint against the EU before the Compliance Committee of the Aarhus Convention (the 'Compliance Committee'), to which the European Community became a party in 2005.[84] In December 2008, the NGO ClientEarth, supported by a number of other environmental NGOs,[85] lodged a complaint before the Compliance Committee arguing that the EU had infringed Article 9 of the Aarhus Convention and, in particular:

- Article 9(2), which relates to access to justice for challenges to Article 6 decisions, i.e. public participation in decisions on specific activities;[86]
- Article 9(3), which relates to access to justice for challenges to other acts and omissions by private persons and public authorities which contravene national environmental law provisions;[87]
- Article 9(4), which requires that the access to justice procedures provided for under the above provisions shall provide 'adequate and effective remedies' and be 'fair, equitable, timely and not prohibitively expensive';[88] and
- Article 9(5), which requires that information be provided to the public on access to administrative and judicial review procedures and that

---

84 See Communication to the Aarhus Convention's Complaint Committee of 1 December 2008, ACCC/C/2008/32 (EC), available at www.unece.org. See also, Decision 2005/370 on the conclusion, on behalf of the European Community, of the Convention on access to information, public participation in decision-making and access to justice in environmental matters OJ 2005 L 124/1.

85 For a list of supporting NGOs, see www.unece.org/env/pp/compliance/C2008–32/communication/SupportingNGOs.pdf.

86 Article 9(2) provides that, 'Each Party shall, within the framework of its national legislation, ensure that members of the public concerned (a) Having a sufficient interest or, alternatively, (b) Maintaining impairment of a right, where the administrative procedural law of a Party requires this as a precondition, have access to a review procedure before a court of law and/or another independent and impartial body established by law, to challenge the substantive and procedural legality of any decision, act or omission subject to the provisions of article 6 and, where so provided for under national law and without prejudice to paragraph 3 below, of other relevant provisions of this Convention.'

87 Article 9(3) provides that, 'In addition and without prejudice to the review procedures referred to in paragraphs 1 and 2 above, each Party shall ensure that, where they meet the criteria, if any, laid down in its national law, members of the public have access to administrative or judicial procedures to challenge acts and omissions by private persons and public authorities which contravene provisions of its national law relating to the environment.'

88 Article 9(4) provides that, 'In addition and without prejudice to paragraph 1 above, the procedures referred to in paragraphs 1, 2 and 3 above shall provide adequate and effective remedies, including injunctive relief as appropriate, and be fair, equitable, timely and not prohibitively expensive. Decisions under this article shall be given or recorded in writing. Decisions of courts, and whenever possible of other bodies, shall be publicly accessible.'

appropriate 'assistance mechanisms' be established to remove or reduce barriers to access to justice.[89]

The complainant pointed to the following separate alleged breaches of Article 9:

i)   the restrictive interpretation given to the concept of 'individual concern' under Article 263 TFEU;

ii) the limitations present in Regulation 1367/2006 implementing the Aarhus Convention provisions on access to information, public participation and access to justice in environmental matters in relation to EU institutions and bodies (the 'Aarhus Regulation').[90] In particular, while Articles 10–12 of that Regulation provide that NGOs[91] are entitled to make a request for internal review of an administrative act (or omission) under environmental law, and can bring a follow-on action before the EU Courts, the complainant argued that this is not sufficient to ensure access to justice because the Regulation specifies that such proceedings may be instituted 'in accordance with the relevant provisions of the Treaty'.[92] Further, such right to judicial review is not open to individuals or Member State regions, and only applies to appeals against individual acts of an administrative nature;

iii) The potentially prohibitive nature of the costs to which the losing party would be exposed in any action for judicial review at EU level.

In March 2010, the complainant, in response to a request for clarification from the Compliance Committee, confirmed that it did not view the Lisbon Treaty as bringing the EU into compliance with its Aarhus obligations.[93]

In its defence, the Commission argued that Article 9(2) of the Convention does not apply to the EU, as the EU does not, in its view, take decisions falling under Article 6 of the Convention. More broadly, in relation to Article

---

89 Article 9(5) provides that, 'In order to further the effectiveness of the provisions of this article, each Party shall ensure that information is provided to the public on access to administrative and judicial review procedures and shall consider the establishment of appropriate assistance mechanisms to remove or reduce financial and other barriers to access to justice.'

90 Regulation (EC) No 1367/2006 of the European Parliament and of the Council of 6 September 2006 on the application of the provisions of the Aarhus Convention on Access to Information, Public Participation in Decision-making and Access to Justice in Environmental Matters to Community Institutions and Bodies OJ 2006 L 264/13.

91 Article 11 provides that a qualifying NGO must meet the following conditions: (a) it is an independent non-profit-making legal person in accordance with a Member State's national law or practice; (b) it has the primary stated objective of promoting environmental protection in the context of environmental law; (c) it has existed for more than two years and is actively pursuing the objective referred to under (b); (d) the subject matter in respect of which the request for internal review is made is covered by its objective and activities.

92 *Ibid.*, Article 12.

93 Letter from ClientEarth to the Secretary to the Aarhus Convention of 1 March 2010, available at www.unece.org.

9(3), the Commission made the classic argument relied upon consistently by the EU Courts to the effect that it is not only for the EU Courts to ensure access to justice via Article 263 TFEU, but also for national courts via the Article 267 TFEU preliminary reference procedure.

The complaint raised far-reaching issues about the interplay between EU and international law, not least because the Committee was effectively being asked to adjudicate on the effectiveness of judicial protection in environmental matters within the EU before the EU Courts had themselves had an opportunity to pronounce on a number of highly relevant matters, including the scope of Article 12 of Regulation 1367/2006, the scope of Article 263(4) TFEU, and the potential effect of the post-Lisbon binding nature of the EU's Charter of Fundamental Rights.

Unsurprisingly, the Compliance Committee's first set of findings and recommendations, adopted on 14 April 2011, aimed to avoid 'jumping the gun' in this manner as far as possible. Thus, the Committee avoided making a formal finding of incompatibility with the Convention, on the ground that the EU Courts had not yet had the opportunity to rule on the effect of the Aarhus Regulation,[94] an opportunity that will arise in the pending *Stichting Natuur en Milieu and Pesticide Action Network Europe v Commission* case.[95] The Committee's April 2011 findings do not, therefore, cover the issue of the compatibility of the Aarhus Regulation with the Aarhus Convention. The Committee also avoided dealing with the compatibility of the post-Lisbon situation in relation to standing (on which, at the time of the Committee's findings, the EU Courts had yet to pronounce), focusing instead on the compatibility with Article 9(3) and (4) of the Convention of the EU Courts' test of *locus standi* applying the pre-Lisbon version of the Treaty.

Despite the limited scope of the findings, the Compliance Committee was very clear that the pre-Aarhus Regulation EU jurisprudence, which restricted standing to applicants satisfying the *Plaumann* test, would contravene Article 9(3) and (4) of the Convention as it effectively meant that no member of the public is ever able to challenge a decision on environmental or health grounds in such a case before the ECJ.[96] Nor, in the Committee's view, would the system of preliminary rulings compensate for these limitations.[97] While it avoided making a finding of incompatibility prior to the EU Courts' ruling on the Aarhus Regulation, therefore, the Committee nonetheless indicated that a 'new direction of the jurisprudence of the EU Courts should be established in order to ensure

---

94 Note Case T-16/04 *Arcelor v European Parliament and Council*, judgment of the General Court of 2 March 2010, at para. 89.

95 Case T-338/08 OJ 2008 C 301/40 (pending). See also, Case T-396/09 *Vereniging Milieudefensie and Stichting Stop Luchtverontreiniging Utrecht v Commission* OJ 2009 C 297/28, which also raises issues of interpretation of the Aarhus Regulation. The hearings for both cases before the General Court were held on 13 September 2011.

96 Case T-16/04 *Arcelor v European Parliament and Council*, judgment of the General Court of 2 March 2010, at para. 86.

97 *Ibid.*, at para. 90.

compliance with the Convention'.[98] The Committee was particularly critical of the *WWF-UK* judgments (at General Court and ECJ levels), noting its 'regret' that the EU Courts in these judgments 'did not account for the fact that the Convention had entered into force'.[99]

These findings are remarkable, and form part of a new phase in European environmental governance whereby the EU Courts can no longer accurately be viewed as the supreme instance in environmental matters within Europe. The EU's ratification of the Aarhus Convention changes matters – as does its upcoming accession to the European Convention on Human Rights (ECHR),[100] given the growing body of jurisprudence of the European Court of Human Rights (ECtHR) on environmental matters.[101] The EU, Aarhus and ECHR jurisdictions may intersect in cases where the EU finds itself before the Compliance Committee or, in the future, the ECtHR.

The potential for jurisdictional conflict is particularly evident in cases where, as with the matter before the Compliance Committee in the above instance, the question at issue is whether the jurisprudence of the EU Courts (rather than, say, EU legislation) is in compliance with the Aarhus Convention. In theory, the relationship between the Compliance Committee and the EU Courts could be described as hierarchical, in the sense that the Committee is competent to assess the legality of the EU Courts' jurisprudence under the Convention. The Committee, however, is not a 'court' and its findings not formally binding on the Parties to the Convention.[102] The reality, therefore, is more nuanced, as the Committee's findings in the EU case illustrate. While the Committee did not shirk away from stating that the EU's pre-Aarhus Regulation jurisprudence was incompatible with the Convention, it carefully avoided having to make any finding on the compatibility of EU law in its present (post-Regulation and post-Lisbon) form.[103]

98　*Ibid.*, at para. 97.

99　*Ibid*, at para. 95. The Committee expressly did not consider the question whether the *WWF* judgments in themselves constituted breaches of the Convention.

100　As made possible by the Treaty of Lisbon (Article 6(2) TEU). Negotiations for accession began in July 2010 but, at the time of writing, no accession agreement had been signed.

101　See, for instance, *Lopez Ostra v Spain* (1994) 20 EHRR 277; *Guerra v Italy* (1998) 26 EHRR 357; *Fadeyeva v Russia* [2005] ECHR 376; *Taskin v Turkey* [2006] 42 EHRR 50.

102　The compliance procedure pursuant to the Aarhus Convention is expressly *not* a judicial one, and the Compliance Committee is not a court (Article 15, Aarhus Convention), but it nonetheless has jurisdiction to make findings on how the Convention applies to individual cases brought before it. However, it is the Meeting of the Parties that ultimately has the final say on the 'appropriate measures to bring about full compliance with the Convention'. See Report of the First Meeting of the Parties to the Aarhus Convention, Addendum, Decision 1/7 Review of Compliance, ECE/MP.PP/2/Add.8, setting out the structure and functions of the Compliance Committee (esp. paras. 36 – 37). To date, the Meeting of the Parties has generally endorsed all of the Compliance Committee's findings (with certain notable exceptions: see, for instance, Communication ACCC/C/2008/24 (Spain)).

103　It should be noted that the Lisbon Treaty amendment does not in itself fully solve the concerns raised by the Committee. It certainly improves access to justice in the case of '*regulatory acts*', and therefore may rectify problems pursuant to Article 9(2) of the Aarhus Convention, which excludes bodies acting in a 'legislative capacity' from its scope (see Article 2(5) of the Convention). However, Article 9(3) of the Convention does not contain any similar limitation.

Indeed, perhaps one of the most notable features of the findings is their timing. *Prima facie*, it might have seemed natural for the Committee to have delayed publishing any findings until after the General Court's interpretation of the Aarhus Regulation in *Stichting Natuur en Milieu*.[104] The choice not to do so is significant; in fact, the Committee's findings appeared well before the oral hearing in *Stichting* (which took place in September 2011). This decision as to timing made it possible for the Committee to avoid making any declaration of non-compliance, while at the same time sending a clear signal to the EU Courts that their jurisprudence needs to change in order to avoid such a declaration in the future. The findings also contain a rather signal to the General Court that a broad interpretation of the Aarhus Regulation might in principle offer a solution to the matter ('if the examined jurisprudence of the EU Courts on access to justice were to continue, *unless fully compensated for by adequate administrative review procedures,* the Party concerned would fail to comply with article 9, paragraph 3, of the Convention … ') (emphasis added).[105] Ultimately, therefore, the Committee's findings may be viewed as an attempt to enter into a dialogue with the EU Courts,[106] deliberately avoiding direct confrontation and, with that, a hierarchical solution. In that sense, the findings are an example of multi-level, networked European environmental governance in action in the (quasi-)judicial sphere.[107]

Nonetheless, the Commission has rejected the findings outright, declaring itself 'baffled' by them and that, as no breach was found, there can be no obligation for the EU Courts to establish a new direction of jurisprudence.[108] This failure to engage with the Compliance Committee's reasoning is disappointing, particularly given the EU's own actions (via the Commission and ECJ) requiring greater access to environmental justice at national levels, discussed below. It is perhaps explicable (although not excused) by the fact that, while the Commission is charged with participating in the Compliance Committee's procedure, it is effectively powerless to remedy the breach in the present case. This task falls to the EU Courts alone or, if Treaty amendment is required, the Member States.

---

104 It should be noted that, unlike many (more) well-established international judicial dispute resolution mechanisms such as the European Court of Human Rights, there is no strict requirement that 'domestic' remedies be exhausted prior to the lodging of a complaint with the Committee. See United Nations, Guidance Document on the Aarhus Convention Compliance Committee, at p. 34 (exhaustion of domestic remedies does not constitute a 'strict requirement'; it is at the 'discretion of the Committee to decide not to examine the substance of a communication if in its view the communicant has not sufficiently explored the domestic administrative or judicial procedures, especially at times of particularly increased workload.')

105 Case T-16/04 *Arcelor v European Parliament and Council*, judgment of the General Court of 2 March 2010, para. 88.

106 Indeed, the findings are addressed to 'all relevant EU institutions' competent to 'take the steps to overcome the shortcomings reflected in the jurisprudence of the EU Courts in providing the public concerned with access to justice in environmental matters' (*ibid.*, para. 98).

107 See the discussion in the Introduction to this volume.

108 Letter from the European Commission to the Compliance Committee, 20 July 2011.

7.4.2 Access to environmental justice before national courts

In parallel to this pressure exerted by one level of environmental governance (the Compliance Committee) on the other (the EU Courts), the EU Courts have themselves been busy instructing national courts to adopt broader approaches to access to environmental justice for matters falling within the scope of EU law. This is especially evident from the ECJ's judgments in the recent cases *Lesoochranárske zoskupenie ('LZ')* and *Bund für Umwelt und Naturschutz Deutschland*, delivered in March and May 2011, respectively.[109]

Directive 2003/35 instituted a broadly two-tier approach to access to environmental justice within the EU, with matters falling within the scope of that Directive – namely, challenges to the EIA and IPPC (now Industrial Emissions) Directives – benefiting from its access to justice provisions, but matters falling outside its scope left to rely on national law rules on access to justice.[110] The EU Courts' jurisprudence has, overall, reflected this legislative distinction, interpreting Directive 2003/35 in a broad and purposive manner, but unable to make much headway in improving access to environmental justice in national courts outside the scope of that Directive, where conditions of access to justice vary significantly.[111]

The ECJ's desire to maximise the *effet utile* of the access to justice provisions of Directive 2003/35 is particularly evident in two recent judgments, *Bund für Umwelt und Naturschutz Deutschland* and *Commission v Ireland* (Case C-427/07).[112] *Bund für Umwelt und Naturschutz Deutschland* arose from German proceedings in which an environmental NGO sought to challenge an authorisation to construct and operate a coal-fired power station, on the ground that this authorisation had been granted in breach of Article 6(3) of the Habitats Directive. The question raised was whether Article 10a of the EIA Directive, which (along with the IPPC Directive)[113] is one of the few areas where the Aarhus access to justice provisions

---

109 Case C-240/09 *Lesoochranárske zoskupenie*, judgment of 8 March 2011, and Case C-115/09 *Bund für Umwelt und Naturschutz Deutschland*, judgment of 12 May 2011.

110 Directive 2003/35/EC of the European Parliament and of the Council of 26 May 2003 providing for public participation in respect of the drawing up of certain plans and programmes relating to the environment and amending with regard to public participation and access to justice Council Directives 85/337/EEC and 96/61/EC OJ 2003 L 156/17.

111 See generally, E. Pozo Vera, *An Inventory of EU Member States' Measures on Access to Justice on Environmental Matters*, study commissioned by the European Commission, June 2008, available at http://ec.europa.eu/environment, which identified Austria, Belgium, Germany and Malta as the jurisdictions with the most restrictive standing rules for civil society organisations, only permitting those parties directly affected to take action. The report identified prohibitive costs as a barrier to access to justice as a particularly acute problem in Ireland, the UK, Hungary, Italy and Latvia. It also pointed to Ireland's very limited legal aid scheme as a barrier to access to justice. See also, N. de Sadeleer et al., *Access to Justice in Environmental Matters and the Role of NGOs* (Groningen: Europa Law Publishing, 2005).

112 See the discussion in the Introduction to this volume. See also the contribution of Ryall in Chapter 9 of the present volume.

113 See now, Directive 2010/75/EU of the European Parliament and of the Council of 24 November 2010 on industrial emissions (integrated pollution prevention and control) OJ 2010 L 334/17, Article 25.

have been implemented into EU law, has direct effect in a jurisdiction such as Germany, where the claimant must normally show impairment of a substantive individual right in order to have standing to bring an action for judicial review of an administrative measure. The matter was also brought before the Compliance Committee, which stayed proceedings pending the outcome of the EU case.[114]

Following her approach in *Djurgården* (in which the Court did not have to decide the matter),[115] Advocate General Sharpston took the view that a national legal rule under which an environmental NGO seeking to challenge a decision likely to affect the environment must be able to maintain the impairment of a substantive individual right in order to enjoy *locus standi* is not compatible with Article 10a of the EIA Directive. Following its Advocate General, the Fourth Chamber of the ECJ underlined that Article 10a of the EIA Directive must be interpreted 'in the light of, and having regard to, the Aarhus Convention', with which EU law should be 'properly aligned'.[116] This Article states that environmental NGOs should be deemed to have 'rights capable of being impaired' such as to allow them access to a review procedure to challenge the legality of decisions, acts or omissions subject to the public participation provisions of that Directive. Interpreted in the light of the Aarhus Convention, the Court held this to mean that the 'rights capable of being impaired' which environmental NGOs enjoy 'must necessarily include the rules of national law implementing EU environment law and the rules of EU environment law having direct effect'.[117] This included the rules contained in Article 6 of the Habitats Directive. As a result, the German rule precluding environmental NGOs from challenging the authorisation was contrary to Article 10a of the EIA Directive.

This case is of great potential significance for those jurisdictions which typically condition standing on the existence of a right.[118] More broadly, the case demonstrates the possibilities that the Aarhus Convention can offer in cases where EU legislation (in this case, the EIA Directive) exists: in line with the EU Courts' case law in the case of international agreements concluded by the EU in non-environmental spheres, a duty of consistent interpretation arises to interpret the applicable EU law insofar as possible in conformity with the Convention and its aims.[119] The case is also of interest as an example where the Aarhus Convention's Compliance Committee chose – in contrast to

---

114 Opinion of Advocate General Sharpston of 16 December 2010 in Case C-115/09 *Bund für Umwelt und Naturschutz Deutschland.*

115 In Case C-263/08 *Djurgården* [2009] ECR I-9967, the ECJ held *inter alia* that a national measure that restricted access to a review procedure to challenge decision-making procedures under Article 2(2) of the EIA Directive to NGOs with at least 2,000 members did not allow an effective remedy and ran counter to the objectives of the EIA Directive.

116 Para. 41.

117 Para. 48.

118 For instance, Italy and Germany. See further, E. Pozo Vera, *An Inventory of EU Member States' Measures on Access to Justice on Environmental Matters,* study commissioned by the European Commission, June 2008, available at http://ec.europa.eu/environment.

119 See, for instance, Case C-53/96 *Hermès* [1998] ECR I-3603.

the EU case discussed above – to suspend its proceedings pending the outcome of an ECJ judgment.

A similar reliance on the *effet utile* of the Aarhus Convention in the context of the EIA Directive is evident in the Grand Chamber's judgment of September 2011 in *Boxus*.[120] In holding that Belgian rules whereby planning consents were 'ratified' by legislation could not *per se* exclude such consents from the scope of application of the Aarhus principles, the Court reasoned on the basis of the need to ensure the effectiveness of Article 10a of the EIA Directive and Article 9 of the Aarhus Convention.[121]

Bund für Umwelt und Naturschutz Deutschland and *Boxus* were preceded by the ECJ's 2009 ruling in *Commission v Ireland* (Case C-427/07), which demonstrates that the Court, as ever, will not tiptoe around rules which are argued to be inherent to particular legal systems (in that case, judicial discretion as to costs). In particular, the Court found Ireland's costs regime, whereby unsuccessful parties generally pay the other side's costs, subject to a judicial discretion to order otherwise, to be contrary to Article 10a of Directive 2003/35.[122] However, due to an error of pleading on the Commission's part, Ireland avoided any ruling on the compatibility of its requirement to demonstrate a 'substantial', rather than a 'sufficient', interest to challenge certain planning measures under section 50A(3) of the Irish Planning and Development Act, as well as on the compatibility of the high threshold set for judicial review of the substantive legality of acts.[123] *Commission v Ireland* led to statutory amendment of the costs rules for EIA, IPPC and SEA cases in Ireland such that unsuccessful environmental plaintiffs will not generally be obliged to pay the costs of the defendant, while defendants may be ordered to pay the costs of successful environmental plaintiffs.[124] As a result, the Commission closed its non-communication case against Ireland, while continuing its analysis of the compatibility of the legislation with EU law.[125] Subsequently, the Commission has lodged an infringement action against the UK for breach of the access to justice provisions of Directive 2003/35 due to the prohibitive expense involved in going to court in the UK.[126] This follows adverse findings by the Aarhus Convention Compliance Committee as regards the cost of accessing environmental justice in the UK, discussed further below.

---

120 Case C-128/09 *Boxus*, judgment of the Grand Chamber of 18 October 2011 (followed in Case C-182/10 *Solvay*, judgment of the Fourth Chamber of 16 February 2012).

121 *Ibid.*, para. 53.

122 Case C-427/07 *Commission v Ireland* [2009] ECR I-6277, paras. 91–94. The Court also held that Ireland had breached its obligation to provide practical information to the public on access to judicial review procedures (paras. 96–99).

123 *Ibid.*, paras 82–89.

124 See most recently the Environment (Miscellaneous Provisions) Act 2011, Part 2 and, further, the contribution of Ryall in Chapter 9 of the present volume.

125 See Commission Press Release of 10 November 2010 IP 10/1581. The Commission's case was closed prior to the most recent amendment of the relevant legislation (i.e. the Environment (Miscellaneous Provisions) Act 2011, Part 2).

126 Case C-530/11 OJ 2012 C 39/7.

While *Bund für Umwelt und Naturschutz Deutschland* and *Commission v Ireland* concerned matters falling within the scope of Directive 2003/35, the ECJ in its March 2011 judgment in *LZ* has also demonstrated its willingness to impose the requirement of effective access to environmental justice outside the scope of this Directive, by using the Aarhus Convention to interpret EU law. In *LZ*, the Grand Chamber of the ECJ considered the question whether, as a matter of EU law, Article 9(3) of the Aarhus Convention should be viewed as being directly effective in national legal orders in its own right, even in the absence of any generally applicable Directive on access to environmental justice being passed at EU level.[127] The matter arose in the context of a challenge by a Slovakian environmental NGO to the refusal on the part of the Slovak state to admit the NGO as a party to administrative proceedings concerning the grant, within Slovakia, of derogations to the system of protection, required pursuant to Article 12 of the Habitats Directive, for species such as the brown bear.[128]

Applying the Court's case law on mixed agreements, Advocate General Sharpston had taken the view that, insofar as the EU had not yet legislated on the implications of Aarhus for national provisions on access to environmental justice, the question of the direct effect of Article 9(3) in the national legal order was a matter solely for the national court. Indeed, this was the conclusion that might have seemed natural to anyone seeking to apply the Court's standard reasoning on how far the scope of EU law (and therefore the scope of the doctrine of direct effect) extends. In a complex and far-reaching judgment, however, the Grand Chamber declined to follow its Advocate General, holding that it did in fact have jurisdiction to rule on whether Article 9(3) of the Convention was directly effective. The Court reached this conclusion by reasoning that 'a specific issue which has not yet been the subject of EU legislation is part of EU law, where that issue is regulated in agreements concluded by the European Union and the Member State and it concerns a field in large measure covered by it'.[129] As the dispute at issue concerned the system of species protection required by the Habitats Directive, this test was satisfied and the matter fell within the scope of EU law.[130] The fact that no specific Directive had yet been adopted on access to environmental justice was not, therefore, decisive, as the relevant field was covered 'in large measure' (albeit not exhaustively) by EU law.[131]

This left the Court free to consider the further question whether Article 9 (3) of the Convention satisfied the conditions required to be directly effective as a matter of EU law. Here again, the Court demonstrated considerable creativity of approach in concluding that these conditions were indeed met.

---

127 Case C-240/09 *Lesoochranárske zoskupenie*, judgment of 8 March 2011. Viz. the failed Commission Proposal for a Directive on access to justice, COM (2003) 624 final.

128 For the conditions of derogation, see Article 16 of the Habitats Directive (Council Directive 92/43/EEC of 21 May 1992 on the conservation of natural habitats and of wild fauna and flora OJ 1992 L 206/7, as amended).

129 Para. 36.

130 Paras 33–38.

131 Para. 40.

The Court acknowledged that Article 9(3) of the Aarhus Convention did not contain any clear and precise obligation capable of directly regulating the legal position of individuals without subsequent implementing measures (as would normally have been required for direct effect):[132] the wording of Article 9(3) itself, after all, makes clear that the requirement of access to environmental justice pursuant to that provision is subject to meeting the 'criteria, if any' laid down in national law. Nonetheless, the Court avoided this difficulty by relying instead on the principle of effectiveness of national procedural remedies, which requires Member States to ensure that rights derived from EU law (in this case, the Habitats Directive) are effectively protected.[133] It followed that national courts were obliged, as regards a species protected by the Habitats Directive, to interpret their national procedural rules 'in a way which, to the fullest extent possible, is consistent with the objectives laid down in Article 9(3) of the Aarhus Convention'.[134]

This judgment is a significant one, demonstrating a willingness on the part of the Grand Chamber to interpret its own jurisprudence creatively with a view to furthering the objectives of access to environmental justice within the EU, even in circumstances where the EU legislator has not been able to achieve this result. In practical terms, the impact of the judgment is potentially very considerable: the Court has created a duty of consistent interpretation for national courts applying national procedural rules to interpret them in conformity with the Aarhus Convention 'to the fullest extent possible'. A comparison with the original (French) version of the text confirms the remarkably strong language employed by the Court in this regard (*'dans toute le mesure du possible'*). Indeed, the Court gave a clear indication as to what it considered the outcome of such interpretation should be in the case at hand, stating that the interpretation should be done 'so as to enable' (*'afin de permettre'*) an environmental protection organisation, such as the one at issue, to challenge before a court a decision taken following administrative proceedings liable to be contrary to EU environmental law.[135] Moreover, while the *LZ* case itself involved a question of standing of environmental NGOs, its implications are far broader, extending to *any* national procedural rule which is open to interpretation in conformity with Article 9(3), as long as the case at hand falls within the scope of EU law.[136] This would include, for instance, rules in relation to costs, where such rules make access to environmental justice impossible or excessively difficult. The full significance of *LZ*, therefore, will become clear in follow-on cases brought over the next years. However, it certainly means that EU law

132 See, e.g., Case C-265/03 *Simutenkov* [2005] ECR I-2579.
133 Paras 44–48.
134 Para. 50.
135 Para. 51.
136 See also, Article 47 of the EU Charter of Fundamental Rights, which guarantees an 'effective remedy', which applies only where the right relied on falls within the scope of EU law.

may be of some assistance in access to justice cases before national courts even in fields outside the EIA and IPPC/Industrial Emissions Directives.

The ECJ's efforts in this area must be viewed, of course, alongside the increasing number of findings of the Aarhus Convention's Compliance Committee on access to environmental justice.[137] Of particular interest from a common-law perspective are the September 2010 findings in three separate cases by the Compliance Committee that features of the UK's judicial review system fail to ensure access to environmental justice as required by Article 9 (4) of the Aarhus Convention.

In *Belfast City Airport*, the Committee found that the costs awarded against the applicant in judicial review proceedings (in that case, £39,454) were prohibitively expensive contrary to Article 9(4) of the Convention, and recommended that the UK review its system for allocating costs in judicial review applications within the scope of the Convention 'and undertake practical and legislative measures to ensure that the allocation of costs in such cases is fair and not prohibitively expensive'.[138] In the Committee's view, where a claimant was pursuing the public interest in bringing an application, this should be taken into account in allocating the costs to be paid.[139]

On the same day, the Committee adopted its findings in *Port of Tyne*, holding once again that the UK's rules on costs contravened Article 9 of the Convention.[140] In that case, the Committee criticised the fact that protective costs orders (PCOs) were, following the Court of Appeal's judgment in *Corner House*, only available in exceptional circumstances and subject to compliance with stringent conditions.[141] The fact that applicants seeking an injunction were required to provide a cross-undertaking in damages also, in the Committee's view, breached Article 9 of the Convention. Overall, the Committee emphasised that in legal proceedings within the scope of Article 9 of the Convention, the public interest nature of the proceedings was not sufficiently taken into account in allocating costs.[142] The Committee also expressed concern about the fact that only limited grounds of review were available to applicants in judicial review procedures, while refraining from holding that this breached Article 9 of the Convention.[143] Further, the Committee held that the requirement that judicial review proceedings should be brought 'promptly' breached Article 9 of the Convention, as it relied on judicial discretion to ensure compliance.[144]

---

137 At the time of writing, Ireland had just become the final EU Member State to ratify the Convention. See further, the contribution of Ryall to the present volume.
138 Communication ACCC/C/2008/27, findings adopted on 24 September 2010, at p. 10.
139 *Ibid.*, p. 9.
140 Communication ACCC/C/2008/33, findings adopted on 24 September 2010.
141 *R (Corner House Research) v Secretary of State for Trade and Industry* [2005] 1 WLR 2600.
142 Communication ACCC/C/2008/33, findings adopted on 24 September 2010, p. 30. See, however, *R (Garner) v. Elmbridge Borough Council* [2011] 1 Costs L.R. 48 (8 September 2010), which was not considered in the Compliance Committee's findings.
143 *Ibid.*, para. 127.
144 *Ibid.*, para. 139.

Finally, the Committee's findings against the UK in *Hinton Organics* were also adopted in September 2010, holding that, while the fact that the applicant in that particular case had been ordered to pay all of the costs breached Article 9 (4) of the Convention, the quantum of £5,130 was not in itself prohibitively expensive within the meaning of that provision.[145]

In the wake of these findings, the UK has entered into a consultation process on plans to institute a cost-capping scheme for cases falling within the scope of the Aarhus Convention by which, where environmental PCOs are granted, the default order would be that a cap of £5,000 would be placed on claimants' liability to pay the defendants' costs, and a cap of £30,000 on defendants' liability to pay claimants' costs.[146] This follows two reports of the working group chaired by Sullivan LJ of May 2008 and August 2010,[147] which concluded that, 'a radical change in the Civil Procedure Rules is required, one which recognises the public interest nature of environmental claims'.

It is notable that the Compliance Committee's findings in the UK cases to a significant extent mirror the Commission's arguments in the narrower context of the EIA and IPPC Directives, raising, for instance, the requirement of cross-undertakings in damages for injunctive relief (as per the Commission's action against the UK), and the 'considerable discretion of the courts' in deciding on costs awards (as per the Commission's arguments, upheld by the ECJ, in *Commission v Ireland*). The Committee's findings also echo the ECJ's approach in judgments such as *LZ*, *Commission v Ireland* and *Bund für Umwelt und Naturschutz* which, taken together, constitute major steps towards improving access to environmental justice in national courts within the sphere of EU law in circumstances where the conditions and extent of access to environmental justice presently differ substantially across the Member States. In this way, as more decisions are handed down by the Committee and as the Aarhus compliance mechanism matures, so one sees the beginning of a mutually reinforcing and supporting dialectic between the EU and Aarhus jurisdictions, of a similar kind to that which has developed over the years between the EU and Strasbourg courts. From the perspective of ensuring effective access to environmental justice, this would be an extremely promising development. Yet the Commission's refusal to accept the Committee's findings in the context of the test of *locus standi* before its own

---

145 Communication ACCC/C/2008/23, findings adopted on 24 September 2010.

146 See UK Ministry of Justice, Consultation Paper CP16/11, *Cost Protection for Litigants in Environmental Judicial Review Claims*, 19 October 2011.

147 Sullivan LJ et al., *Ensuring Access to Environmental Justice in England and Wales*, Report of May 2008 and Update Report of August 2010, available at www.unece.org/env/pp/compliance/C2008–33/correspondence/FrCAJE_updatedSullivanReport_2010.09.14.pdf. See also the Report of Jackson LJ, *Review of Civil Litigation Costs*, January 2010, which recommends a solution of 'qualified one-way costs shifting' to the problem of prohibitive costs, by which costs ordered against the claimant in, *inter alia*, judicial review claims shall 'not exceed the amount (if any) which is a reasonable one for him to pay having regard to all the circumstances including (a) the financial resources of all the parties to the proceedings; and (b) their conduct in connection with the dispute to which the proceedings relate'.

Courts, discussed above, will undoubtedly hamper this burgeoning dialectic and, more broadly, may diminish the authority of the Committee's findings.

7.5 Conclusions

It is impossible seriously to dispute that a significant improvement in environmental enforcement would have a major impact on the EU's ability to deliver on its environmental policy objectives. Yet what is also clear is that there is no silver bullet for tackling this complex area, not least because the overall level of enforcement is a factor of how well *each* of the three pillars – the European Commission, national authorities and private parties – is functioning in practice, but also because this is an area where international law, EU law and national law overlap and, at times, send out conflicting signals. In part, the complexity of the task of improving environmental enforcement within the EU is due to the fact that this requires empowering civil society to play a greater role in this area, by increasing access to environmental justice at national and EU levels. In this sense, EU environmental enforcement forms a classic instance of networked governance, whereby centralised bodies 'have become increasingly dependent upon the cooperation and joint resource mobilization of policy actors outside their hierarchical control'.[148]

While substantial efforts have been made at certain levels to improve matters in recent years – notably, by certain sections of the Commission, the EU Courts and civil society and by certain, though not all, Member States – such efforts have consistently come up against the same essential obstacle: a lack of political will to commit sufficient resources to enforcement. This is evident at EU level (lack of resources for DG Environment for bringing infringements; lack of agreement by Member States on a separate environmental enforcement agency; EU Courts' highly restrictive approach to access to justice) as well as national level (significant continuing restrictions on access to justice in many Member States, as well as restrictions on public environmental enforcers' powers and resources). At its heart, this amounts to a prioritisation of non-environmental over environmental policy goals.

Changing the status quo will not happen overnight, yet the following seem, at the very least, important steps in the right direction:[149]

---

148 See A. Jordan and A. Schout, *The Coordination of the European Union* (Oxford: Oxford University Press, 2006), at p. 6, and the emphasis of Commissioner Potočnick on 'partnership' with national authorities in implementation (note 57 *supra*). See also, Jordan, 'The Implementation of EU Environmental Policy', at p. 87, who concludes that, 'Implementation is at the sharp end of the EU policy process, where a burgeoning supranational legal order meets a decentralised policy delivery system dominated by states.'

149 See, for a comparison of pressing issues in environmental enforcement from the late 1990s, the analogous 'wish lists' in the conclusions of Jordan, 'The implementation of EU environmental policy' and of Dillon, 'The mirage of EC environmental federalism in a reluctant member state jurisdiction'. A comparison of those lists with the present list demonstrates that progress in this area in the interim has been remarkably slow, but not non-existent.

- a commitment from the Commission that it will not renege on its duty to ensure the application of EU environmental law in non-priority areas, and that it will examine Member State responses under the EU Pilot scheme thoroughly prior to dismissing a complaint. In practice, this will necessitate a commitment to invest additional resources in the units responsible for enforcement and compliance within DG Environment;
- a willingness by Member States to accede to a certain level of minimum harmonisation in key areas of environmental enforcement by national authorities, such as inspections in relation to the application of all major pieces of legislation;
- a willingness on the part of the EU to engage with the findings of the Aarhus Convention's Compliance Committee in relation to access to environmental justice before its own courts. Adopting a position of denial would be counter-productive, risking seriously damaging the Committee's authority and, with it, the authority of a vital instrument of international environmental law;
- a confirmation by the EU Courts in cases such as *Stichting Natuur en Milieu and Pesticide Action Network Europe v Commission*[150] that, at the least, qualifying environmental NGOs under the Aarhus Regulation have the right to challenge decisions taken pursuant to internal review, without the need to satisfy any further standing tests;
- a continuation on the part of the EU Courts of the drive to improve access to environmental justice at national levels as witnessed by judgments such as *LZ*, *Commission v Ireland* and *Bund für Umwelt und Naturschutz*;[151]
- ultimately, the passing of a Directive (whether or not in the form of the 2003 proposal)[152] ensuring a minimum level of access to environmental justice in all Member States.

7.6 Postscript

On 14 June 2012, the General Court handed down its judgments in Case T-338/08 *Stichting Natuur en Milieu, Pesticide Action Network Europe v Commission* and Case T-396/09 *Vereniging Milieudefensie and Stichting Stop Luchtverontreiniging Utrecht v Commission*. In finding against the Commission, the Court ruled that Article 10(1) of the EU's Aarhus Regulation is unlawful, in so far as it limits the concept of 'acts' in Article 9(3) of the Aarhus Convention to 'administrative act(s)', defined in Article 2(1)(g) of the Aarhus Regulation as 'measure(s) of individual scope'. The implications of the judgments for access to justice within the EU are far-reaching, and they are currently under appeal by the Commission to the ECJ.

---

150 Case T-16/04 *Arcelor v European Parliament and Council*, judgment of the General Court of 2 March 2010, para. 89.

151 See the discussion in the Introduction to this volume and Case C-128/09 *Boxus*, judgment of the Grand Chamber of 18 October 2011.

152 See note 127.

8 Commission enforcement of EU environmental legislation in Ireland

A 20-year retrospective

*Liam Cashman**

8.1 Introduction

Ireland's membership of what has become the European Union broadly coincides with the emergence and development of a European environmental *acquis*. Despite this, Ireland's environment has benefited only belatedly or incompletely from the safeguards put in place at EU level.

The period since the 1970s has been marked by, amongst other problems, a serious decline in the extent of pristine water bodies, widespread bacteriological contamination of drinking water, lack of timely compliance with urban waste-water treatment requirements, inadequate protection of wildlife sites and endangered species, and impact-assessment rules that are left without a meaning in practice.

As guardian of the Treaty, the European Commission has had to address these problems, just as it has had to address comparable problems elsewhere. In doing so, the Commission has adapted its policy and practice over time, both to respond to Irish specificities[1] and to follow a broader direction that encompasses other Member States.[2]

8.2 The Irish environment

Ireland is a middle-sized European country located entirely within the Atlantic biogeographical region,[3] reflecting its wet, temperate climate. There are abundant freshwater and groundwater resources. Terrestrial vegetation cover and habitat types are typical of the wetter part of the region, including, for example, an

---

* The author is a Commission official. The views expressed are entirely personal and do not represent those of the Commission or any of its services.

1 Systemic problems associated with peat extraction on protected sites are largely specific to Ireland.

2 The importance that is given to the conformity of national implementing legislation extends to all Member States.

3 For purposes of habitat protection under the Habitats Directive, Council Directive 92/43/EEC of 21 May 1992 on the conservation of natural habitats and of wild fauna and flora OJ 1992 L 206/7, as amended, Europe has been divided into several biogeographic regions. This reflects a wish to have, on the one hand, a broadly consistent approach across frontiers and, on the other, a recognition of the habitat differences that result from climatic variations.

extensive surface area of blanket bog. The country has a large off-shore area and is significant for the conservation of whales and dolphins and cold-water reefs. Over the ten thousand or so years of human settlement, vegetation cover has been greatly altered by humans. Clearance for agriculture means that Ireland now has one of the smallest percentages of native woodland of any Member State.

Agriculture is by far the dominant land-use. Much of the country consists of a patchwork of fields enclosed by hedgerows or – more rarely – stone boundaries. Notwithstanding the disappearance of native woodland, traditional low-intensity farming has had its compensations – species-rich grassland, for instance, and practices that allowed species such as the corncrake to thrive.

The period since accession has been one of agricultural intensification. Many environmental pressures stem from the presence of high livestock numbers. During the 1980s, fragile and unstable upland peat soils came to be severely eroded as a result of very heavy stocking with sheep. Changing patterns of husbandry, in particular, winter livestock housing, have generated large volumes of slurry for land-spreading. This, combined with more intensive forms of grassland management – involving greater levels of fertilisation – has increased nutrient run-off into rivers and lakes. At the same time, the countryside has become much less hospitable to species such as the corncrake which have been unable to adapt to new agricultural practices.

Afforestation and peat extraction are other activities that have had major surface area impacts from the middle of the twentieth century to date.

During this period, a drive to increase forest cover has transformed many semi-natural areas or areas of marginal agricultural importance into plantation forests. Although sometimes discussed as though they were indistinguishable, plantation forests, overwhelmingly made up of North American conifers, are very different from the broadleaved indigenous woodland that represented Ireland's original forest estate. Drainage, fertilisation and encroachment associated with these plantations have been a major factor in the loss of intact peatlands and a decline in the quality of pristine rivers and streams.

Since time immemorial, Ireland's peatlands have been subject to local-scale exploitation as a fuel source. However, up to modern times, very extensive tracts of intact raised bog – the deep, dome-shaped areas of peat typical of the Irish midlands – survived. Beginning in the 1930s, a state company, Bord Na Móna, has largely destroyed these through industrial extraction for fuel and horticultural peat. Mechanised exploitation outside of the state sector continues to damage and reduce the active[4] raised bogs that remain.

Other activities with a significant transformative impact include quarrying and aquaculture.

As for settlements and infrastructure, Irish land-use policy – or, perhaps more accurately, practice – has favoured dispersed settlement in the countryside. One-off houses figure prominently in new construction over the past twenty

---

4 That is, still capable of laying down new peat.

years. The significance of one-off houses is evident in an estimated 400,000 septic tanks – and in the number of small drinking water supplies, which runs to several hundred. Widespread bacteriological contamination of the groundwater relied on by many of these supplies makes the provision of safe drinking water a considerable challenge.

Over the past twenty years, Ireland has sought to catch up with other Member States, making major investments in roads, drinking water supplies, waste-water collection and treatment, and waste facilities. Linear infrastructure such as new motorways has criss-crossed the landscape. Very significant low-density urban expansion has been noted by the European Environment Agency, especially in the hinterland of Dublin.

8.3 Parts of the *acquis* of special relevance to Ireland

Space does not allow full justice to be done to a very extensive *acquis* but the following instruments deserve particular mention:

- *Impact Assessment Directive (Directive 85/337/EEC) and Strategic Environmental Assessment Directive (Directive 2001/42/EC).*[5] These seek to incorporate an element of environmental foresight into decision-making across a very wide range of project types and plans. The project categories include ones with special significance in an Irish context – afforestation and peat extraction, for example. The required assessments relate to a very broad concept of the environment: in addition to nature and the environmental media, they cover aspects of the cultural heritage such as archaeologically significant landscapes. The required assessment procedures include public consultation and there are related access-to-justice provisions introduced by Directive 2003/35/EC to align EU law with the Aarhus Convention.[6] The latter promotes public participation, access to information and access to justice in the field of the environment. The preventive requirements have proved incompatible with the permissive approach that Ireland has sought to retain for many forms of physical development.
- *Access to Information Directive (Directive 2003/4/EC).*[7] This provides for the disclosure on request, and in some cases the active dissemination, of environmental

---

5 Council Directive 85/337/EEC of 27 June 1985 on the assessment of the effects of certain public and private projects on the environment OJ 1985 L 175/40; Directive 2001/42/EC of the European Parliament and of the Council of 27 June 2001 on the assessment of the effects of certain plans and programmes on the environment OJ 2001 L 197/30.

6 Directive 2003/35/EC of the European Parliament and of the Council of 26 May 2003 providing for public participation in respect of the drawing up of certain plans and programmes relating to the environment and amending with regard to public participation and access to justice Council Directives 85/337/EEC and 96/61/EC OJ 2003 L 156/17.

7 Directive 2003/4/EC of the European Parliament and of the Council of 28 January 2003 on public access to environmental information and repealing Council Directive 90/313/EEC OJ 2003 L 41/26.

information held by public authorities. It replaces an earlier directive, Directive 90/313/EEC.[8] Until the adoption of Ireland's own Freedom of Information Act, the earlier directive served to open up an Irish administration traditionally averse to putting information and documents into the public domain.

- *Wild Birds Directive (Directive 2009/147, previously Directive 79/409/EEC).*[9] This covers all naturally occurring wild bird species. It requires Member States to control hunting, establish a network of special protection areas (SPAs) for migratory species and listed resident species and adopt conservation measures in the wider countryside.
- *Habitats Directive (Directive 92/43/EEC).*[10] This foresees the creation of a Europe-wide network of protected nature sites called Natura 2000. Examples of Irish habitat types and species earmarked for protection include active blanket bogs, active raised bogs, old oak woodland, limestone pavement, grey sand dunes and the freshwater pearl mussel, *Margaritifera margaritifera*.
- *Drinking Water Directive (Directive 98/83/EC, previously Directive 80/778/EEC).*[11] This sets standards for the drinking water supplied to consumers, including a requirement that drinking water be completely free of bacteria. There are public information requirements and requirements to address supply-quality problems.
- *Nitrates Directive (Directive 91/676/EEC).*[12] This aims at reducing nitrate pollution from agricultural sources. Its rationale is that the amount of artificial and organic fertilisers applied to land should not exceed crop needs or contribute to water pollution. Translating this rationale into practice can be challenging, especially where intensive livestock farming generates more waste than can be safely used on the land-holding concerned.[13] Where waters are affected or likely to be affected by nitrate pollution, Member States are required to designate the areas draining into them as nitrate vulnerable zones; alternatively they can treat their whole territory as requiring pollution controls. In nitrate vulnerable zones, the Directive prohibits land-spreading of organic fertilisers such as slurry during winter months – when pollution risks are greatest. As a consequence, there must be sufficient storage for animal wastes. Although specifically targeted at nitrates, the Directive

---

8 Council Directive 90/313/EEC of 7 June 1990 on the freedom of access to information on the environment OJ 1990 L 158/56.

9 Directive 2009/147 of the European Parliament and the Council on the conservation of wild birds, OJ 2010 L20/7; Council Directive 79/409/EEC of 2 April 1979 on the conservation of wild birds OJ 1979 L 103/1.

10 Council Directive 92/43/EEC on the conservation of natural habitats and of wild flora and fauna, OJ 1992, L 206/7.

11 Council Directive 98/83/EC of 3 November 1998 on the quality of water intended for human consumption OJ 1998 L 330/32; Council Directive 80/778/EEC of 15 July 1980 relating to the quality of water intended for human consumption OJ 1980 L 229/11.

12 Council Directive 91/676/EEC of 12 December 1991 concerning the protection of waters against pollution caused by nitrates from agricultural sources OJ 1991 L 375/1.

13 See further the contribution of Joseph McMahon in Chapter 5 of this volume.

indirectly serves to reduce pollution from another nutrient, phosphorous, since this too is found in the animal wastes that are subject to controls. In many Irish river catchments, agriculture is the main source of phosphorous and the main cause of freshwater eutrophication.

- *Urban Waste Water Treatment Directive (Directive 91/271/EEC).*[14] This complements the Nitrates Directive by requiring that larger human settlements, referred to as agglomerations, collect and treat urban waste water – the other main source of nutrient pollution. Inadequate treatment of urban waste water has been one of the chief causes of water quality problems in Irish rivers, lakes and coastal waters.

- *Water Framework Directive (Directive 2000/60/EC) and precursor instruments.*[15] This creates an overarching system – involving water quality objectives, monitoring, river basin management plans, programmes of measures and stakeholder involvement – aimed at ensuring that all water bodies enjoy good water quality. Its water pricing provisions have a particular topicality, given recent Irish Government moves to introduce domestic water charges (the current absence of such charges is an instance, by no means the only one, of Ireland's exceptionalism in relation to the *acquis*). The Directive builds on the earlier Dangerous Substances Directive (Directive 76/464/ EEC, later Directive 2006/11/EC).[16] Much of the content of Ireland's recent river basin management plans under the Water Framework Directive reflects measures adopted to comply with the earlier instrument (after Commission litigation).[17] These include water-quality objectives specific to rivers designated for the protection of the freshwater pearl mussel, one of Ireland's most pollution-sensitive aquatic species.

- *Waste Framework Directive (originally Directive 75/442/EEC, now Directive 2008/98/EC).*[18] This establishes a basic set of rules for the safe disposal and treatment of waste. Unauthorised disposal is prohibited. Disposal and recovery operations must be carried out under permit and without harm to the environment and human health. Waste collectors need to be registered or authorised. Member States must inspect and control waste operations and waste collection. The polluter pays principle is incorporated in a clause requiring that the holders of waste pay for its disposal.

---

14 Council Directive 91/271/EEC of 21 May 1991 concerning urban waste-water treatment OJ 1991 L 135/40.

15 Directive 2000/60/EC of the European Parliament and of the Council of 23 October 2000 establishing a framework for Community action in the field of water policy OJ 2000 L 327/1.

16 Council Directive 76/464/EEC of 4 May 1976 on pollution caused by certain dangerous substances discharged into the aquatic environment of the Community OJ 1976 L 129/23; Directive 2006/11/EC of the European Parliament and of the Council of 15 February 2006 on pollution caused by certain dangerous substances discharged into the aquatic environment of the Community OJ 2006 L 64/52.

17 See Case C-282/02, *Commission v Ireland* [2005] ECR I-4656.

18 Council Directive 75/442/EEC of 15 July 1975 on waste OJ 1975 L 194/39; Directive 2008/98/EC of the European Parliament and of the Council of 19 November 2008 on waste and repealing certain Directives OJ 2008 L 312/3.

- *Landfill Directive (Directive 99/31/EC).*[19] This complements the Waste Framework Directive by setting detailed standards for the operation of landfills. Requirements include provisions for the diversion of biodegradable waste – which generates polluting methane gas. The Directive is important in an Irish context given the country's reliance on landfills.

8.4 Commission work on implementation and enforcement: evolution from an *ad hoc* to a more strategic approach

Commission enforcement work on the environment has had a strategic own-initiative aspect from the 1980s on. More specifically, it has consistently addressed the lack of transposition of directives into national law, with infringement proceedings systematically opened against Member States for failing to notify binding measures on time. At the outset, this put a spotlight on an Irish practice – since discontinued – of resorting to circular letters rather than binding legislation.

Such own-initiative enforcement was limited in scope and ambition and, in the late 1980s, the Commission took an interest in citizen complaints as a means of ascertaining how well the *acquis* was being implemented in practice.

The volume of complaints grew rapidly and, by the mid-1990s, complaints about the environment dominated the Commission's overall complaint load. Ireland accounted for a disproportionately high number relative to its population size. Submissions came from a broad cross-section of society – individuals, local communities, NGOs, and occasionally business interests.

Complaints about chronic winter smog in Dublin, the result of widespread use of bituminous coal for home-heating, represent an early example from the 1980s. Over subsequent years, complaints were received on a plethora of concerns: threats to important wildlife sites from proposed infrastructure projects; micro-biological contamination of drinking water; nutrient enrichment of rivers and lakes from agricultural run-off and untreated sewage; encroachment of monocrop forestry plantations into blanket bog; uncontrolled quarrying and peat extraction; erosion of uplands as a result of sheep overgrazing; destruction of limestone pavement in the Burren; and polluting local authority tipheads. A significant number concerned projects or activities benefiting from EU funding.

In addition to complaints sent directly to the Commission, a steady stream of environmental petitions was directed to the European Parliament's Petitions Committee.

The propensity to submit complaints to the Commission has persisted. At the end of 2010, Ireland still accounted for a disproportionately high number of registrations in the new Commission complaint registration system, CHAP.

The early tendency – not only with regard to Ireland – was for Commission enforcement to be *ad hoc*. Where complaints focused on an isolated breach, so

19 Council Directive 1999/31/EC of 26 April 1999 on the landfill of waste OJ 1999 L 182/1.

too did the Commission's response. This is evident in the case-law of the European Court of Justice (ECJ) – for example, Case C-355/90 *Commission* v *Spain*[20] concerns the failure to classify a single Spanish wetland, Santoña Marshes, under the Wild Birds Directive and Case C-45/91 *Commission v Hellenic Republic*[21] concerns the failure to regulate properly a single landfill on the island of Crete.

Several factors contributed to a gradual shift towards a more strategic approach.

To begin, some complaints were themselves strategic in character; for example, a complaint on Irish drinking water focused on the entire supply network of approximately 1000 public and private supplies.

Further, a number of complaints raised the issue of the way in which national legislation transposed directives; for example, Ireland's initial transposition of the Environmental Impact Assessment Directive was followed by complaints focusing on defects in the statutory instruments concerned. This coincided with a growing Commission recognition that the quality of national transposing measures needed to be systematically checked in order to ensure that objectives agreed at European level were not diluted or disregarded at national level.

Independently of complaints, the Commission realised that the implementation of directives varied widely. Certain directives became the subject of Commission studies – for example, to verify whether Member States had correctly fulfilled the zoning requirements of the Nitrates Directive. The study prepared for Ireland challenged Ireland's approach of not recognising any parts of the country as being vulnerable to nitrate pollution from agriculture – and of not having in place the mandatory controls that must accompany the designation of nitrate vulnerable zones.

Individual complaints began to disclose wider patterns of deficient – or absent – oversight and accountability. For example, a succession of complaints highlighted poorly managed local authority waste disposal sites – and, coincident with an upsurge in private waste disposal activities, private waste sites as well. Examples included the tiphead for Limerick at Longpavement beside the River Shannon – which spilled waste into the river – and the tiphead for Tramore in County Waterford which – with the acquiescence of the Irish Environmental Protection Agency (EPA) – encroached without authorisation into the internationally important wetland at Tramore Back Strand.

Some individual complaints had a prophetic or early-warning character. A complaint from County Wicklow in the late 1990s drew attention to an absence of controls on private waste collection. Examination of the Irish legislation confirmed that, contrary to the Waste Framework Directive, waste collectors were not subject to registration or authorisation or related controls. The full seriousness of this weakness only became evident with the uncovering a few years later of significant illegal trafficking in Irish domestic waste – collected

---

20 [1993] ECR I-4221.
21 [1992] ECR I-2509.

by private waste collectors and clandestinely transferred for illegal disposal in Northern Ireland. The sequel is still unfolding with the Irish taxpayer having to meet the cost of repatriating the waste under EU trans-frontier waste shipment rules.

The scale of the implementation gap highlighted the infeasibility of tackling it in a piecemeal way. For example, the number of important bird areas left unclassified across the EU was too high to allow for each one to be addressed individually as the Santoña Marshes had been.

The European *acquis* continued to grow, adding to the number of instruments that the Commission had to monitor. At the same time, the longer laws were in place, the less excusable became an absence of intended results. Implementation was increasingly stressed in policy documents. As a small organisation, the Commission needed to reflect on how to undertake its guardianship role more efficiently.

The Commission is used to developing initiatives at a European scale – that is part of its *raison d'être*. Taking account of a political and legal imperative to better integrate environmental protection into other policy areas, during the 1990s it put an increased emphasis on strategic initiatives to support the environmental *acquis* – notably, agri-environmental spending to support nature conservation and spending under the Regional and Cohesion Funds to establish environmental infrastructure.

The strategic approach ultimately found expression in a Commission communication on implementation adopted in 2008,[22] the policy contained in which, had before then come to be reflected in the case-law, including decisions concerning Ireland.[23]

8.5 Difficulties encountered by the Commission in respect of Ireland

It is understandable that academic interest in Commission enforcement is often based on analysis of case-law. Case-law represents a public record of disputes and a structured and reasoned endorsement or rejection of the Commission's approach by the other key EU institution involved in enforcement. However, obtaining ECJ rulings is seldom the Commission's primary objective and most enforcement activities result in outcomes other than court decisions. Furthermore, time-lags mean that court decisions are usually delivered long after a problem has first been encountered.

It was only in 1999 that the first ECJ judgment against Ireland was handed down,[24] i.e. almost at the mid-point in this twenty-year retrospective, but the

---

22 COM (2008) 773.
23 See, for example, Case C-494/01 *Commission v Ireland* [2005] ECR I-3331 which illustrates how the Commission addresses a systemic failure in the implementation of rules.
24 Case C-392/96 *Commission v Ireland* [1999] ECR I-5901.

preceding period was marked by significant exchanges, with Commission interventions being a factor in several Irish reforms. In 1990, for example, Ireland's European presidency – which had been announced as a 'green' presidency – saw the outlawing of use of bituminous coal in Dublin. A Commission infringement for breach of European air-quality norms had already been launched and the coal ban allowed this to be closed. Similarly, the 1996 Waste Management Act resolved an important infringement concerning the absence of a requirement for Irish local authority waste sites to hold a waste permit.

By the late 1990s, however, it was apparent that, under several headings, insufficient progress was being made.

8.5.1 *Quality of national implementing legislation*

As an initial Commission focus on the form of transposing legislation gave way to a more critical focus on content, Ireland became more reluctant to respond with legislative change. In particular, a willingness to replace circular letters with primary legislation or (more commonly) statutory instruments was not matched by a similar willingness to revisit binding legislation once this was adopted.

Many of the non-conformity difficulties have related to national rules that leave the intended scope of European provisions without a meaning in practice. Such rule-making might be considered to follow a 'business-as-usual' rationale. The need to transpose is respected in terms of there being a rule to satisfy the requirements of outward form, but the rule as designed carries no practical consequences for the sectors ostensibly addressed: it is hollow. For example, the first non-conformity ruling in 1999 related to national rules for the impact assessment of afforestation and peat extraction that, in practice, left projects within these categories completely unconstrained by the need to assess environmental impacts, or consult the public, in advance.

Perhaps reflecting this underlying rationale, a pattern formed of Ireland allowing Commission proceedings for non-conformity of legislation to take their course. The first judgment in 1999 was followed by others until Ireland became subject to one of the highest number of ECJ decisions on the environment.

Ireland is not, of course, the only Member State to allow Commission non-conformity proceedings to take their course, but – amongst new Member States in particular – there is now a marked tendency to try to resolve non-conformity problems in the pre-litigation phase.

Factors that have differentiated Ireland include an absence within the Department of the Environment and Local Government of the corps of environmental lawyers typically found in environmental ministries elsewhere. Although the Department has drawn on legal advice from the Attorney General's office, which leads Ireland's defence in the Court of Justice, the lack of in-house legal expertise has arguably slowed the process of recognising and responding to transposition shortcomings. A further differentiating factor is an internal departmental management weakness[25] in timely delivery on commitments sometimes offered during the pre-litigation phase – and indeed the Article 260 TFEU phase. Several ECJ judgments concern legislative defects that were the subject of promised action that simply never materialised.[26]

8.5.2 Reluctance to recognise areas needing special environmental management

Four ECJ rulings against Ireland relate to a failure to recognise areas for environmental management purposes.

The ruling of 11 September 2001 in Case C-67/99[27] concerns Ireland's failure to propose a meaningful set of sites for the conservation of Europe's most endangered habitat types and species under the Habitats Directive. Ireland's contribution was due in 1995 but remained the most nugatory of any Member State when the Commission court proceedings were lodged.

The factors that caused the delay are worth noting. Unlike almost all other Member States, Ireland did not have a territorially significant existing network of national parks and protected nature sites to begin with. Put bluntly, Ireland since independence showed scant interest in protecting its natural heritage. An inventory of areas of scientific interest – modelled on Britain's sites of special scientific interest – was compiled during the 1970s by an environmental research body, An Foras Forbartha, but the expected national statutory regime to protect the sites concerned never materialised. The status of the inventory fell victim to judicial review because of lack of landowner consultation and An Foras Forbartha was abolished in 1993, being replaced by the Environmental Protection Agency (which however did not take up its predecessor's role in habitat identification).[28] A later effort to create a statutory network of Natural Heritage Areas (NHAs) also faltered, with the only NHA orders to date being adopted to help resolve an ECJ ruling.[29]

The establishment of an Irish contribution to Natura 2000 therefore had little to build on in terms of a pre-existing statutory network or a recognised need to protect. Using Community funds, Ireland's National Parks and Wildlife Service (NPWS) reviewed the earlier inventory and compiled a new one but formalisation of this encountered the same factors that had militated against any meaningful national protection – landowner mistrust and resulting political

---

25 Not confined to the Irish Department of the Environment, Community and Local Government.

26 See, for example, Case C-418/04 *Commission v Ireland* [2007] ECR I-10947 which *inter alia* concerns several shortcomings in Irish nature legislation. The nature legislation in question had long been subject to intended revision but this did not materialise until 2011.

27 Case C-67/99 *Commission v Ireland* [2001] ECR I-5757.

28 S.I. No. 215/1993—Environmental Protection Agency Act, 1992 (Dissolution of An Foras Forbartha Teoranta) Order, 1993.

29 Case C-392/96, *op. cit.* NHA orders were adopted in respect of a set of peatlands to operationalise certain EIA rules.

caution. The Irish authorities sought to achieve domestic acceptance by, on the one hand, instituting a non-statutory appeals mechanism for landowners and, on the other, targeting European agri-environmental payments at the selected sites. However, the process dragged on for over a decade.

Similar factors were at work in Case C-418/04,[30] which, to a significant extent, concerns a failure to classify SPAs under the Wild Birds Directive. Despite the fact that the duty to classify was supposed to have been met in 1981, Ireland still had the tiniest and most incomplete SPA network of any of the EU-15 Member States when the ECJ pronounced in 2007 – indeed, nearly all of the Member States that acceded in 2004 had already by then surpassed Ireland in classification coverage.

There were corresponding delays in recognising areas for purposes of better controlling water pollution.

At the time that the Commission made its referral in Case C-396/01[31] Ireland was the only Member State not to have recognised any part of its territory as requiring mandatory control measures under the Nitrates Directive. Ireland's approach reflected a wider reluctance to impose mandatory environmental measures on the farming sector.

Similarly, Case C-148/05[32] reflects the mismatch between Ireland's development of a shellfish industry and its willingness to recognise areas used for shellfish culture in order to prevent or reduce water pollution.

Although the matter was ultimately resolved without need for a Court judgment, Ireland was initially reluctant to recognise a significant number of sensitive areas for purposes of the Urban Waste Water Treatment Directive.

8.5.3 Environmental infrastructure deficits

The Urban Waste Water Directive requires Member States to collect and treat urban waste water by set deadlines related to the sensitivity of the receiving water and the size of the settlement. So far as Ireland is concerned, the first deadline expired at the end of 1998, the second at the end of 2000 and the final one at the end of 2005. Despite heavy investments, many co-financed, Ireland struggled to comply. Certain – but far from all – compliance delays are reflected in the Court ruling in Case C-316/06,[33] which found that six Irish agglomerations had missed the 2000 deadline. The Commission's action was part of a wider exercise that took in other Member States, and the Court ruling against Ireland is not unique.

Inadequate infrastructure for supplying drinking water is reflected in the Court ruling in Case C-316/00.[34] This found that, across Ireland's extensive

---

30 Case C-418/04 *Commission v Ireland* [2007] ECR I-10947.
31 Case C-396/01 *Commission v Ireland* [2003] ECR I-2315.
32 Case C-148/05 *Commission v Ireland* [2007] ECR I-82.
33 Case C-316/06 *Commission v Ireland* [2008] ECR I-124.
34 Case C-316/00 *Commission v Ireland* [2002] ECR I-10527.

supply network, there were chronic problems of non-compliance with the microbiological parameters set out in the Drinking Water Directive. These problems reflected source contamination, underinvestment in treatment and monitoring equipment and poor or absent management and supervision.

A final judgment of note in relation to inadequate environmental infrastructure is Case C-494/01,[35] which followed an underinvestment in waste facilities to treat Irish domestic waste. The background to the Commission litigation was one of Ireland's reliance on a large – if steadily reducing – number of local tipheads that were usually poorly engineered and managed and often located on environmentally sensitive wetlands. There are close parallels with the situation in new Member States prior to accession: in these too, the past decade has been marked by a process of radical reduction in the number of individual waste disposal sites and the emergence of networks consisting of fewer and larger landfills.

8.5.4 Reluctance to put in place effective oversight and enforcement mechanisms

For problems such as infrastructure deficits, the question arises as to why Commission enforcement action should be necessary at all, given that the relevant requirements ought to be subject to adequate oversight and enforcement requirements at national level.

It was steadily borne in on the Commission that, in Ireland, effective oversight and enforcement mechanisms were lacking.

Historically, responsibility for environmental infrastructure has rested with Irish local authorities. The environmental functions of these have their roots in pre-independence Victorian sanitary legislation that is still vestigially extant.[36] From Victorian times, local authorities collected rubbish, disposed of it at tipheads, collected and – to a limited extent – treated waste water, and took care of supplying drinking water to the larger settlements. In the 1960s, they acquired responsibilities in relation to land-use planning.

During the 1970s, the revenue-raising powers of local authorities were curtailed as a result of abolition of domestic rates, and, later, water charges. Local authorities became more dependent on central government transfers, especially for infrastructure. So far as compliance with EU law is concerned, this created a problem of accountability. Typically, the Department of Environment and Local Government transposed relevant legal requirements by placing responsibility for their compliance on local authorities. Although the Department retained control of funding, the minister was statutorily shielded from any domestic legal responsibility. The result was that, domestically, the

---

35 Case C-494/01 *Commission v Ireland* [2005] ECR I-3331.
36 Ireland sought to rely on Victorian sanitary legislation in Case C-188/08 *Commission v Ireland* [2009] ECR I-172.

minister – and Department – could treat lack of compliance as being exclusively a matter for the local authorities, while the latter could treat themselves, financially at least, as departmental dependencies.

A further problem was an absence of oversight at an operational level.

Between the 1970s and 1990s, significant administrative changes occurred. In the 1970s, the Planning Appeals Board was set up to process appeals from local authority land-use decisions. In the 1990s, the EPA was set up to take care of licensing of industrial plants and state-of-the-environment reporting. The Agency's statute provided for a limited oversight role in respect of local authorities.

Notwithstanding these changes, local authorities were essentially free agents in terms of how they managed their infrastructure. No prior authorisation requirements – or corresponding controls – applied. Sub-standard facilities and poor performance could go unchallenged.

The Commission was in a position to directly challenge infrastructure deficits and did so. As *de facto* interlocutor, the Department of the Environment and Local Government was obliged to confront problems that had been statutorily side-stepped at domestic level. The missing infrastructure was itself the subject of Commission enforcement, but the Commission also addressed the account-ability deficit. It contended that, under the Waste Framework Directive, it was necessary for local authority waste facilities to hold a waste permit and be subject to external inspection. This was eventually conceded in the Waste Management Act, 1996. Later, the Commission contended that the waste-water discharges of local authorities ought to be authorised under the Dangerous Substances Directive. Following a Court judgment in the Commission's favour,[37] an authorisation regime was introduced. In both instances, the EPA became the licensing authority.

Hollow national rules are one reason why commitments made at EU level go unfulfilled. Another is that, even where rules appear satisfactory, effective administration may be lacking.

The case-law concerning Ireland provides several illustrations. Although the EPA assumed responsibility for licensing and controlling local authority waste facilities, in practice it operated a licensing 'go-slow' policy. Facilities were left in a legal limbo, with licence applications submitted but not decided. This may have been the result of a pragmatic calculation that, before any licensing decision was taken, such facilities would close. The problem was that this prolonged the period of unaccountability – new landfill cells were constructed without authorisation at Tramore on previously undeveloped salt marshes, for instance. The Commission decided to address this by way of an infringement that argued that implementation of the Waste Framework Directive was characterised by systemic failures.[38]

---

37 Case C-282/02 *Commission v Ireland* [2005] ECR I-4653.
38 Case C-494/01 *Commission v Ireland* [2005] ECR I-3331.

The failure to enforce statutory requirements was a much wider phenomenon highlighted by complainants and petitioners. This failure has had many dimensions:

- failure of local authorities to seriously investigate illegal waste sites, quarries and other unauthorised developments;
- local authority conflicts of interest, in particular in relation to quarries. In their role as enforcement bodies, local authorities were supposed to control quarrying – *inter alia* for purposes of the Environmental Impact Assessment Directive. At the same time, in their capacity as road developers, local authorities were major customers of aggregate suppliers;
- failure to employ any serious sanctions to deter illegal development. Although Irish environmental codes allow for hefty criminal sanctions, in practice criminal enforcement – to the extent that it took place at all – took place at the level of Ireland's District Courts where the maximum penalties are very low. Only the Director of Public Prosecutions had entitlement to prosecute in the higher courts but in practice did not do so;
- absence of, or serious delays in, any resort to civil remedies such as injunctions;
- the existence of a range of statutory devices to facilitate illegal developments. These included provision for retrospective development consent for projects already executed in whole or in part,[39] and a statute of limitations that allowed inactive local authorities to eventually plead that the possibility for enforcement action was statute-barred.

This phenomenon of circumvention at the stage of application has been – and still is – very difficult for the Commission to address.

8.5.5 Obstacles to an effective role for civil society

The drawn-out Commission enforcement process is open to criticism. However, the Commission cannot itself compel an unwilling Member State to comply. It must lodge proceedings and bears the burden of proof in doing so. An examination of the case-law on what is termed 'bad application' – i.e. inadequate implementation in practice – shows just how heavy that burden can be, and hints at how much time and effort may be required to satisfy it, especially for a small organisation like the Commission without any environmental inspection powers. Member States reluctant to take measures can rely on this, especially where there are few domestic deterrents – such as an effective system of judicial review.

Within this context, EU law has sought to facilitate private enforcement through case-law doctrine, environmental rights legislation and, more recently, the Treaty-endorsed Charter of Fundamental Rights.

---

39 So-called 'retention permission' under Irish planning legislation.

Ireland's exceptionalism in this area has been pronounced.

To begin, for an extended period, Ireland was the only Member State out of twenty-seven not to have ratified the Aarhus Convention, ratification only being completed in June 2012.

It was also the only Member State to introduce participatory fees for members of the public wishing to participate in development consent procedures. A Commission ECJ challenge to this failed in respect of Directive 85/337/EEC before it was aligned with the Aarhus Convention through Directive 2003/35/EC.[40]

Further, the loser pays principle has meant that unsuccessful environmental litigants have been exposed to adverse cost orders – sometimes running to hundreds of thousands of euros – that have no equivalent in their severity elsewhere in the EU. By way of contrast, the EPA has reported that, in the three-year period 2006–2008, the total amount of fines and costs imposed for all breaches of environmental law prosecuted by the EPA amounted to €684,782.[41] Individual environmental litigants have been ordered to pay sums that approach or exceed this, the financial hazards of judicially challenging the legality of a development proving greater than those of unlawfully polluting. Ireland has argued that the cost provisions of the Environmental Impact Assessment Directive – which, in line with the Aarhus Convention, stipulate that the costs of judicial review should not be prohibitive – did not require any modification of Irish law, existing judicial discretion being sufficient and cost orders not being prohibitive in an Irish context. The implications of the Aarhus Convention stirred reflection and initiative within the British judiciary, the UK having had a comparable – though more mitigated – system of cost orders: and a preliminary reference to the ECJ was also recently decided there.[42] The issue of prohibitive costs did not stir similar judicial initiative in Ireland and, although the Irish courts were seized,[43] no preliminary reference was considered necessary.

The unlikelihood of any preliminary references in environmental cases is a feature of the Irish system[44] and it has been left to the Commission to bring important matters of interpretation arising in Ireland to the ECJ's attention. Following Commission legal action against Ireland, the ECJ ruled that legislative transposition was necessary for the cost provisions of the Environmental Impact Assessment Directive.[45]

---

40 Case C-216/05, *Commission v Ireland,* [2006] ECR I-10787.
41 *Focus on Environmental Enforcement in Ireland: A Report for the Years 2006-2008* (Wexford, Environmental Protection Agency, 2009), p. 13.
42 Case C-260/11, *Edwards* OJ 2011 C 226/16.
43 *Friends of the Curragh Environment Ltd v An Bord Pleanála & Ors* [2006] IEHC 243.
44 The Irish courts decided to ask for a preliminary reference in an environmental case for the first time in 2010, see Case C-258/11 *Sweetman and others* OJ 2011 C 226/15. To its credit, the Irish state supported the move.
45 Case C-427/07 *Commission v Ireland* [2009] ECR I-6277.

8.6 State of play

Over the past twenty years, Commission enforcement of EU environmental law in Ireland has been characterised by two fundamental objectives. The first has been to secure outcomes that, at a strategic level, protect or improve the state of the environment in accordance with the *acquis*. The second has been to make the governance structure in Ireland as dependable as possible and so reduce the long-term need for Commission intervention.

Measured against these objectives, the current picture is a mixed one.

So far as the state of the environment is concerned, improved air quality in Dublin represents an early success. Investments in waste-water treatment have alleviated water pollution pressures in many parts of the country. Further, Ireland's decision, in response to an ECJ ruling, to take a whole-territory approach to the Nitrates Directive has strengthened safeguards against diffuse water pollution: slurry-spreading in winter has been prohibited and major investments have been made in farmyard waste storage.

An important network of protected nature sites has been established. Site protection is assisted by the availability of agri-environmental payments. Afforestation has been ended in protected peatlands. Sheep overgrazing has been made subject to sophisticated control measures across the estimated 400,000 hectares of commonage that were adversely affected. Taken as a whole, Ireland's network of landfills is better managed than during the 1990s and – although fly-tipping remains a problem – significant-scale clandestine landfilling appears to be a thing of the past. Finally, drinking water supplies benefit from a set of greater safeguards, including chlorine alarms that alert operators to treatment malfunctions.

On the other hand, urban waste-water collection and treatment still falls short of what the Urban Waste Water Treatment Directive requires. Improved controls on septic tanks remain a work in progress. In addition, it is not evident that the situation of once pristine Irish water bodies – which were still declining over much of the last two decades – has yet been turned around. The status of a key indicator species, the freshwater pearl mussel, remains highly precarious, with most of its populations unable to reproduce themselves because of impaired water quality. Intended controls on peat extraction in protected sites have been disapplied in practice[46] and the area of active raised bog has continued to shrink.

So far as the governance structure is concerned, administrative reforms mean that the EPA has assumed overall supervision of Ireland's waste, waste-water and drinking water infrastructure. Provided the EPA exercises this role effectively, this should reduce the need for the Commission to be involved over the longer term. The EPA's periodic drinking water reports are a very creditable example of its action – and one of the reasons that persuaded the Commission to close its case on polluted Irish drinking-water supplies.

---

46 Following Commission legal action, illegal peat extraction on Natura 2000 raised bog sites was subject to official surveillance and intervention during 2012.

Ireland has deployed a relatively sophisticated and multi-faceted approach to illegal waste activities. A complaint system has been instituted and an Office of Environmental Enforcement created within the EPA to oversee local authority compliance with waste management requirements. A network has been established to support local enforcement officials and the Director of Public Prosecutors has recently undertaken a number of high-profile waste prosecutions.[47] There have been some very tentative moves towards a similar approach in the area of planning. Further, there are occasional rulings of the Irish courts that illustrate how complementarity can be achieved with ECJ rulings.[48] Ireland has introduced provision for back-to-back costs for certain categories of judicial review, so removing the deterrent represented by previous application of the 'loser pays' principle.[49]

On the other hand, Ireland remains very slow to address non-conformity issues raised by the Commission. This is the case even after the ECJ has ruled. For example, over three years after the ruling, legislation still remained outstanding to correct most of the non-conformity problems that figure in Case C-427/07 in relation to SPAs. On 16 February 2011, the Commission announced a second referral and a proposed daily penalty of €33,000 in respect of the ECJ ruling in Case C-66/06 as Ireland had failed to adopt legislation to comply with a 2008 ECJ ruling: the Commission's file dated back ten years.[50] The tentative moves to improve planning enforcement are far from assured. Enforcement of requirements related to nature legislation and the Environmental Impact Assessment Directive remains weak. Finally, notwithstanding the lifting of the loser pays principle, the costs of judicial review remain enormous. There is no legal aid and a consequence of back-to-back cost provision is that, even where successful, environmental litigants may still end up very significantly out of pocket.[51]

8.7 Conclusions and looking ahead

Recent observations of Ireland's Heritage Council in relation to landscape protection seem pertinent:[52]

> The last ten to fifteen years have witnessed dramatic changes in the manner in which the Irish landscape is perceived and used. These changes are evident throughout our rural, urban and peri-urban environments.

---

47 See, for example, the report in the Wicklow People, 3 August 2006, of a significant fine imposed in respect of an illegal landfill at Whitestown, County Wicklow.

48 For example, *An Taisce v Ireland & Ors* [2010] IEHC 415 addresses issues of control of unauthorised quarrying that feature prominently in complaints to the Commission.

49 Planning and Development (Amendment) Act, 2010. In the subsequent Environment (Miscellaneous Provisions) Act, 2011, Ireland adopted provisions that also allow for possible recovery of costs by a successful plaintiff.

50 Commission Press Release IP/11/168, 16 February 2011.

51 This consequence may be mitigated by the 2011 legislation referred to in note 49.

52 Available at: www.heritagecouncil.ie/landscape/publications/article/proposals-for-irelands-landscapes-2010.

The speed and scale of the changes have stretched our legislative frameworks and structures to the limit. They have also heralded a new orthodoxy that championed an almost exclusively utilitarian perception of the landscape as a blank, a-historical canvas whose value could only be realised through development (i.e. building).

Experience in implementing the *acquis* suggests that the utilitarian orthodoxy referred to by the Heritage Council is not confined to the aspect of new construction. Case C-494/01 refers to the infill of three rare valley fens in County Waterford. These were ancient features of the landscape between Waterford City and Tramore and lent it a distinct character. Despite this, they were vulnerable to being quite casually destroyed and no instances in Ireland moved to protect them. Similarly, there are echoes of the a-historical canvas in the case-study on destruction of archaeological remains from the early Christian era in County Kerry referred to in Case C-66/06.[53]

The utilitarian orthodoxy arguably goes back more than fifteen years. For example, Ireland did not value after independence its inheritance of an intact, planned eighteenth-century Dublin in the way that, say, Estonia has valued its inheritance of an intact medieval Tallinn.

Utilitarian orthodoxy is not, of course, unique to Ireland – nor is 'utilitarian' always the most apt description since acting as though there is an a-historical canvas may result in a poor economic return on finite assets.

Be that as it may, utilitarian orthodoxies are embedded phenomena and likely to continue to have a determinative influence on outcomes. There are few objective reasons to suppose that – bar areas such as waste management – the patterns that have applied in Ireland over the past twenty years are about to appreciably change.

To a significant extent, further improvements are likely to depend on final resolution of still-outstanding Article 260 cases which remain the subject of ongoing bilateral exchanges between Ireland and the Commission.

At EU level, the environmental Directorate-General of the Commission has in recent years entered into a programme of cooperation with European organisations representing national judges: the latter have expressed a keen interest in improving awareness of the environmental *acquis* amongst their membership. This cooperation has led to seminars on specific topics such as EU nature conservation and environmental impact assessment legislation. In some jurisdictions, judges have assumed a greater role in upholding the *acquis,* thus alleviating part of the burden that falls on the Commission and the ECJ. A trend in that direction in Ireland would certainly be welcome.

Against this background, the following are suggestions on how Ireland's implementation of the *acquis* might be improved:

53 [2008] ECR I-158, para. 71.

- *Greater recognition of the underlying purposes and objectives of EU environmental legislation.* The environmental *acquis* is ultimately about safeguarding public goods: unpolluted water sources, clean air, a healthy and rich biodiversity to hand on to future generations. Clear articulation at a sufficiently high level of the underlying purposes and objectives of EU environmental legislation – as well as its long-term benefits – is likely to assist the process of implementation. In the case of peatlands – to give just one example – it would draw attention to their importance for storing carbon and alleviating flood risks as well as to their intrinsic importance as part of Europe's natural heritage.
- *Greater care and foresight in the drafting of implementing legislation.* There is a temptation for those charged with transposition to reproduce the words – or an approximation of the words – of a directive without thinking too hard about the mechanics of effective implementation. However, if problems are to be avoided, crafting effective administrative arrangements is essential. A basic question drafters should ask themselves is: will this work under Irish conditions? Drafters should also assume that there will be individuals – or even instances – with a disinclination to comply and include provisions that anticipate that.
- *Creativity in the design and deployment of implementing measures.* Member States have a considerable margin to craft specific approaches and solutions. Ireland has, on occasion, shown creativity and originality – for example, in relation to the plastic bag levy and the arrangements for improving implementation of waste legislation. In the area of nature legislation, benefits may result from a closer alignment of regulatory, incentive and educational approaches.
- *Greater emphasis on long-term strategic approaches and tools such as strategic environmental assessment.* A recent petition to the European Parliament argues the plight of homeowners in County Galway who purchased new houses built in areas of high flood risk. A strong sense of grievance is expressed about the zoning of such areas for housing. Strategic environmental assessment (SEA) under Directive 2001/42/EC now offers an important tool and safeguard for highlighting such risks in advance rather than *ex post*. However, a strong sense of public goods remains essential if SEA is not to end up as a *pro forma* exercise.
- *Greater coherence and targeting of implementing measures.* Environmental problems are often interconnected and a joined-up approach to addressing them is therefore very desirable. For example, poorly located or poor-performing septic tanks and careless slurry-spreading are major risk factors for contamination of drinking-water sources. It therefore makes sense to design septic tank and slurry-spreading checks so that they are closely related to drinking-water abstractions at risk from microbiologically contaminated groundwater. Another example concerns flood risks. It is incoherent to argue for stronger flood control measures while at the same time arguing for a high degree of permissiveness in zoning decisions and in relation to actions such as reclamation of callow land and wetlands that can help absorb flood waters.

- *An emphasis on outcomes in enforcement action.* Results-based obligations make up a significant part of the *acquis*. For this reason, it is important that enforcement action at national level is also results-oriented. Enforcement authorities should consider the range of tools available to them, selecting those most likely to achieve the required results. Civil remedies may sometimes be the most effective, for example injunctions in the case of unauthorised activities.
- *Further improvements in oversight of and assistance to local authorities.* Many compliance problems arise at the level of local authorities. The increased oversight role of the EPA has already been mentioned. However, the EPA has no function in relation to planning legislation and there is arguably scope for the Irish Ombudsman to exercise a greater rule in ensuring that local authority environmental decision-making is adequately informed, reasoned and properly recorded. It is worth noting that the Ombudsman represents part of Ireland's implementation framework for Article 10a of the Impact Assessment Directive (the access to justice clause). At the same time, the assistance given to local authorities through the enforcement network for waste legislation offers valuable lessons in the area of planning.
- *Further improvements in relation to role of civil society.* Completion of ratification of the Aarhus Convention is a positive signal.

9 Delivering the rule of environmental law in Ireland

Where do we go from here?

*Áine Ryall**

9.1 Introduction

Effective enforcement lies at the very heart of environmental governance. Without it, environmental laws are meaningless in practice and the rule of law is undermined. Notwithstanding significant developments in the law in recent years, including new access to justice obligations, a substantial implementation deficit persists and the quality of the environment remains under constant threat. This state of affairs is the result of a lack of political will to strengthen legal and other mechanisms to promote compliance, together with a parallel failure to resource the enforcement effort adequately. Drawing on Ireland as a case study, this chapter considers current issues and problems around environmental enforcement. It charts likely future directions and puts forward a number of suggestions for improving compliance in the Irish context. Above all, it calls for stronger environmental leadership from government and a more proactive stance on the part of the judiciary.

9.2 The challenge of delivering the rule of environmental law in Ireland

There have been long-standing and well-founded concerns over arrangements for access to environmental justice in Ireland. Individuals and environmental non-governmental organisations (ENGOs) seeking to enforce environmental law face formidable obstacles including a notoriously deferential standard of judicial review and high legal costs.[1] Access to the courts is further impeded

* I thank Declan Walsh, Phyllis Comerford and Suzanne Kingston for helpful comments on an earlier draft of this chapter.
1 There have been many environmental cases over the years where unsuccessful challengers have been faced with enormous costs. See Á. Ryall, *Effective Judicial Protection and the Environmental Impact Assessment Directive in Ireland* (Oxford: Hart Publishing, 2009) pp. 211–214. For a recent example consider *Klohn v An Bord Pleanála* [2011] IEHC 196, where the High Court refused to quash a decision of the Taxing Master of the High Court to allow the respondent's legal team costs of approximately €86,000. The High Court took the view that the Taxing Master's allowance was not 'excessive' in the context of judicial review proceedings that ran for four days in the High Court. Rather tellingly, Hedigan J noted that the costs as

by the fact that legal aid is not generally available for environmental matters in Ireland and no Irish court has seen fit to make a Protective Costs Order (PCO) in any environmental challenge to date. In the cases that have reached the courts, the reluctance of the judiciary (and of the Supreme Court in particular), to refer points of interpretation to the Court of Justice meant that the implications of European Union (EU) environmental law for the national legal system were not clarified at an early stage. This resulted in unnecessarily protracted uncertainty about the scope and content of EU environmental rights and obligations, in particular in the context of the Environmental Impact Assessment (EIA) Directive[2] and the Habitats Directive.[3]

There were also wider concerns about the judiciary's willingness to engage with arguments based on EU law, especially where the preventive outlook championed by Europe clashed with the more permissive approach to development adopted at national level.[4] Dissatisfaction with the Irish authorities' enforcement efforts, and the enormous costs involved in embarking on litigation at national level, prompted a disproportionately high number of complaints to the Commission alleging breaches of EU environmental law.[5] Infringement proceedings against Ireland have resulted in significant victories for the Commission before the Court of Justice which have highlighted serious (and, at times, genuinely shocking) implementation gaps.[6]

---

assessed 'appeared to reflect the economic reality for litigants in the State'. It is notable, however, that in the course of his judgment Hedigan J commented obiter that 'it might well be the case' that if the planning application in question had been made post-25 June 2005 (the date by which Member States were obliged to have implemented Directive 2003/35/EC), then the applicant 'would have an arguable case' that the costs in these proceedings violated Art 10a of the EIA Directive.

2 Directive 85/337/EEC on the assessment of the effects of certain public and private projects on the environment OJ 1985 L 175/40 (as amended).
3 Directive 92/43/EEC on the conservation of natural habitats and of wild fauna and flora OJ 1992 L 206/7.
4 S. Dillon, 'The Mirage of EC Environmental Federalism in a Reluctant Member State Jurisdiction' (1999) 8 *New York University Environmental Law Journal* 1 and Á. Ryall, *Effective Judicial Protection and the Environmental Impact Assessment Directive in Ireland* (Oxford: Hart Publishing, 2009), in particular chapters 5 and 6. For a recent example of the High Court's failure to accept that the EIA Directive has direct effect see G. Simons, 'EIA Directive, Direct Effect and the Irish Courts' (2011) 18 *IPELJ* 67 (commentary on *Lackagh Quarries Ltd v Galway County Council* [2010] IEHC 479).
5 See further the contribution by Cashman in Chapter 8 of the present collection.
6 Noteworthy examples from the substantial body of Court of Justice jurisprudence on Ireland's numerous failures to meet environmental obligations include: Case C-392/96 *Commission v Ireland* [1999] ECR I-5901 and Case C-66/06 *Commission v Ireland* [2008] ECR I-158* (EIA Directive and setting of thresholds for Annex II projects); Case C-494/01 *Commission v Ireland* [2005] ECR I-3331 ('general and persistent' breach of obligations under Waste Directive); Case C-418/04 *Commission v Ireland* [2007] ECR I-10947 (failure to fulfil obligations under Wild Birds Directive and Habitats Directive); Case C-215/06 *Commission v Ireland* [2008] ECR I-4911 (EIA Directive and retrospective planning permission); Case C-427/07 *Commission v Ireland* [2009] ECR I-6277 (EIA Directive and demolition works; EIA and IPPC Directives and rules governing the cost of review proceedings); and Case C-50/09 *Commission v Ireland*, [2011] ECR I-0000 (EIA Directive and split decision-making in the planning/pollution control context). Many other examples are noted in Cashman's contribution to this collection.

The 'Irish' case law has also made a valuable contribution to the general principles underpinning Commission enforcement activity. The landmark ruling in *Commission v Ireland*,[7] where the Court pioneered the concept of systemic default and identified a 'general and persistent' breach of obligations under the Waste Directive,[8] strengthened the Commission's hand considerably and provided a much needed fillip for its enforcement agenda. Notwithstanding these important rulings, however, the Commission's efforts to police EU environmental law are far from perfect. The enforcement mechanism under Articles 258 and 260 TFEU is highly political, opaque, slow-moving and resource-intensive. Kingston's contribution in this collection highlights recent significant shifts in Commission enforcement policy and explores the consequences of these developments for environmental complainants. The Commission's pursuit of a more 'strategic' approach to enforcement, involving the formal prioritization of certain categories of infringements, is particularly striking in this context.[9] This development is obviously aimed at achieving the best return for the Commission from its scarce resources. From the complainant's point of view, however, it simply confirms that there is little prospect of the Commission bringing infringement proceedings in respect of non-priority matters.

Moreover, the emergence in April 2008 of the 'EU Pilot'[10] scheme has resulted in the Commission diverting a significant number of complaints back to the national authorities for investigation and appropriate action. The Commission's inability to pursue all genuine environmental complaints, and the growing tendency to rely on the 'EU Pilot' as a dispute resolution mechanism, highlights the significant resource deficit within the Commission when it comes to environmental enforcement. It also demonstrates the obvious lack of political will to resource Environment Directorate-General appropriately and to sharpen its enforcement powers. It is difficult, therefore, to disagree with Kingston's conclusion that it is 'ironic', given the current enthusiasm for network-based, multi-level environmental governance, that many complainants are, in reality, excluded from the enforcement process at EU level.[11]

Even in cases where infringement proceedings are instituted, it usually takes considerable time, effort and persistence on the Commission's part (and indeed on the complainant's part) to secure the required outcomes. As Cashman's chapter in this collection demonstrates, there is no guarantee of prompt compliance by a Member State following an adverse ruling from the Court of Justice. Ireland provides a good example of this type of inertia. It is

---

7 Case C-494/01 *Commission v Ireland* [2005] ECR I-3331.
8 Directive 75/442/EEC OJ 1975 L 194/39 (as amended).
9 European Commission Communication, *Implementing European Community Environmental Law* COM (2008) 773 final (18 November 2008).
10 European Commission Communication *A Europe of Results – Applying Community Law* COM (2007) 502 final (5 July 2007) and http://ec.europa.eu/eu_law/infringements/application_monitoring_en.htm.
11 See Kingston's contribution in Chapter 7 of this book, in the section 'National authorities as enforcers: the pressure of harmonisation'.

disheartening to note that, at the time of writing, there are two (environment) cases before the Court of Justice alleging breach of Article 260 TFEU by Ireland[12] (these are proceedings where the Court of Justice may impose financial penalties on a Member State for failure to comply with the terms of a previous Court ruling).[13] The obvious weaknesses in the centralised enforcement process confirm the fundamental importance of accessible and effective remedies at local level if EU law rights are to be delivered in a timely manner in practice. This basic point has particular resonance in the Irish context where the national enforcement effort has traditionally been considered weak.

9.2.1 Aarhus Convention: a catalyst for change

Effective oversight and enforcement mechanisms have been inordinately slow to emerge in the Irish context, notwithstanding unrelenting efforts on the part of the Commission, as well as vocal demands from individuals and communities keen to see the national authorities take firm action against polluters. The emergence of the Aarhus Convention,[14] which is widely regarded as a ground-breaking environmental Treaty, raised high expectations in Ireland (especially among seasoned campaigners and the more established ENGOs), that arrangements for access to environmental justice would be overhauled. Although Ireland signed the Convention in 1998, 13 years on it remains the only Member State of the EU that has failed to ratify it. One obvious consequence of Ireland not being a Party to the Convention is that the Aarhus Convention Compliance Committee (ACCC)[15] does not have jurisdiction to deal with communications (complaints) concerning alleged non-compliance with Convention obligations. This remains a source of considerable frustration for individuals and ENGOs in Ireland who are currently limited to pursuing their grievances with the national authorities and/or lodging a complaint with the Commission in the (often faint) hope of triggering infringement proceedings.

The ACCC operates in an admirably open and transparent manner with the documentation concerning each communication posted online for all to see.[16]

---

12 Case C-279/11 *Commission v Ireland* OJ 2011 C 282/13, action brought on 1 June 2011 alleging breach of Art. 260 TFEU in failing to take the necessary measures to comply with the judgment in Case C-66/06 *Commission v Ireland* [2008] ECR I-158* (concerning obligations arising under the EIA Directive) and Case C-374/11 *Commission v Ireland* OJ 2011 C 226/18, action brought on 13 July 2011 alleging breach of Art. 260 TFEU in failing to take the necessary measures to comply with the judgment in Case C-188/08 *Commission v Ireland* [2009] ECR I-172* (concerning obligations arising under the Waste Directive, specifically domestic waste water disposed of in the countryside through septic tanks and other individual waste water treatment systems).

13 A number of other Art. 260 TFEU cases are at the pre-litigation stage.

14 United Nations Economic Commission for Europe, *Convention on Access to Information, Public Participation in Decision-making and Access to Justice in Environmental Matters* (Aarhus Convention) 38 ILM 517 (1998) text available at http://live.unece.org/env/pp/treatytext.html.

15 See generally http://live.unece.org/env/pp/ccBackground.html.

16 http://live.unece.org/env/pp/ccBackground.html.

This approach stands in sharp contrast with the generally opaque nature of infringement proceedings against Member States pursued by the Commission where, for example, letters of formal notice and reasoned opinions are not made available to the public or even to the complainant.[17] Recent findings of the ACCC, confirming that the United Kingdom (UK) (a Party to the Convention since 2005) must go further to ensure compliance with its access to justice obligations, have sparked considerable interest in Ireland given the similarities between the legal systems in these two common law jurisdictions.[18] In particular, the ACCC's findings in the UK cases suggest that there must be doubts as to whether the deferential standard of review deployed by the Irish courts,[19] and the high levels of legal costs that prevail in Ireland, are compatible with the requirements of the Convention. It is unfortunate therefore that the enforcement mechanism offered by the ACCC is not available to deal with communications concerning Ireland at the present point in time. This additional level of independent and transparent oversight would supplement Commission enforcement activity and would, no doubt, exert a positive influence on Irish environmental law and policy.

9.2.2 EU law access to justice obligations: the Irish response

Notwithstanding the fact that it has yet to ratify the Aarhus Convention, Ireland is of course bound by EU law measures that purport to give effect to the Convention within the EU legal order. The relevant provisions here include Directive 2003/4/EC on public access to environmental information[20] and Directive 2003/35/EC,[21] which introduced important amendments to the EIA and IPPC[22] Directives, including access to justice clauses. The Irish authorities' response to the new access to justice obligations articulated in Article 10a of the EIA Directive and Article 15a of the IPPC Directive provides a stark example of just how protracted, confused and frustrating the process of implementing EU environmental obligations can prove to be in practice.

---

17 Case T-105/95 *WWF v Commission* [1997] ECR II-313; Case T-191/99 *Petrie v Commission* [2001] ECR II-3677 and *Sweetman v An Bord Pleanála* [2009] IEHC 174.

18 Findings and Recommendations with regard to ACCC/C/2008/27 adopted by the ACCC on 24 September 2010 and Findings and Recommendations with regard to ACCC/C/2008/33 adopted by the ACCC on 24 September 2010. Full text of documentation available at: http://live.unece.org/env/pp/pubcom.html.

19 *O'Keeffe v An Bord Pleanála* [1993] 1 IR 39.

20 Directive 2003/4/EC on public access to environmental information and repealing Council Directive 90/313/EEC OJ 2003 L 41/26. For a critique of the Irish response to the access to justice obligations arising under Directive 2003/4/EC see Á. Ryall, 'Access to Environmental Information in Ireland' (2011) 24 *Journal of Environmental Law* 45.

21 Directive 2003/35/EC OJ 2003 L 156/17.

22 Directive 96/61/EC concerning integrated pollution prevention and control (IPPC Directive) OJ 1996 L 257/26.

Member States were required to implement Directive 2003/35/EC (usually described as 'the public participation Directive') by 25 June 2005. The Irish authorities initially adopted the position that the existing system of judicial review met the access to justice obligations set down in the EIA and IPPC Directives. Special rules were subsequently introduced in 2006, however, which relaxed standing requirements in the case of certain ENGOs seeking to challenge planning decisions.[23] It appears that this measure was prompted by the express requirement in Article 10a of the EIA Directive that ENGOs meeting any requirements specified under national law are *automatically* deemed to have standing to invoke judicial review procedures.[24] Infringement proceedings taken by the Commission led to a ground-breaking ruling from the Court of Justice in July 2009 which found that Irish costs rules did not meet the access to justice obligations in the EIA and IPPC Directives.[25] Specifically, the Court determined that a judicial discretion to depart from the general rule that costs follow the event (i.e. the loser pays principle) did not constitute adequate transposition of the obligation that the costs involved in review procedures must not be 'prohibitively expensive'.[26] In summer 2010, the Irish legislature responded to this ruling by introducing a new costs rule in the form of section 50B of the Planning and Development Act 2000 (as amended).[27] It is striking that there was only minimal consultation with interested parties at the very last minute before this measure was enacted in purported compliance with the Court of Justice ruling. The essence of the new costs regime was that in judicial review proceedings involving the EIA Directive, the IPPC Directive or the Strategic Environmental Assessment (SEA) Directive,[28] each party was to bear its own costs.[29] However, provision was made for an award of costs in favour of a party 'in a matter of exceptional public importance and where in the special circumstances of the case it is in the interests of justice to do so'.[30] Costs could also be awarded against a party where the court considered it appropriate to do so: because the claim was frivolous or vexatious; because of the manner in which the party had conducted the proceedings; or where a party was in contempt of court.[31]

The new costs rule attracted immediate and strong criticism from a variety of sources, including ENGOs and a number of lawyers.[32] The blatant lack of

---

23 Planning and Development (Strategic Infrastructure) Act 2006 s. 13, which inserted a new s. 50A(3)(b)(ii) into the Planning and Development Act 2000.

24 It is curious, however, that the 2006 Act contains no reference to Art 10a of the EIA Directive.

25 Case C-427/07 *Commission v Ireland* [2009] ECR I-6277.

26 Contrast the analysis presented by Advocate General Kokott in her Opinion in Case C-427/07 *Commission v Ireland* [2009] ECR I-6277 paras 97–99.

27 Inserted pursuant to s. 33 of the Planning and Development (Amendment) Act 2010.

28 Directive 2001/42/EC on the assessment of the effects of certain plans and programmes on the environment OJ 2001 L 197/30.

29 Planning and Development Act 2000 (as amended) s. 50B(1) and (2).

30 S. 50B(4).

31 S. 50B(3).

32 See, for example, 'President urged to intervene as late change to planning Act sparks fears', *Irish Times*, 19 July 2010.

consultation on the fundamental question of costs liability was also widely condemned. The main thrust of the concerns expressed by critics of section 50B was that the new regime actually risked undermining access to the courts in that it removed any incentive for lawyers to become involved in environmental litigation on a 'no win – no fee' basis. Furthermore, as legal costs in Ireland are so high, the new rule meant that even a successful challenger could still be faced with a substantial bill for their own costs. Doubts were also raised about the constitutionality of section 50B in the context of the right of access to the courts.

These concerns prompted modifications to the new costs rule under amendments introduced via the Environment (Miscellaneous Provisions) Act 2011 (the 2011 Act). Specifically, section 21 of the 2011 Act, which entered into force on 23 August 2011,[33] modified section 50B by inserting a new provision which expressly empowers the courts to award costs in favour of a person seeking judicial review, but only to the extent that they succeed in obtaining relief. This innovation seeks to dilute the severity of the original section 50B and potentially increases the possibility of a successful challenger recovering some element of their costs. It is noteworthy, however, that the new provision only confers the courts with a *discretion* in this regard; there is no guarantee that a successful challenger will, in fact, recover any of their costs. It is difficult to reconcile a broad discretion as to the award of costs with the unambiguous ruling from the Court of Justice in *Commission v Ireland*[34] which insists that a judicial discretion does not provide sufficient certainty as to potential costs liability in this particular context.

Beyond the question of whether the new costs provisions actually go far enough to meet the requirements of EU law, in the absence of case law interpreting section 50B (either in its original form or as amended by the 2011 Act), it is impossible to predict its true impact in practice and the extent to which the statutory restrictions on a successful challenger recovering their costs will operate to impede access to the courts. There is a conspicuous lack of publicly available data on costs in environmental matters generally in Ireland; for example what proportion of such cases are taken on a 'no win – no fee' basis and to what extent has the advent of section 50B impacted on this practice? These important practical questions should be explored as a matter of urgency to obtain a clear picture of how costs rules operate in practice and to identify accurately the true cost of environmental litigation in Ireland.

In the absence of a timely response to EU access to justice obligations on the part of the Irish legislature, the national courts were called upon to give effect to the rights conferred on individuals and ENGOs under the public participation Directive (Directive 2003/35/EC). The national courts' response can, at best, be described as mixed. In the early case law, the High Court refused

33 Environment (Miscellaneous Provisions) Act 2011 (Commencement of Certain Provisions) Order 2011 (SI No. 433 of 2011).
34 Case C-427/07 *Commission v Ireland* [2009] ECR I-6277.

categorically to accept that Article 10a of the EIA Directive could have direct effect in the national legal order in the absence of implementing measures.[35] This conclusion was based on the view that the terms of the Directive lacked the clarity, precision and unconditionality to support direct effect. As a result, the High Court refused to deploy Article 10a to support the grant of a PCO in favour of an ENGO seeking to challenge a planning decision.[36] It also rejected the ENGO's argument, again based on Article 10a, that it should be recognised as having standing to challenge the decision in question.[37] One High Court judge even went so far as to state that if Directive 2003/35/EC were applied literally, then it had the potential to underpin what he described as a 'crank's charter' – in the sense that 'every litigant no matter how vexatious should have carte blanche to engage without risk of basic responsibility [for legal costs]'.[38]

There are other High Court rulings, however, where the judges have displayed greater willingness to engage with Article 10a with a view to teasing out its implications for national judicial review procedures, in particular by engaging the doctrine of consistent interpretation. In *Sweetman v An Bord Pleanála*,[39] for example, Clarke J adopted a flexible approach to the (usually very restrictive) 'substantial interest' standing test[40] in order to accommodate the obligation to provide 'wide access to justice' under Article 10a.[41] In similar vein, in *Klohn v An Bord Pleanála*,[42] McMahon J observed, *obiter*, that Article 10a may require a recalibration of the traditionally deferential standard of review deployed by the courts in planning cases.

In *Hands Across the Corrib Ltd v An Bord Pleanála*,[43] Birmingham J relied on Article 10a in determining the question of liability for costs in a case where

---

35 *Friends of the Curragh Environment Ltd v An Bord Pleanála (No 1)* [2006] IEHC 243; *Friends of the Curragh Environment Ltd v An Bord Pleanála (No 2)* [2006] IEHC 390; and *Sweetman v An Bord Pleanála (No 1)* [2007] IEHC 153.

36 *Friends of the Curragh Environment Ltd v An Bord Pleanála (No 1)* [2006] IEHC 243.

37 *Friends of the Curragh Environment Ltd v An Bord Pleanála (No 2)* [2006] IEHC 390.

38 *Kavanagh v Ireland* [2007] IEHC 389.

39 *Sweetman v An Bord Pleanála (No 1)* [2007] IEHC 153.

40 First introduced pursuant to s.50 of the Planning and Development Act 2000, the 'substantial interest' test set a very high threshold for access to the courts. Although the concept of a 'substantial interest' is not defined in any detail in the 2000 Act, the High Court generally adopted a strict interpretation which required an applicant seeking leave to bring judicial review proceedings to demonstrate how they would be directly affected by the proposed development. The Supreme Court endorsed a narrow approach to the 'substantial interest' test in *Harding v Cork County Council* [2008] IESC 27. See Á. Ryall, *Effective Judicial Protection and the Environmental Impact Assessment Directive in Ireland* (Oxford: Hart Publishing, 2009) pp. 203–207. A restrictive approach to standing at national level is difficult to reconcile with the obligation under the Aarhus Convention and Directive 2003/35/EC to deliver 'wide' access to justice.

41 It is noteworthy that s. 20 of the Environment (Miscellaneous Provisions) Act 2011, which came into force on 23 August 2011, amended s. 50A of the Planning and Development Act 2000 by substituting 'sufficient interest' for 'substantial interest'. In other words, the law has reverted to the pre-2000 Act position and the traditionally more generous standing test of a 'sufficient interest' has been reinstated.

42 *Klohn v An Bord Pleanála* [2008] IEHC 111.

43 *Hands Across the Corrib Ltd v An Bord Pleanála and Galway County Council,* unreported, High Court, 21 January 2010 (ruling on costs).

an ENGO had mounted unsuccessful judicial review proceedings. Birmingham J noted that having regard to the requirement in Article 10a that procedures must not be 'prohibitively expensive', it might be problematic for a court to make the usual order for costs (i.e. an unqualified provision for payment of costs by the losing party with provision for taxation of costs in default of agreement). The High Court took judicial notice of the fact that 'a single issue' ENGO (as was the case here), which is concerned with a particular project in a particular area, 'is very unlikely to have recourse to any substantial funds'. Overall, Birmingham J was satisfied that the ENGO had established that there were 'sufficient grounds' to justify a departure from the normal rule that the losing party should bear the costs of the proceedings. The High Court therefore concluded that 'the justice of the situation' was met in this case by making no order as to costs (with the result that each party was left to bear its own costs).

This ruling provides a good example of how Article 10a can be deployed to mould national procedural rules to EU requirements in the absence of implementing legislation. It is disappointing, however, that the High Court did not explore the perplexing notion of costs that are not 'prohibitively expensive' in any detail. The ban on prohibitive expense has been the subject of considerable judicial scrutiny in the UK. It is telling that the UK Supreme Court has seen fit to refer a series of important questions concerning the interpretation of this ambiguous aspect of Article 10a to the Court of Justice.[44] Given the persistent controversy over allegedly prohibitive costs in the context of environmental litigation in Ireland, it is remarkable that an Irish court did not make such a reference as far back as 2005/2006.

The (Irish) Supreme Court has been required to consider the implications of Article 10a for national law on only one occasion to date.[45] It is notable that the flexible approach to standing adopted by the High Court in *Sweetman* contrasts sharply with the line of analysis pursued in the Supreme Court in *Harding v Cork County Council*.[46] On this occasion, Kearns J concluded that a narrow interpretation of the 'substantial interest' test was mandated by the restrictive nature of the (domestic) statutory scheme governing judicial review of planning decisions. Although Kearns J was prepared to accept that the Planning and Development Act 2000 fell to be interpreted in light of the terms and the objectives of the public participation Directive (Directive 2003/35/EC), the obligation of consistent interpretation under EU law did not require the court to interpret national law *contra legem*. This approach is open to criticism in that a 'substantial interest' is not defined in the 2000 Act and is therefore plainly susceptible to different interpretations. So it is difficult to

---

44 *R (Edwards) v Environment Agency* [2010] UKSC 57 and Case C-260/11 *R (Edwards) v Environment Agency* OJ 2011 C 226/16.

45 The possibility of an appeal to the Supreme Court from a decision of the High Court in planning judicial review cases is severely restricted by statute: Planning and Development Act 2000 (as amended) s. 50(4)(f). In practice, therefore, very few planning cases reach the Supreme Court.

46 *Harding v Cork County Council* [2008] IESC 27.

see why Kearns J determined that adopting a flexible approach to the statutory standing test would involve a *contra legem* interpretation of national planning law.

Overall, the Irish judiciary's response to Article 10a of the EIA Directive to date has been disappointing. The jurisprudence reveals a striking lack of consistency in the approaches adopted by different judges. While some judges were prepared to deploy the doctrine of consistent interpretation in an effort to align domestic law with EU law requirements, others failed to engage with Article 10a in any meaningful way and preferred to leave implementation matters exclusively in the hands of the legislature. The legislature's belated and inadequate response to Article 10a (confirmed in *Commission v Ireland*)[47] resulted in a serious implementation gap as regards access to environmental justice which the national courts failed to address effectively.

The Court of Justice has persistently confirmed the national courts' mandate to act to ensure the effectiveness of EU law rights at local level.[48] To this end, it has equipped the national courts with the doctrines of direct effect and consistent interpretation and it expects results. The Irish courts' approach falls well short of what is expected. A more robust approach to EU environmental law rights and obligations is required. The timid level of engagement with Article 10a to date has done little to promote the cause of environmental justice at national level. While the legislature has now responded (again belatedly) to the Court of Justice ruling condemning Irish costs rules, the national courts must be alert to ensure that the fundamental obligation – to provide access to environmental justice that is not 'prohibitively expensive' – is delivered in practice. Given the level of discretion as to potential costs liability that remains vested in the national courts under section 50B (as amended), it is clear that the judiciary will continue to have a crucial role to play if the ban on prohibitive costs is to have any meaning in practice.

9.3 Future directions: where do we go from here?

9.3.1 Environmental enforcement in context

Effective oversight of planning and environmental decision-making by way of judicial review is a cornerstone of the rule of law. Moreover, there is an obvious public interest in ensuring that such decisions are taken lawfully. A positive step forward would be to work towards improving the quality of planning and environmental decision-making at first instance, thereby potentially reducing the need for judicial review. A long-standing problem in Ireland is the

---

47 Case C-427/07 *Commission v Ireland* [2009] ECR I-6277.
48 For example Case 26/62 NV *Algemene Transport-en Expeditie Onderneming van Gend en Loos v Netherlands Inland Revenue Administration* [1963] ECR 1; Case 222/84 *Johnston v Chief Constable of the Royal Ulster Constabulary* [1986] ECR 1651; and Case C-72/95 *Aannemersbedrijf PK Kraaijeveld BV v Gedeputeerde Staten van Zuid-Holland* [1996] ECR I-5403.

fragmented nature of the legislative framework in the area of planning and environmental law. This substantial body of legal rules is the subject of regular amendments and the result is a complex jumble of provisions spread over a range of different instruments. The law is therefore far from being user-friendly and it is difficult for even experienced lawyers to disentangle the current disorganised legislative scheme. In *O'Connell v Environmental Protection Agency*,[49] Fennelly J in the Supreme Court described the EIA provisions at issue in that case as 'a statutory maze' and commented that it was 'regrettable' that rules of law intended to provide for public participation were not written in 'a more accessible form'. Consolidation of primary and secondary planning and environmental legislation is long overdue and should be progressed as a matter of urgency in the interests of facilitating access to the law for everyone concerned. If the public is to be in a position to exercise its rights to participate in planning and environmental decision-making, an accessible legislative scheme is essential. Article 3(1) of the Aarhus Convention demands that Parties take the necessary 'legislative, regulatory and other measures', to establish and maintain 'a clear, transparent and consistent framework' to implement the Convention's provisions. As the Aarhus Convention Implementation Guide explains, 'the applicable rules must be clear and consistent'.[50] It appears beyond doubt, therefore, that Parties are obliged to deliver coherent and comprehensible legislation to underpin the rights guaranteed in the Convention. A similar obligation arises as regards provisions designed to transpose EU (environmental) obligations into the national legal order. The Court of Justice has ruled consistently that:

> [T]he provisions of a directive must be implemented with unquestionable binding force and with the specificity, precision and clarity required in order to satisfy the need for legal certainty, which requires that, in the case of a directive intended to confer rights on individuals, the persons concerned must be enabled to ascertain the full extent of their rights.[51]

In addition to a coherent legislative framework, appropriate (legal and technical) expertise, accurate information on environmental rights and obligations, together with regular updates and effective training programmes, are an essential component of any drive to improve the quality of decision-making and to improve public confidence in the regulatory system. It is vital that the Department of Environment, Community and Local Government[52] communicates the principles emerging from the contemporary planning and environmental jurisprudence to decision-makers and the public in a timely manner so that

---

49 *O'Connell v Environmental Protection Agency* [2003] ISEC 14 paras 2 and 54.
50 *The Aarhus Convention: An Implementation Guide* (New York and Geneva: United Nations, 2000), p. 42.
51 Case C-427/07 *Commission v Ireland* [2009] ECR I-6277 para. 55 and the authorities cited therein.
52 Or the relevant Government Department, depending on the subject matter of a particular judgment.

these principles may be incorporated into day to day practice at the earliest opportunity.

The expectations generated by the ban on 'prohibitively expensive' costs in judicial review proceedings has, at times, tended to overshadow other dimensions of the access to environmental justice debate in Ireland. Judicial review proceedings are, of course, only one aspect of the national environmental enforcement landscape. Once a planning or (environmental) licensing decision is taken by the relevant public authority, that decision must be implemented correctly and, where necessary, enforced effectively. Weak enforcement of planning law remains a pressing concern in Ireland. While significant strides have been made in the area of environmental enforcement in recent years, particularly following the establishment in 2003 of the Office of Environmental Enforcement, adequate resources must be made available to the various authorities involved in enforcement, including the Environmental Protection Agency (EPA) and local authorities. The resources issue poses an enormous challenge in the current economic climate. It is incumbent on the Irish government to rise to this challenge and to ensure that the quality of our environment is not compromised through lack of resources to support enforcement. It is plain that the effectiveness of environmental rules will be undermined in the absence of a robust and adequately resourced environmental enforcement programme. The ruling in *Commission v Ireland*[53] (concerning *inter alia* alleged breach of the EIA Directive in the context of the Derrybrien windfarm project) provides strong authority that Member States are obliged to operate an effective planning control system in order to deliver the aims of the EIA Directive.[54] Notwithstanding that the EIA Directive is silent on the question of enforcement (apart from Article 10a concerning the right to judicial review), a purposive interpretation of the Directive leads to the conclusion that an effective enforcement regime is essential if the underlying objectives of the Directive are to be delivered in practice. A similar argument may be deployed in the context of other environmental directives including, for example, the IPPC Directive and the Habitats Directive.

In times of economic crisis, there is a real danger that environmental protection will slip down the political agenda. This would be a retrograde and short-sighted development. Now, more than ever, we need strong environmental leadership from government. The forthcoming Irish Presidency of the EU (January to June 2013) presents the government with an important opportunity to play a leadership role in furthering the 'green' agenda at international and EU levels and to capitalise on the political momentum for change which will (hopefully) follow in the wake of the United Nations Conference on Sustainable Development in summer 2012 (the Rio+20 Earth Summit).

---

53 Case C-215/06 *Commission v Ireland* [2008] ECR I-4911 paras 74–79.
54 See Á. Ryall, 'Case Note: Case C-215/06 *Commission v Ireland*, Judgment of the European Court of Justice, 3 July 2008' (2009) 18 *RECIEL* 211.

Early ratification of the Aarhus Convention by Ireland (as promised in the *Programme for Government 2011*)[55] would be an important indicator of the government's commitment to improve Ireland's track record on environmental protection matters and it is heartening to see definite movement in this direction.[56] In particular, Part 2 of the Environment (Miscellaneous Provisions) Act 2011, which came into force on 23 August 2011, contains a series of measures aimed at giving effect to Article 9(3) of the Aarhus Convention. Put simply, the new provisions aim to align Irish law with the Aarhus-based obligation to ensure that (qualified) members of the public have access to administrative or judicial procedures to challenge acts and omissions by private persons, and public authorities, which contravene provisions of national environmental law. The main thrust of Part 2 of the 2011 Act[57] is that where proceedings are brought to enforce a statutory requirement or condition attached to a planning permission or other development consent (or in respect of the contravention of, or failure to comply with, such a permission or consent), each party to the proceedings is to bear its own costs. The template set down in Part 2 therefore mirrors the costs provisions in section 50B of the Planning and Development Act 2000 (as amended) which were noted earlier above in the specific context of judicial review proceedings. The rationale behind the new provisions in Part 2 is to address the costs barrier usually faced by individuals and/or ENGOs who wish to call on the courts to enforce planning permissions or environmental licences/consents. As with section 50B, however, it is not clear at this early stage what impact the new costs provisions will have on the level of environmental litigation in Ireland and whether they go far enough to ensure that costs are not 'prohibitively expensive' in practice. Another noteworthy aspect of Part 2 of the 2011 Act is that section 8 provides that judicial notice is to be taken of the Aarhus Convention. So, notwithstanding Ireland's failure to ratify the Convention, the judiciary is now required to take account of its provisions – as a matter of domestic law. As explained earlier in this chapter, the national judiciary has a crucial role to play in ensuring that Ireland delivers on the access to justice obligations set down in the Aarhus Convention and related EU law measures.

Beyond strong environmental leadership from government and an environmentally aware judiciary, the potential contribution of an active ENGO sector and an informed media should not be overlooked. Irish ENGOs have made significant

---

55 *Programme for Government 2011*, p. 60, text available at: www.taoiseach.ie/eng/Publications/Publications_2011/Programme_for_Government_2011.html.

56 In response to a parliamentary question posed by Catherine Murphy TD, as regards when the Government proposes to ratify the Aarhus Convention, the Minister for the Environment, Community and Local Government replied, on 14 September 2011, that he intended to proceed with ratification 'in the near future, following an analysis of all implementation measures by [his] Department in conjunction with the Office of the Attorney General'.

57 A detailed account of all of the provisions contained in Part 2 of the 2011 Act lies beyond the scope of this chapter.

advances in recent years. They are now much more organised, articulate and well-informed. Their contribution to the environmental policy debate is invaluable, particularly in the current stringent economic climate. The ENGO sector generates pressure for positive change and helps to keep the environment on the political agenda. Plus it provides a critical voice advocating on behalf of environmental interests and performs an important 'watchdog' role by highlighting breaches of planning and environmental law, and in particular infringements of EU law. As regards the media, it is both surprising and disappointing that environmental matters attract limited media attention in Ireland. The media is a powerful force for informing and influencing public opinion. It plays an important role in supplementing the education and awareness efforts of public authorities, including the EPA. Well-researched, informative, interesting and timely reports on contemporary environmental issues are vital to increase public awareness of current challenges and to support active environmental citizenship. A lot more could be done to inform the public of enforcement activities undertaken by public authorities and of significant environmental decisions from the courts, including the Court of Justice. Surely environmental matters merit as much media attention as health and education?

There has been little, if any, public debate around access to environmental justice in Ireland and, in particular, around how best to respond to the obligations set down in the Aarhus Convention and the related (Aarhus-inspired) EU law measures. Even more puzzling is the fact that when legislative measures were eventually brought forward to address deficiencies in Irish law (in particular the costs involved in seeking to enforce environmental law via the courts), these measures were rushed through the legislative process with minimal opportunity for consultation and discussion. It is not surprising, therefore, to find that environmental campaigners and ENGOs are disappointed at how Ireland has responded to the challenge of ensuring effective access to the courts in environmental matters.

9.3.2 Complexity, frustration and unfulfilled expectations

The extremely complex nature of the contemporary enforcement landscape is striking, as is the rapid pace at which the law continues to evolve. Any attempt to identify the basic rules governing access to environmental justice involves an examination of the Aarhus Convention together with the relevant provisions of EU and national law. Teasing out the intricacies of the provisions in the Convention which govern access to justice, and the various EU measures designed to give effect to these obligations, is no easy task. Moreover, predictable tensions have arisen between the (potentially) generous model of access to justice articulated in the Convention and the more restrictive approach pursued at national level. The net result is that it is difficult to articulate the rules governing access to environmental justice with any degree of certainty in advance of authoritative interpretation from the ACCC and the Court of

Justice. This state of affairs raises obvious problems when it comes to enforcing access to justice obligations. As long as the scope of these obligations remains in a state of flux, any attempt to enforce them will be a fraught, protracted and largely unpredictable process. The extent to which national systems may validly restrict access to the courts in environmental matters remains hotly contested. Disputes have arisen over a range of practical issues including standing requirements, the standard of review to be applied where decisions are challenged before the courts and the cost of court proceedings. At the time of writing, these disputes continue to be played out before the ACCC, the Court of Justice and national courts. Important points of interpretation are gradually beginning to emerge in the case law,[58] but it is clear that it will be some time yet before there are definitive answers on what exactly the Aarhus Convention and EU access to justice obligations mean for national legal orders.

9.3.3 A promising outlook?

It is heartening to note that the Court of Justice has pursued a consistently forceful approach when called upon to interpret the access to justice clauses in the EIA and IPPC Directives. It is clear from the jurisprudence concerning Article 10a to date that the Court is determined to do all in its power to sharpen the impact of the access to justice obligations within the national legal orders. For example, the Court of Justice ruled emphatically that Article 10a precluded a Swedish procedural rule that limited access to the courts to ENGOs having at least 2,000 members.[59] Similarly, in a reference from a German court, the Court determined that ENGOs enjoy a directly effective right of access to the courts to enforce EU environmental rules, notwithstanding a national procedural law purporting to limit this right to situations where individual rights (rather than the interests of the general public) have been impaired by the contested decision.[60] The Court of Justice has also ruled that Article 10a falls to be interpreted 'in the light of, and having regard to, the objectives of the Aarhus Convention'.[61] The rapidly developing body of jurisprudence on Article 10a emerging from the Luxembourg Court should prompt the Irish courts to take a firm stance when called upon to give effect to access to justice obligations at national level. Moreover, a number of potentially ground-breaking references for preliminary rulings are pending before the Court of Justice at the time of writing, thus guaranteeing the

---

58 See, for instance, the judgments of the Court of Justice discussed in the section below.
59 Case C-263/08 *Djurgården-Lilla Värtans Miljöskyddsförening v Stockholms kommun genom dess marknämnd* [2009] ECR I-9967.
60 Case C-115/09 *Bund für Umwelt und Naturschutz Deutschland, Landesverband Nordrhein-Westfalen eV v Bezirksregierung Arnsberg, Trianel Kohlekraftwerk Lünen GmbH & Co KG* [2011] ECR I-0000, also discussed in Kingston's contribution to the present volume.
61 Ibid., para. 41.

Court further opportunities to strengthen the right of access to environmental justice.[62]

Beyond Article 10a, the Court of Justice has adopted a similarly robust approach to the access to justice obligations set down in Article 9(3) of the Aarhus Convention. As noted above, Article 9(3) obliges Parties to ensure that (qualified) members of the public have access to administrative or judicial procedures to challenge acts and omissions of private parties, and of public authorities, which contravene national environmental law. The EU has not, as yet, adopted any specific measures to give effect to Article 9(3) as regards the Member States' obligations.[63] However, because the EU is a Party to the Aarhus Convention, its provisions, including Article 9(3), 'form an integral part' of EU law.[64] A reference for a preliminary ruling from the Supreme Court of the Slovak Republic provided the Court of Justice with the opportunity to send a clear message to the national courts regarding their duty to uphold the rule of EU environmental law.[65] Although the Court determined that Article 9(3) of the Convention did not have direct effect in the EU legal order, its provisions 'are intended to ensure effective environmental protection'.[66] It fell to the Member States to lay down procedural rules to ensure the effective protection of EU law rights, including rights arising under the Habitats Directive.[67] The Court seized the opportunity to deliver what must surely be one of its most emphatic commands to national courts to date in the area of environmental protection. In the words of the Court:

> [I]f the effective protection of EU environmental law is not to be undermined, it is inconceivable that Article 9(3) of the Aarhus Convention be interpreted in such a way as to make it in practice impossible or excessively difficult to exercise rights conferred by EU law.
>
> It follows that, in so far as concerns a species protected by EU law, and in particular the Habitats Directive, it is for the national court, in order to ensure effective judicial protection in the fields covered by EU environmental law, to interpret its national law in a way which, to the fullest

---

62 Joined Cases C-128/09, C-129/09, C-130/09, C-131/09; C-134/09 and C-135/09 *Boxus and Roua et al v Région wallonne* [2009] OJ C 153/18, Opinion of Advocate General Sharpston delivered on 19 May 2011; Case C-177/09 *Le Poumon vert de la Hulpe ASBL, Jacques Solvay de la Hulpe, Marie-Noëlle Solvay, Jean-Marie Solvay de la Hulpe, Alix Walsh v Région wallonne* OJ 2009 C 180/30; Case C-260/11 *R (Edwards) v Environment Agency, First Secretary of State, Secretary of State for Environment, Food and Rural Affairs* OJ 2011 C 226/16 and Case C-416/10 *Križan and Others v Slovenská inšpekcia životného prostredia* OJ 2011 C 301/11.

63 A Commission proposal for a Directive on access to justice in environmental matters (COM (2003) 264 final) failed to gain traction due to persistent resistance from the Member States.

64 Case C-240/09 *Lesoochranárske zoskupenie VLK v Ministerstvo životného prostredia Slovenskej republiky* [2011] ECR I-0000 para. 30, also discussed in Kingston's contribution to the present volume.

65 Case C-240/09 *Lesoochranárske zoskupenie VLK v Ministerstvo životného prostredia Slovenskej republiky* [2011] ECR I-0000.

66 *Ibid.*, para. 46.

67 *Ibid.*, para. 47.

extent possible, is consistent with the objectives laid down in Article 9(3) of the Aarhus Convention.[68]

Following this uncompromising line of analysis, the Court of Justice concluded that the referring court was obliged to interpret domestic procedural rules on access to the courts, to the fullest extent possible, in the light of the objectives of Article 9(3) and the objective of effective judicial protection, so as to enable an ENGO to challenge a decision that had potentially been taken in breach of EU environmental law.[69] This unambiguous edict from Luxembourg should leave the national courts in no doubt as to what is expected of them. More significantly, it provides them with a firm jurisprudential basis on which to tackle domestic procedural rules that may impede access to the courts in environmental matters falling within the scope of EU environmental law.

9.4 Closing observations

The access to environmental justice case law continues to evolve at international (ACCC), EU and national levels. The advent of Article 47 of the Charter of Fundamental Rights of the European Union,[70] under which Member States are bound 'to provide remedies sufficient to ensure effective legal protection in the fields covered by Union law', provides yet another express basis on which to bolster the right of access to justice more generally. And, of course, the European Court of Human Rights continues to develop its innovative jurisprudence based on Article 6 and Article 13 of the ECHR. There is no doubt that interesting developments are inevitable into the future as the complex interplay between the different sources of legal authority begins to crystallise in practice. The strong external pressure for improvement, driven primarily by the Aarhus Convention and EU law obligations, means that the outlook is promising, notwithstanding that Ireland got off to a very slow start. But it is the national judiciary who hold the key to unlocking access to the courts and delivering effective judicial protection. The time has come for the Irish courts to rise to this challenge; to cast off the shadow of past failures and vigorously enforce the rule of EU environmental law.

This chapter examined current issues and problems around environmental enforcement in Ireland, with particular emphasis on the Irish response to access to justice obligations arising under the Aarhus Convention and EU law. It charted the tardy and initially inadequate legislative response in Ireland and the disappointingly timid stance taken by the national judiciary. Notwithstanding the advent of section 50B of the Planning and Development Act 2000 (as amended), and the new measures introduced in Part 2 of the

---

68 *Ibid.*, paras. 49–50.
69 *Ibid.*, para. 51.
70 Charter of Fundamental Rights of the European Union OJ 2000 C 364/1.

2011 Act, important questions remain as to how these provisions will operate in practice. It is not surprising therefore, to find that individuals and ENGOs remain frustrated with the lack of tangible progress on access to justice in environmental matters in Ireland. It should not be necessary for the Commission to secure a Court of Justice ruling before Ireland moves to fulfil its EU law obligations. The legislature should act promptly to ensure that obligations are implemented correctly and in a timely manner. Where the legislature fails to deliver, the national courts are under an obligation to do all in their power to address implementation gaps. The recent series of strong rulings from the Court of Justice interpreting Article 10a of the EIA Directive should embolden the national judiciary to take a firmer approach when called upon to uphold rights flowing from this provision.

9.5 Postscript

There have been a number of significant developments since this chapter was concluded including the following:

On 20 June 2012, Ireland finally ratified the Aarhus Convention. The GMO Amendment to the Convention (amendment on public participation in decisions on deliberate release into the environment and placing on the market of genetically modified organisms) and the Protocol to the Convention on Pollutant Release and Transfer Registers were also ratified. The three agreements will enter into force on 18 September 2012.

On 21 June 2012, the Commission decided to refer Ireland back to the Court of Justice with a view to the imposition of a lump sum fine and a daily penalty payment for failure to comply with an adverse judgment on EIA matters delivered in March 2011 (Case C-50/09 *Commission v Ireland* [2011] ECR I-0000).

10 Environmental enforcement in Ireland

The need to get a piece of the multi-party action

Joanne Blennerhassett*

10.1 Introduction: environmental enforcement in Ireland and the potential role of multi-party actions

As the environment is a diffuse interest, it does not fit naturally within the framework that is traditionally recognised by the law for the protection of individual rights. Ireland's environmental law-enforcement landscape is currently lacking in several areas in relation to both the formal and informal enforcement mechanisms available to citizens. In both law and practice, private individuals and NGOs are inclined to have a secondary role in the regulation of environmental matters, as compared to public authorities. There is considerable acknowledgement by the Irish legislature that individuals or groups can have an interest in the environment, despite the more prominent role played by the regulatory authorities in this area and the adjustments that have been made to deal with problems of legal standing and cost. Existing tools for citizen enforcement are, however, hampered by issues of accessibility and cost. One of the longstanding lacunae in the area of access to environmental justice is the lack of a procedural mechanism to enable multi-party action (MPA) for mass harm. Such actions could be similar to the US 'class action' type lawsuit. The absence of such a mechanism impedes citizens' access to justice for environmental mass harm in Ireland.

MPAs, by enabling victims of mass harm to combine their legal actions, are a key tool in achieving the overall objectives of expanding access to justice, procedural efficiency and fairness. They can enable litigants to overcome many of the impediments facing citizens who take legal actions individually. These themes will be explored throughout this chapter. As other contributions in this volume explore,[1] international conventions such as Aarhus[2] highlight the

---

* This contribution draws on and develops my chapter in J. Kalajdzic (ed.), *Accessing Justice: Appraising Class Actions – Ten Years After Dutton, Hollick, & Rumley* (Ontario: LexisNexis Canada, 2011).

1 See, for instance, the contributions of Kingston and Ryall in Chapters 7 and 9, respectively, of the present volume.

2 The United Nations Convention on Access to Information, Public Participation in Decision-making and Access to Justice in Environmental Matters.

need for access to justice as a key facet of the aim of improving environmental governance in Europe.

10.2 Overview of the use of MPA mechanisms in common law jurisdictions[3]

Outside Ireland, the use of MPA mechanisms is seen quite often in other common law jurisdictions. In the United States environmental 'class action' type lawsuits can be taken for personal injury based on exposure to an environmental hazard.[4] Unlike individual personal injuries, it is often the case that numerous victims are affected by exposure to such a hazard, often hundreds or thousands of people may be exposed. Instead of each of these people suing individually, they often join together in an environmental class action lawsuit. In England and Wales, the tool of the 'Group Litigation Order' (GLO) has been adopted to enable a similar form of mass harm litigation.[5] The GLO, however, is a case-management system, not a collective or class action *per se*.[6] Moreover, the English courts, seem to emphasise the primacy of public law in environmental matters and they seem to prefer not to deal with environmental matters via private law (such as by use of common law remedies), as they regard this area as highly regulated.[7] In jurisdictions such as Canada, there has been limited class action activity in the area of environmental law.[8] Therefore, it seems that even though environmental cases may be well suited to the class action

---

3 This chapter will focus on the possibilities for use of MPAs in common law jurisdictions and will not deal with civil law jurisdictions, for reasons of space and the major procedural differences that exist between the two groups.

4 An environmental class action lawsuit is a large lawsuit brought by a group of similarly situated plaintiffs. This means that a lot of people who suffered similar injuries get together and bring one lawsuit. There is usually a lead plaintiff, or group of plaintiffs, who first brought the case to a lawyer. There may be one law firm handling the class action lawsuit, or a series of lawyers who team up together. This law firm and lead plaintiff go to court to speak for all of the other people in the class. Other victims are given the opportunity to join the class, which means be represented by this plaintiff and attorney, or opt out. If you choose to join the class, then you can't sue the company yourself and you are bound by whatever happens in the class action lawsuit.

5 For example a Group Litigation Order was made in respect of the Corby Litigation which has recently been settled after a first instance judge found in favour of the claimants on the subject of the breach: *Corby Group Litigation* [2009] EWHC 1944. This was an action against a local authority that the claimants argued was responsible for birth defects, given the manner in which it cleaned up contaminated land in the area. This however is a rare success for claimants in an environmental 'toxic torts' case in the UK. A much less successful claim was *Hunter v Canary Wharf* [1997] AC 655 brought by various residents of the London Docklands, which was eventually heard by the House of Lords.

6 A GLO is a court order which permits a number of claims which give rise to common or related issues (of fact or law) to be managed collectively. The GLO procedure was added to the Civil Procedure Rules in May 2000 (r. 9 Civil Procedure (Amendment) Rules 2000 SI 2000/221)

7 See Lord Goff in *Cambridge Water v Eastern Counties Leather plc* [1994] 2 AC 264, at p. 305

8 Presently, only four provinces have enacted class action legislation establishing class action proceedings as an alternative litigation tool: Quebec (1979), Ontario (1992), British Columbia (1995) and Saskatchewan (2002).

format, there is no guarantee that such cases will be certified as suitable for this in jurisdictions where class action mechanisms exist.[9]

Ireland, also a common law jurisdiction, is still somewhat at sea procedurally between the class action mechanisms seen in the US and the emerging group litigation approach in England. This is because Ireland, at present, has no formal statutory or court rules for MPAs, so neither multi-party nor specifically 'class' action is yet permitted, save for very limited representative actions. These possibilities are rarely invoked because they are of such restricted use. This is a major distinguishing factor in Ireland and is a gap in the Irish legal framework. Under the existing statutory framework MPAs seem to be actively discouraged. While Ireland does not yet have a mechanism for MPAs as such, a confusing array of alternative methods has occasionally been used by the courts, in cases where MPAs would have played an obvious role. In recent years there have been a number of cases of mass harm, including contaminated blood products, army deafness and asbestos-related ill health. Such cases usually draw widespread public interest due to the nature of their claims, the scale of the potential class or the prospect of state liability. Normally, however, due to the lack of an appropriate mechanism, those with cases potentially suited to an MPA must pursue them in another way. Great injustices and inefficiencies have resulted from these improvisations.

10.3 The Irish approach: no MPAs

The Irish Law Reform Commission (LRC), Ireland's principal public body for the investigation of law reform, has recognised the procedural gap that results from the absence of MPAs.[10] In a major study in 2005, it explored the prospects for MPAs in Ireland and has recommended their introduction.[11] The key recommendations of this pivotal report are described further below. In England and Wales, GLOs were introduced as a form of multi-party litigation in May 2000, yet, despite the LRC recommendations, there has not yet been any such major change in Ireland.

---

9 For instance, pollution claims usually require extensive and expensive expert evidence of cause and effect. Further, potentially large groups of persons might be adversely affected by a contaminating event, such as the release of a noxious gas cloud from an industrial facility or the pollution of a river with toxic effluents.

10 The Law Reform Commission was established by the Law Reform Commission Act 1975 as an independent statutory body whose main aim is to keep the law under review and to make practical proposals for its reform. It has published over 100 documents containing proposals for law reform which are available online at www.lawreform.ie. The Commission usually publishes in two stages: first, a Consultation Paper and then a Report. This occurred with the Multi-Party Litigation recommendations. The Consultation Paper is intended to form the basis for discussion and its recommendations, conclusions and suggestions are therefore provisional. The Consultation Paper on Multi-Party Litigation was published by the Commission in July 2003.

11 Report on Multi-party Litigation (LRC 76-2005), available online at www.lawreform.ie/_fileupload/Reports/rMultipartylitigation.pdf.

This raises a number of questions. It is possible to speculate that there are policy reasons for the lack of MPAs. It seems that there is almost a *de facto* prohibition on them, because of the lack of a mechanism for them and because of the presence of rules that effectively prohibit them, including, for example, the prohibition on damages awards for representative actions.[12] Despite the LRC's recommendations for multi-party actions in mass tort and personal injury litigation – where the state has been, and is likely to be, a regular defendant – the state is very slow to introduce a multi-party action system.[13] Irish policy-makers may be exercising caution for fear of opening apocryphal litigation floodgates by having a full-blown class action procedure, bringing with it the risks that some have alleged this mechanism can unleash where a class action procedure is abused and is not accompanied by adequate controls.[14] Perhaps there is a concern regarding competitiveness or attractiveness as a location for foreign investors wishing to set up business in Ireland. However, the MPA procedure, as recommended by the LRC, is designed to minimise such risks.

Irish Supreme Court Judge Susan Denham, when launching the LRC Report in 2005, commented:

> It is probable that the less well off, those disadvantaged in our society, would be the main beneficiaries of a new procedure enabling multi-party action … . It is no easy task – the challenge is to find a just balance in multi-party litigation between procedural efficiency and fairness. The Law Reform Commission has met this challenge successfully. Implementation of this Report would bring us a step closer to succeeding in this task.[15]

In these words, Denham J. identified the *raisons d'être* of the MPA. She highlighted the three key benefits that they are designed to achieve: (1) access to justice; (2) procedural efficiency; and (3) fairness. Ireland's lack of MPAs cannot be explored in a vacuum and the situation here must be examined in light of these objectives. This contribution examines the limited arrangements currently available in Ireland to see to what extent they meet these three requirements.

---

12 There is no explicit reason for this prohibition; it is likely to discourage the taking of such actions to achieve a monetary award. Remedies are limited to injunctive or declaratory relief. The bar on the bringing of representative actions in tort currently exists in Order 6 rule 10 of the Circuit Court Rules 2001.

13 See further, Opinion of Lisa Broderick, available online at www.accountancyireland.ie/Archive/2005/October-2005/Class-Actions—Opting-in-or-out-of-the-bandwagon/.

14 Arthur Miller, 'Of Frankenstein Monsters and Shining Knights: Myth, Reality and the "Class Action Problem" ' (1979) 92 *Harv. L. Rev.* 664 (outlining these problems while defending class actions and asserting that the problems are overstated).

15 *Ibid.*

10.3.1 *Overview of current Irish mechanisms for dealing with mass harm*

Multi-party litigation can arise in a variety of situations that can be broadly categorised as follows.

10.3.1.1 *Public actions*

This denotes a category of actions whereby certain public officials are empowered to institute litigation on behalf of a wide group of affected individuals. For example, regulatory bodies (or a given regulator) and the Director of Public Prosecutions may institute public actions for the prosecution of regulatory offences, such as those in the financial sector.[16] Another example is that the Attorney General may sue on behalf of the public and bodies such as NGOs using section 6 of the Ministers and Secretaries Act 1924 for the assertion of public rights.[17] In the environmental context, one might include prosecutions or other enforcement action taken by the Environmental Protection Agency within this category.

10.3.1.2 *Organisation actions*

It may be possible for certain organisations to institute proceedings that could otherwise be taken by a number of individuals. Such organisations are often public interest groups or pressure groups that are deemed to have a sufficient interest in the case to qualify for standing. In this way an action by an appropriate organisation could effectively dispose of multiple potential individual cases.[18] However, the issue of *locus standi* could operate as an obstacle and also the possibility of damages does not exist, as only declaratory or injunctive relief may be given. This may be a deterrent to such actions being used in environment-related cases (although, in the case of actions to enforce the EIA or IPPC Directives, the fact that environmental NGOs enjoy automatic standing avoids some of these difficulties).[19]

10.3.1.3 *Litigation avoidance*

Occasionally it may be best to deal with a group of individual actions together in a way that avoids litigation and to facilitate a remedy in a more sensitive and

---

16 See also, the jurisdictions of the Competition Authority and the Director of Consumer Affairs to institute proceedings on behalf of consumers.

17 For example, the case of *Attorney General (SPUC) v Open Door Counselling Ltd* [1988] I.R. 593 (this case was taken by the Attorney General on behalf of the Society for the Protection of the Unborn Child to challenge the distribution in Ireland by Open Door Counselling of information on abortion services abroad).

18 An example of this is the case of *Irish Penal Reform Trust v Minister for Justice, Equality and Law Reform* [2005] IEHC 305.

19 See Directive 2003/35 OJ 2002 L 156/17, amending the EIA Directive to implement the Aarhus Convention.

efficient way, particularly where a question of public interest is involved. An obvious example of this is special mechanisms such as statutory no-fault compensation schemes that deal with mass cases of personal injury (for example, injuries arising from infected blood products supplied by state bodies,[20] and injuries suffered by those who had been in residential institutional care).[21] In situations of serious injury or widespread mismanagement, usually for which there is some state accountability, there have been cases in which a public inquiry is necessitated, for example the call for a state inquiry into recent banking malpractice. The aim of a public inquiry is to determine facts relating to a particular incident or series of incidents of public interest and to ascertain whether a wrong has been committed against society or the public interest. Its aim is *not* to deliver judgment on legal rights. Depending on the results of such inquiry this may lead to claims for compensation by victims or their relatives, such as occurred with the Hepatitis C tribunal and the Institutional Redress Board under the no-fault compensation schemes discussed above.

Other methods of litigation avoidance, which have been used particularly in consumer actions, include the use of Alternative Dispute Resolution (ADR). In the US, ADR has recently been endorsed in the US Supreme Court's decision in *AT&T Mobility LLC v Concepcion*.[22] In this case, the court invalidated a Californian law that attempted to limit contract arbitration clauses considered unfair to consumers. The court held that if there is an arbitration clause in a contract, parties must be held to that. If this approach is followed in other courts and jurisdictions, this will strengthen the use of ADR as an alternative to class action litigation.

Prevention through regulation may be another method of potentially avoiding litigation. While the function of regulation in the domain of multi-party litigation may not be immediately obvious, the influence of effective regulatory mechanisms will often function to prevent the wrong arising in the first place and therefore preclude the need for any type of multi-party litigation.[23] Regulation often relates to areas in which there is great potential for multiple parties, for example consumer regulation and the safety of pharmaceutical products. In such circumstances, regulation plays an essential role in multi-party litigation. There is an important background role played by certain Irish regulatory and standards agencies in this area; the Office of the Director of Consumer Affairs and the Irish Medicines Board, for example, are particularly active and effective. Also, the State Claims Agency is charged with the function of identifying risks that could lead to future claims against public bodies. It is empowered to liaise with these bodies to ensure that these foreseeable risks are

---

20 See Hepatitis C Compensation Tribunal Act 1997 (No. 34/1997), available online at www.bailii.org/ie/legis/num_act/1997/0034.html.
21 See Residential Institutions Redress Act 2002 (No. 13/2002), available online at www.bailii.org/ie/legis/num_act/2002/0013.htm.
22 584 F.3d 849 (9th Cir., 2009), rev'd 131 S.Ct. 1740, 79 U.S.L.W. 4279 (2011).
23 Report on Multi-party Litigation (LRC 76-2005), at p. 7.

managed and controlled appropriately. In this way it carries out an important preventative role. This Agency was established as a direct result of the state's largest litigation experience, the army deafness claims (discussed below).[24] In the environmental context, this regulatory role is carried out by the Department of the Environment, Community and Local Government in conjunction with the EPA and local authorities.

10.3.1.4 EU initiatives

Several EU instruments, for example those provided for consumer protection, permit a nominated competent authority (in Ireland's case the Director of Consumer Affairs) to initiate proceedings on behalf of consumers.[25]

10.3.1.5 Private actions

This is the main focus of this contribution and refers to procedures that enable a group of individuals to institute proceedings to deal with that group collectively. Unlike the public action or organisation action, in private litigation the decision to pursue an action rests solely with the group of individuals. As mentioned at the outset, Ireland has a confusing array of mechanisms that have occasionally been used for cases of mass harm. These are rarely invoked and are private multi-party procedures that currently fall short of MPAs. They comprise the following:

10.3.1.5.1 REPRESENTATIVE ACTIONS

Irish courts have taken a very restrictive attitude toward these: they are permitted in very limited circumstances in which parties have the same interest and where certain prerequisites are met. They cannot be used for tort claims[26] and it is not possible to get damages. It is not possible to get legal aid for these cases. This type of representative action is a long way from the class action procedure seen on the other side of the Atlantic.

10.3.1.5.2 JOINDER

This is a process whereby the court can simply join additional litigants to an action where it is necessary in the interests of justice and in this way it can hear related cases together. The joinder system is used regularly to combine

---

24 For further detail see *ibid.*

25 See, e.g., Council Directive 93/13/EEC of 5 April 1993 on unfair terms in consumer contracts OJ 1993 L 95/29.

26 Order 6 rule 10 of the Circuit Court Rules 2001 expressly excludes representative actions founded on tort. No further explanation can be found of why this is so but this was also stated by the Supreme Court in *Moore v Attorney General (No. 2)* [1930] I.R. 471.

actions involving two or more parties and can, on occasion, broaden to multi-party actions with many parties.[27]

10.3.1.5.3 CONSOLIDATION

This is an alternative to a joinder. It occurs where the court rules that disputes must be tried or consolidated together by a plaintiff uniting several causes of action in the same proceedings.[28] This rule further provides that where such causes of action cannot be tried together conveniently, the court may order separate trials or make such other order as may be necessary or expedient to dispose of the matters.[29] Where a plaintiff does not take steps to unite several causes of action in the same proceedings, matters pending in the High Court may be consolidated by order of the court on the application of any party and regardless of whether or not all the parties consent to the order.[30] Aside from the provisions in the Rules, the court has an inherent jurisdiction to order that cases be heard simultaneously.[31] The difference between joinder and consolidation is that consolidation does *not* involve making all the claimants parties to a single set of proceedings. Instead, the plaintiff litigates the consolidated claims on the premise that he represents the class, and any judgment is deemed to be binding on the members (i.e. the plaintiffs in the parallel proceedings, with which his claim has been consolidated). In this way consolidation resembles the representative action and is a less flexible system for managing large class claims.

10.3.1.5.4 TEST CASES

These are currently used in Ireland as the favoured means of dealing with multi-party actions. Quite often a plaintiff proceeds on an individual basis. The test case establishes a benchmark and, while subsequent actions by other litigants are not bound by the result, the test-case outcome gives an indicator of the outcome of future litigation both in terms of formal precedent and the similarity of subsequent proceedings.[32] This is uncomplicated where the test

---

27 See, e.g., *Abrahamson v Law Society* [1996] 1 I.R. 403 (Law students challenged the Law Society's decision to deny them exemption from the entrance examination to the Law Society. Their individual actions were combined in a single action before the High Court as plaintiffs were a defined group with identical claims for declaratory and injunctive relief, represented by one legal team.)

28 Order 18 rule 1 of the Irish Rules of the Superior Courts (RSC) provides that a plaintiff may unite several causes of action together in the same proceedings.

29 Order 18 rule 9 RSC provides that where it appears to the court that causes of action are such that they cannot all be conveniently disposed of together, the court may order any of such causes of action to be excluded and consequential amendments to be made to such order as to costs may be just.

30 Order 4 rule 6 RSC; *Duffy v News Group Newspapers Ltd* [1992] 2 IR 369.

31 *O'Neill v Ryanair Ltd* [1992] 1 IR 160.

32 G. Whyte, *Social Inclusion and the Legal System* (Dublin: Institute of Public Administration, 2002), at p. 104.

case pronounces an administrative or legislative action unconstitutional,[33] but is less straightforward where an individual assessment of damages is necessary. Test cases were used to deal with the many army deafness claims taken against the state and also in private actions.[34] These are unduly costly and result in procedural inefficiencies and unnecessary duplication as illustrated in the examples discussed further below.

10.3.1.5.5 OTHER DISCRETE AREAS

Certain specific provisions under Irish law provide for representative proceedings to be brought under the law relating to trusts and estates and derivative actions on behalf of shareholders in company law and in relation to fatality claims.

10.3.2 Cases exemplifying the problems of mass harm litigation in Ireland

The following cases are a clear illustration of what occurs when some of the above private action procedures are used and there is no appropriate multi-party procedure. They support the contention that by proceeding on the basis of such fragmented and piecemeal procedures, access to justice is impeded, and gross procedural inefficiencies and procedural unfairness result. They fall far short of the three objectives of MPAs identified by Denham J. above.

10.3.2.1 Social welfare equality cases

An early example is the two cases of *Cotter and McDermott v Minister for Social Welfare and Attorney General.* These resulted from the failure by Ireland to implement the 1978 Directive on Equal Treatment in Social Welfare.[35] The two cases were test cases for 11,200 married women who instituted proceedings, out of a total 69,000 who had been disadvantaged by this failure.[36] The state

---

33 See G. Hogan and G. Whyte, *Kelly: Irish Constitution* (4th edn, Dublin: Butterworths, 2003), at pp. 487–97 (such a declaration nullifies the impugned act or legislation in all situations including those where litigation is pending).

34 See, e.g., *Gough v Neary* [2003] 3 IR 92, [2003] IESC 39 (successful negligence claim against an obstetrician for an unnecessary hysterectomy during childbirth, in advance of a further 65 similar cases pending against him).

35 Council Directive 79/7/EEC of 19 December 1978 on the progressive implementation of the principle of equal treatment for men and women in matters of social security OJ 1979 L 6/24.

36 *Cotter and McDermott v Minister for Social Welfare (No. 1)* [1987] E.C.R. 1453 and *Cotter and McDermott v Minister for Social Welfare (No.2)* [1991] 1 E.C.R. 1155. These cases arose from the fact that until 1986 Ireland's social welfare policy had discriminated against married women. Married men were the automatic recipients of child benefit and received higher rates of welfare payment based on a presumption that their wives were dependent on them. For married women to receive these payments, they had to prove that their spouses were incapable of supporting themselves. In 1984, a Directive obliged Ireland to remove these practices of sex discrimination, but they did not do so until 1986. The Free Legal Advice Centre (FLAC) (a *pro bono* NGO) took a case arguing their entitlement to back-payments during the two-year period where Ireland's discriminatory policy was in breach of EU Law. Their victory had far reaching consequences, making it possible for 69,000 women to claim their entitlement.

settled these two cases along with another 2,700 without admission of liability. However, this ignored approximately 8,500 claims initiated as well as the remaining 58,000 married women who had not yet initiated proceedings. This was followed by the case of *Tate v Minister for Social Welfare* involving 70 of these women, in which Carroll J. ruled in the High Court that they too were entitled to relief.[37] This decision resulted in the government announcing that the required payments would be made to the entire group of 69,000 women, with this amount totalling £265 million including interest.

10.3.2.2 Army deafness claims

The army deafness litigation is the best example of multiple, similar claims over a period of thirteen years, resulting from hundreds of individual army deafness cases. Claims of hearing loss were brought by serving and former members of the Defence Forces. It was found that the Defence Forces, and consequently the state, were liable for negligence in failure to prevent noise-induced hearing loss of serving and former members of the Defence Forces. The state's alleged negligence resulted in approximately 14,650 soldiers claiming partial or total loss of hearing.[38]

10.3.2.3 Pyrite construction dispute

The Irish High Court in 2011 finished hearing a case that had been running for over two years against the Irish construction industry with claims of more than €100 million. These claims were brought by 550 homeowners who had purchased houses that developed structural faults, due to the use of pyrite infill during construction. This was the longest running case in the history of the Commercial Court and one of the most expensive court cases in the history of the state. The plaintiffs took separate actions and the same lawyers did not represent them all. The action was settled when a €25.5 million repair fund was agreed. This case typifies the problems inherent in the current procedure whereby plaintiffs must initiate separate and individual claims seeking damages particular to his or her situation. The cost, delay and wasteful inefficiencies of this system speak for themselves and work only to the advantage of lawyers, whose fees are mounting as long as the litigation continues.

While these examples are not necessarily environment related, they suggest that it is in the interests of the state, in the interests of litigants and in the interests of justice to embrace some form of MPA procedure to avoid the anomalous situations illustrated above. Cases where environmental harm is

---

37 [1995] 1 I.R. 418.
38 So far the total cost of the litigation for final claims amount to a cost of €278 million, of which €184.5 million comprises awards or settlements and €94 million was paid by the state in legal costs. The overall cost borne by the Irish taxpayer has been €300 million.

suffered by numerous victims and caused by an identifiable defendant or group of defendants are an obvious further example of where an MPA procedure would be of great assistance. Such a procedure would enhance access to justice and help surmount prohibitive obstacles such as high litigation costs faced by individuals. These constitute gaps in Ireland's current litigation system, which arguably falls short in this respect of that of other European Member States, particularly when viewed in light of the requirements of the Aarhus Convention.

10.4 Particular difficulties with multi-party litigation in Ireland

Ireland does not have a very high level of private civil litigation because legal costs can be prohibitive. The issue of lawyers' fees is controversial in Ireland. There have been recent recommendations for reform in this area from Ireland's Competition Authority[39] and further reform is envisaged in the pending Legal Services Regulation Bill 2011, by formalising an obligation for lawyers to outline costs to clients in advance.[40] Funding cases is a crucial area, and one with which litigants have difficulty dealing. Due to the failure of the Irish authorities to invest public resources in facilitating private civil litigation, the question of funding is central not only to the issue of access to justice but also to considerations of fairness and the efficiency of the civil court system. Recognising that funding is so central, it is useful to look at key elements related to this issue.

10.4.1 *Legal aid*

Ireland does not have a comprehensive and effective system for civil legal aid as it is limited to means-tested parties in family law and some limited civil litigation matters.[41] It is possible, in theory, under the guidelines for civil legal aid, to get funding for personal injury litigation where the criteria for assistance are met.[42] However, the means-testing level set under the financial eligibility requirement test that applies to the funding available to the Legal Aid Board has meant that any such application would almost certainly fail. As a result, a body of so-called Middle Income Not Eligible for Legal Aid (MINELA) has developed in Ireland, and even those fulfilling the financial criteria for civil legal aid are very unlikely to succeed in securing it unless their case falls within a limited number of categories, notably family law and asylum law.[43] Environmental law areas fall outside these categories, although, arguably, it is

---

39 See www.tca.ie/images/uploaded/documents/2010-03-25%20Opening%20Statement%20to%20 PAC.pdf.

40 No. 58 of 2011.

41 See www.legalaidboard.ie/lab/publishing.nsf/Content/ Civil_Legal_Aid_Services.

42 The Civil Legal Aid Act 1995 (No. 32/1995) does not expressly exclude personal injury litigation.

43 MINELA is a term coined under the civil legal aid system in England and Wales.

an area that requires civil legal aid, as parties who wish to bring actions are often acting in the public interest and not just on their own behalf. As such, the tradition of civil legal aid is significantly less generous and efficient than that which prevails in England and Wales (although this is itself presently under review). The Irish civil legal aid scheme specifically excludes test cases and MPAs of any sort, so it is not available for representative actions.[44]

In order to avoid the risk of ruinously expensive legal costs, litigants commonly proceed by using the device of 'men of straw'[45] for challenges under the Planning Acts and in common law and nuisance. There is a very limited additional funding scheme for those not eligible for civil or criminal legal aid called the Attorney General's Scheme, but this is not applicable to most civil legal cases.[46] Perhaps the Civil Legal Aid Act 1995 should be amended to allow funding of some of the improvised mechanisms of MPAs, for example representative actions, even if only on grounds of efficiency. The LRC recommended in its 2005 Report on Multi-party Litigation that this Act be amended to make provision for the funding of an otherwise eligible group member for his proportion of an eventual costs order. As for other litigants who are not eligible for civil legal aid, it seems that in order to avoid costs their best option remains to await a similar case, to be used as a test case, where litigants are willing to proceed despite lack of legal aid funding.

10.4.2 Insurance

Litigation insurance is not generally available in Ireland. 'Before the Event' (BTE) insurance is very uncommon in jurisdictions where, as a rule, costs follow the event and it is unheard of that anybody would take on 'after the event' insurance. If BTE legal expense insurance were to become widespread in this jurisdiction, this could act as a potential means of financing MPA litigation.

10.4.3 Costs follow the event

Finally, but crucially, costs generally follow the event, which means that the award will be made in favour of the successful party. Accordingly, the loser of

---

44 Section 28(9)(a)(ix) of the Civil Legal Aid Act 1995 specifically excludes legal aid for 'matters as respects which the application for legal aid is made by or on behalf of a person who is a member and acting on behalf of a group of persons having the same interests in the proceedings concerned'.

45 I.e., those with extremely limited financial means, hence, no assets to risk losing if costs are awarded against them. It is possible to speculate that the more relaxed approach of the Irish courts to the proprietary interest requirement for *locus standi* in nuisance actions is a tacit recognition of the 'man of straw' plaintiff.

46 See www.attorneygeneral.ie/ac/agscheme.html. This Scheme provides payment for legal representation in certain types of legal cases not covered by the civil legal aid or criminal legal aid schemes. It is an *ex gratia* scheme set up with funds available from the Oireachtas. The Chief State Solicitor's Office administers application the Scheme. It generally covers: certain types of judicial review (relating to criminal matters); bail applications; extraditions including European Arrest Warrant Applications; and Habeas Corpus.

a case usually has to pay the entire amount of the costs, which is a double financial burden, having to meet both sets of costs in the action. However, this is at the discretion of the presiding judge and is not a statutory requirement. The main problem with this serious litigation risk is that of having to meet the other side's costs as well as one's own. If MPAs were to be introduced there would have to be changes to how costs are currently decided. Further, it should be noted that the standard rule that costs follow the event does not apply for certain environmental cases, as discussed more fully by Kingston and Ryall in this volume, in Chapters 7 and 9, respectively.

10.4.4 Conditional fee arrangements

In Ireland it is illegal for barristers and solicitors to charge based on a percentage or proportion of any award or settlement for a case, despite this being a common practice in other common law jurisdictions.[47] However there are occasions on which lawyers agree to represent clients on the basis of a 'no win no fee' arrangement, which is permitted and is a common method of deferred payment for legal services, including in environmental cases.[48]

10.4.5 Advertising and the Irish legal profession

In relation to advertising, solicitors are allowed to advertise but there are severe restrictions on advertising, for instance in relation to personal injury services.[49] Such restrictions on advertising could certainly impact on solicitors running MPAs.[50] However, notification of potential litigants does not pose too difficult a challenge in Ireland, due to the small size of the jurisdiction.

10.5 Irish Law Reform Commission Report on Multi-party litigation, September 2005 – a closer look

As discussed above, this report followed on from the publication by the Commission in 2003 of a Consultation Paper on Multi-party litigation.[51] The report

---

47 Code of Conduct of the Bar of Ireland, s. 12.1(e), 'Barristers may not accept instructions on condition that payment will be subsequently fixed as a percentage or other proportion of the amount awarded', available online at www.lawlibrary.ie/documents/memberdocs/CodeOfConductAdopted050710. pdf.

48 This label though is potentially misleading and must be explained further. Where costs follow the event, this term suggests that where the client is unsuccessful in the action, the solicitor will absorb the fees and if no damages are awarded then there is no fee. However, in fact, these agreements do not insulate the client from costs in the event that their case is unsuccessful. Instead, they merely defer the payment of these costs until the close of the action. This means that the client does not have to pay for representation at the beginning of the litigation, but the solicitor can later pursue the client for these costs as they remain as a debt due between the client and solicitor, although the solicitor may decide against the pursuit of these costs, which is often the case.

49 The Solicitors Advertising Regulations 2002 (S.I. No. 518 of 2002) were introduced pursuant to s. 4 of the Solicitors (Amendment) Act 2002 (No. 19/2002), which preserves the right of a solicitor to advertise, but severely restricts personal injuries advertising.

50 See www.lawsociety.ie/Documents/committees/conduct2.pdf for these professional conduct rules.

51 Consultation Paper on Multi-Party Litigation, Irish Law Reform Commission (LRC CP 25-2003), at p. 14.

focuses on the potential for reform of private multi-party litigation which, to date in Ireland, is usually proceeded by way of test cases. A comparative review of selected multi-party procedures from a variety of jurisdictions as well as current Irish arrangements for multi-party litigation was undertaken to inform this report. As already noted, the LRC concluded that to date *ad hoc* arrangements have been used to deal with the demands of multi-party litigation and that a more structured approach should be available in the form of the MPA. The LRC stated that its proposals for multi-party litigation are not to be considered as replacements for existing procedures, particularly the test case, but rather as providing an alternative procedure where this is more appropriate. Despite this recommendation, MPAs have yet to be pursued seriously by the legislature.

The LRC recommended that any reform in this area should be based on principles of procedural fairness, efficiency and access to justice. Again, this anchors any reform in this area to the three objectives of MPAs identified by Denham J. In particular, the LRC recommended that there should be active case management by the courts (which is in keeping with the general trend in the reform of civil procedure such as those in the UK Woolf reform recommendations.)[52] This report was welcomed by the Free Legal Advice Centre, an Irish *pro bono* legal service, as well as by several senior members of the judiciary.[53]

The Report recommended, *inter alia*:

- the introduction of a completely new procedure to be called a Multi-Party Action (MPA). The MPA would operate as a flexible tool to deal collectively with cases that are sufficiently similar, to be introduced by way of the Irish Rules of Court, where common issues among the individual actions are involved;
- the MPA procedure should operate on the basis of an opt-in system whereby individual litigants will be included in the group only where they decide to join the group action. This is very different, for instance, from the Canadian class action procedure in which individuals are deemed to be part of the class unless they opt-out;
- MPAs would require certification by a court before they could become established;
- the court would certify the MPA only where it was considered to offer a fair and efficient means of resolving the common issues involved;

---

52 The full text of Lord Woolf's Access to Justice Inquiry 1996 is online at www.dca.gov.uk/civil/final/index.htm.

53 See www.flac.ie/download/pdf/dec04_lrc_class_actions.pdf. In summary, FLAC enthusiastically welcomed the Commission's recommendation to introduce class actions, on the basis that to do so can only strengthen public interest litigation and increase access to justice. In particular it notes the necessity of amending the Civil Legal Aid Act 1995 to allow for legal aid in representative actions. It emphasises that the objective of increasing access to justice should underpin all decisions taken in relation to the specifics of the procedure, including those relating to costs.

- the court would establish an MPA Register containing a list of the cases in the MPA;
- the court would, where appropriate, select lead cases to go forward as representative of those in the group;
- the court would set a general cut-off date for entry into the MPA;
- a single legal representative would be agreed by the MPA members or nominated by the court to deal with the common issues arising in the MPA;
- the cost associated with the MPA would be spread among its members in equal measure;
- where an individual member of the MPA would have been eligible as an individual litigant for civil legal aid, they should continue to be eligible for aid to the extent of their share of the costs under an MPA and they will receive funding for this from the Irish Legal Aid Board.[54]

The LRC drafted an amendment to the Irish Rules of the Superior Courts to provide for the introduction of MPAs and also drafted an amendment bill to provide for civil legal aid for multi-party actions for those eligible for legal aid funding. The Report's recommendations include the distinction between general issues in common and subsidiary issues (that individuals may wish to pursue otherwise) and also how to include small claims.[55] The LRC recommended that costs should be shared equally among a group so, in this way, it did not find a solution to the general problem of funding identified earlier in this chapter. It did, however, address the civil legal aid aspect of this barrier, by providing eligibility requirements for this aid for those who would otherwise qualify for civil legal aid and drafting amendments to provide for this in the Rules of Court.

The government has yet to adopt these recommendations by legislation. To date no changes have been made to the Rules of Court. As mentioned earlier in this contribution, it was predicted that, in circumstances where the state has been and is likely to be a regular defendant, it is likely that the state will be slow to introduce a class action system.

10.6 Evaluation of current Irish mass harm mechanisms and MPA objectives

A consensus has developed worldwide around the key objectives of MPAs. Phair stresses that the aim of the US class action was to provide greater access to the courts, particularly for those who 'individually would be without effective strength to bring their opponents to court at all'.[56] In the absence of

---

54 See further details of this online at www.legalaidboard.ie/lab/publishing.nsf/Content/Civil_Legal_Aid.
55 Note Ireland already has a small claims court for disputes up to a value of €2,000, such as those involving consumers, which parties can take without the need to employ a lawyer.
56 R.P. Phair, 'Resolving the "Choice-of-Law Problem" in Rule 23(b)(3) Nationwide Class Actions' (2000) *U. of Chicago L. Rev.* 838, at p. 839.

formal MPA Rules in Ireland, it is still possible to use existing key mechanisms in combination to provide an alternative framework for MPAs. As noted above, Denham J. has identified three *raisons d'être* of MPAs, against which the current Irish mechanisms may be measured, as follows.

10.6.1 Access to justice

In the opinion of Justice Catherine McGuinness, former President of the LRC, the Irish methods of dealing with multiple cases have led to some 'appalling situations because of the lack of multi-party actions' such as the army deafness litigation.[57] Ireland has had its access to justice record condemned previously in several landmark cases in the European Court of Human Rights. Probably the most significant example of this is the historic judgment in *Airey v Ireland*[58] where the court declared that the right of access to justice must not be 'theoretical and illusory' but 'practical and effective'.[59]

Such issues have also arisen in the ECJ, as discussed by Ryall in Chapter 9. Notably, the UK Supreme Court has recently made an order for reference in *R v (Edwards & Pallikaropoulos) v Environment Agency & DEFRA*, the first case in which that court has had to consider the relationship between Article 9 of the Aarhus Convention, which requires that environmental litigation not be 'prohibitively expensive', and the normal rule under English (and Irish) civil procedure that an unsuccessful judicial review claimant should pay the respondent's costs.[60] The appellant argued in that case that for her to pay the respondent's costs would render the litigation prohibitively expensive.[61]

The Irish Constitution holds the rule of law as a core concept of Ireland's legal system. It provides that everyone is subject to the law and its constitutional structure provides for the right of access to the courts and of access to justice. There has been much discussion recently about the high cost of litigation and a concern expressed that not only those on legal aid and those of considerable financial means should have access, but that many litigants who potentially fall between these two categories should have access as well. The constitutional right of access to the courts was recognised by the Irish Supreme Court in the

---

57 Justice McGuinness, Address to the Globalization of Class Actions international conference at Oxford University, 12–14 December, 2007.

58 (1979) 2 E.H.R.R. 305.

59 (1979) 2 E.H.R.R. 305, at p. 314.

60 *R v (Edwards & Pallikaropoulos) v Environment Agency & DEFRA* [2010] UK SC 57. The House of Lords had rejected Mrs. Pallikarapoulos's application for a protective costs order in advance of her appeal on the basis that, *inter alia*, insufficient information had been provided as to her financial means to conclude that the proceedings would be 'prohibitively expensive' for her. She nonetheless proceeded with her appeal. When it was dismissed, the House of Lords ordered that she pay the respondent's costs (totalling around £88,000). See further, the contributions of Ryall and Kingston to the present volume.

61 [2010] UK S.C. 57.

case of *McAuley v Minister for Posts and Telegraphs*, and the excerpt below was quoted by Denham J. in her speech launching the 2005 LRC Report. In that case, Kenny J. held:

> [t]hat there is a right to have recourse to the High Court to defend and vindicate a legal right and that it is one of the personal rights of the citizen included in the general guarantee in Article 40.3, seems to me to be a necessary inference from Article 34.3.1 of the Constitution ... if the High Court has this full original jurisdiction ... it must follow that the citizens have a right to have recourse to that Court ... [62]

10.6.2 *Procedural efficiency*

In terms of procedural efficiency, case management is an essential element of any state's legal system as it enhances the service provided to the public and minimises inefficiencies. Case management is only a recent phenomenon in the Irish legal system and has been emerging since the mid-1990s. As there has been a surge in the volume of litigation since that period there is a clear need to develop efficiency. This increase in volume of work has been matched by the increased complexity of cases in this period. There has also been an increase in similar case litigation. The need for private MPAs is an obvious corollary in order to ensure the fundamental right of access to justice. A rare example of case management was seen in some of the Irish asbestos litigation.

10.6.3 *Procedural fairness*

The need for procedural fairness is a core element in any reform of multi-party litigation, as detailed by the LRC in its 2005 MPA Report.[63] Further, Article 6 of the European Convention on Human Rights requires protection of the right to a fair trial. In criminal cases and in cases to determine civil rights, Article 6 protects the right to a public hearing before an independent and impartial tribunal within a reasonable time, among other requirements. According to the LRC, as the boundaries of the procedure will be dictated by the individual cases within the collective group, a multi-party procedure should facilitate the resolution of individual actions. Procedural fairness is also important from the defendant's perspective. Current arrangements have an inherent lack of transparency and reforms should remove doubts as to the future potential scope of the litigation and an appropriate reduction of associated costs.

---

62 [1966] I.R. 345. In *State (McCormack) v Curran*, Finlay C.J. stated that '[t]he right of access to the courts, stated in its broadest fashion, is the right to initiate litigation in the courts' (1987) I.L.R.M. 225; see also *Murphy v Greene* [1990] 2 I.R. 566 (McCarthy J.)

63 Report on Multi-party Litigation (LRC 76-2005), at p. 8.

10.7 What may lie ahead

10.7.1 Developments in England and Wales

Perhaps pressure is building in Ireland because our closest neighbour has introduced a mechanism to aid multi-party access to justice. Developments in the UK are likely to be watched very closely by Ireland, particularly developments surrounding the Group Litigation Order. Also, some recent cases in the area of mass harm demonstrate the UK courts taking an innovative approach to such cases and not necessarily relying on the GLO. Hodges, in a historical review of multi-party actions,[64] produces a schedule of 'a succession of major cases since the early 1980s' in England and Wales. More recently, however, few group actions, let alone toxic tort claims, have been successfully initiated in the UK[65] given the complexity of evidence and the consequent costs of funding the action.[66] It should be noted that the LRC's report is in line with the UK's Woolf reforms, so there is a broad consensus regarding the requirements of justice in civil litigation. Ireland may be belatedly following in the footsteps of the English legal system if they do proceed with (some of) the LRC's recommendations, taking the advice of the Woolf Report's primary recommendation for introduction of case management and also new provisions for multi-party litigation. Although, as stated previously, it is quite possible that the state may find itself the defendant in such multi-party litigation and so it may remain averse to its introduction, particularly in the current economic climate.

10.7.2 Aarhus and human rights

The Irish legal landscape may well be forced to change as Ireland formally incorporated the European Convention on Human Rights into its legal system in 2003.[67] As noted above, Article 6 of the Convention provides for the right to a fair trial. Current legal mechanisms for mass harm arguably do not provide this. Furthermore, as the only remaining EU Member State not to have yet ratified the Aarhus Convention, questions of access to justice may well be raised by this lack of legal mechanism.

In examining the Aarhus Convention's implications, as discussed by Kingston and Ryall, in Chapters 7 and 9, respectively, it is notable that the Aarhus

---

64 C. Hodges, *Multi-Party Actions* (Oxford: Oxford University Press, 2001)

65 See R. Mulheron, 'Reform of Collective Redress in England and Wales: A Perspective of Need' (research paper prepared for the Civil Justice Council of England and Wales, 2008).

66 Since the introduction of the GLOs in 2000, although it has been possible for numerous claimants to pursue a group litigation action when there are common or closely related issues of fact and law, there are just 69 such actions listed on Her Majesty's Court Service website for 2010 – about seven each year – across all types of claim. According to Mulheron, the second highest category of these actions was environmental claims at 15 per cent ('Reform of Collective Redress in England and Wales').

67 European Convention of Human Rights Act 2003 (No. 20 of 2003).

Convention Compliance Committee (the ACCC) has handed down findings that the UK government is making it too expensive for environmental campaigners to take cases through the English courts.[68] This statement could open the door to new rules in relation to legal costs and community groups wishing to take cases to the English courts. Under the Convention, which was ratified by the UK in 2005, the English government is obliged to give rights and to remove financial barriers for citizens who wish to mount legal challenges. The ACCC found that the UK was failing to ensure court proceedings were not prohibitively expensive and that measures were required to overcome the financial barriers to environmental justice. These issues, as previously mentioned, have also arisen in the ECJ, such as in the recent referral from the UK Supreme Court in the *Edwards* case.[69]

While Aarhus relates to environmental matters specifically, the culture of procedural rights stemming from its requirements might well inform developments in terms of general litigation. The environmental area has often been a trailblazer for the emergence of such procedural rights. Ireland provides an example of where the introduction of rules on freedom of access to environmental information, introduced to transpose a 1990 Directive on access to environmental information, preceded the introduction of a more general Freedom of Information Act 1997[70] which did not come into effect until 1998.[71] This example of a culture relating to procedural rights could inform the development of rules for general civil litigation.

10.7.3 EU initiatives

Different approaches are emerging about how best to address collective redress in the EU system, and seem to have resulted in the rejection of a court-based procedure in favour of a new integrated model founded on three pillars: the first with a strong ADR focus aiming to merge elements of negotiation and settlement; the second involving external facilitators such as mediators and public authorities; and the third allowing for a court-based process as a supervisory and last resort.[72] Although not yet complete, it represents a new model for collective redress in Europe. This innovative model could be useful in informing collective redress both throughout Europe and internationally.[73] In the meantime, ongoing discussions at the European Commission level for

---

68 ACCC/C/2008/33.
69 *R (Edwards & Pallikaropoulos) v Environment Agency & DEFRA* [2010] UK SC 57.
70 Freedom of Information Act (No. 13 of 1997).
71 Directive 90/313/EEC OJ 1990 L 158/56 provided for access to environmental information. This Directive had been implemented in Ireland by means of various statutory instruments made in 1993, 1996 and 1998.
72 See C. Hodges, 'Collective Redress in Europe: The New Model' (2010) *Civil Justice Quarterly* 370.
73 See C. Hodges, *The Reform of Class and Representative Actions in European Legal Systems: A New Framework for Collective Redress in Europe* (Oxford: Hart Publishing, 2008).

the introduction of an alternative means of resolving mass harm through a new 'collective ADR' based approach seem to be gathering strength and momentum, although conclusions are unlikely to be reached in the very short term. Two Directorates-General of the European Commission have been investigating options for introducing a collective action mechanism across Europe, one in relation to enforcement of competition law[74] and another in relation to the enforcement of consumer protection.[75] Ultimately, Ireland may decide to wait and see in which way the EU wishes to progress this issue before finally making up its mind on MPAs – at which point it may not have the luxury of waiting any longer and may be forced to row in with the European approach.

10.7.4 Developments in the US Supreme Court

Developments on the other side of the Atlantic are continuing apace, particularly with class action cases in the US Supreme Court. The recent Supreme Court decision in the case of *AT&T v Concepcion*,[76] which was moved to arbitration, also indicates a move from the courtroom to ADR for class actions. This could herald the endorsement of an ADR approach to resolving class actions stateside.

10.8 Conclusion

The debate continues on whether class action type procedures should be adopted in Ireland, including in environmental cases. As demonstrated, the Irish legal system currently does not provide a viable mechanism for multi-party litigation. Despite this void, multi-plaintiff personal injury litigation is not alien to Ireland. The army deafness cases and the potential banking inquiry following the recent banking system collapse are examples of mass harm straining to find redress within existing, albeit deficient, litigation mechanisms. The asbestos litigation and pyrite litigation are early examples of environmental-type mass harm litigated in Ireland, but it is only a matter of time that other such mass environmental harm matters will need to be litigated on a large-scale level in Ireland.

In recommending the introduction of a multi-party procedure in the form of an MPA, the LRC's 2005 Report set out a scheme providing for a fair and efficient procedure to be executed under judicial supervision. As discussed, there are many advantages to such a procedural mechanism, including the

74 The Commission published a Green Paper in December 2005 on facilitating private damages claims, especially through a collective mechanism. After extensive debate, the White Paper of 2008 (White Paper on damages actions for breach of the EC antitrust rules, COM (2008) 165) made less expansive proposals but included two mechanisms for collective redress.

75 The EU's Consumer Strategy 2007–2013 highlighted the overhauling of legislation of cross-border shopping rights and the creation of strong systems for enforcement and redress, including collective redress mechanisms (COM (2007) 99).

76 See note 23.

reduction of the cost of litigating an issue and the overall cost of achieving a resolution. Further, scarce court resources could be used more efficiently. By avoiding repetitious court hearings and clogging up the already overburdened court system, the MPA would ultimately result in the saving of legal costs to all involved. Finally and most importantly, access to justice will be available to many who would otherwise have been excluded. It is obvious that the existing system of principally using test cases is ineffective. While it does mitigate against speculative claims, and ensures a full and fair hearing to genuine claims, it is inefficient and results in what McGuinness J. of the Irish Supreme Court termed 'appalling situations' because of the lack of MPAs.[77] It is not user-friendly and needs to go further to provide access to justice for all. Also urgently in need of adjustment in order to facilitate access to justice are the Irish costs and civil legal aid systems, although some reform may be provided in relation to costs if the pending Legal Services Regulation Bill 2011 is passed.

Further, the impediment to access to justice in Ireland as a result of the lack of an effective procedural mass harm mechanism affects Ireland's ability to potentially comply with the Aarhus Convention – although it has as yet notably failed to ratify this Convention. The availability of MPAs is crucial in the context of the overall EU environmental governance debate in terms of increasing access to justice more broadly for citizens, as well as improving procedural fairness and efficiency. This state of flux is not particular to Ireland; Irish commentators will watch with great interest changes that are emerging in the US, UK and at EU level. In the meantime, it seems without doubt that the time has come for Ireland to finally get in on the multi-party action, as without it there is a severe lacuna in the mechanisms for environmental mass harm redress in Ireland.

77 Hon. Catherine McGuinness, former President of the Irish Law Reform Commission, Address to the Globalization of Class Actions conference, Oxford University, December 2007.

Index

Note: The reference to 61n10 refers to footnote 10 on page 61.